Feeling, Valuing, and the Art of Growing: Insights into the Affective

Prepared by the
ASCD 1977 Yearbook Committee

Louise M. Berman and Jessie A. Roderick
Co-chairpersons and Co-editors

Association for Supervision and Curriculum Development
Suite 1100, 1701 K Street, NW
Washington, D.C. 20006

Contents

Part Three. Humankind and Schooling: 201
The Affective in Practice

Acknowledgments

Final editing of the manuscript and publication of this yearbook were the responsibility of Robert R. Leeper, Associate Director and Editor, ASCD publications. The production was handled by Elsa Angell, with the assistance of Teola T. Jones and Polly Larson, with Nancy Olson as production manager. The cover and design of this volume are by Peter A. Nisbet.

A word needs to be said about problems related to sexism. First, the thrust of this book is on the affective. When we speak of the affective we are ordinarily speaking of persons as individuals. Thus more inclusive terms frequently are not appropriate to what the various authors are saying.

Second, language usage usually follows the thrust of an idea. Although most sensitive persons are aware of the problems of sexism in our society, terms which take the place of the generic use of "man," "mankind," and the pronoun "he" are frequently awkward to use. Thus, since language does not yet accommodate to the abolishment of sexism, common generic terms, but perhaps what some may see as sexist ones, were used in order not to unduly distort ideas. We hope the reader will understand the dilemma of the writers and editors and tackle the substantive issues with which the authors were dealing rather than the technicalities of language still to be resolved.

Foreword

*P*eriodically a book is published that makes a difference in American education. *Perceiving, Behaving, Becoming,* published in 1962 by ASCD was just such a book. It made a difference in public and private schools, in teacher education programs, in curriculum development, in supervision, and in teaching. From it, educators learned there is hope for all learners, that a learner's self-concept is important in daily performance, and that self-concept can be enhanced.

The impact of the book was broadened during the 1960's by writings of third-force theorists and others insisting that an intermediate variable between stimulus and response is an important factor in human behavior. Most of these writers can now be grouped as supportive of what we call humanistic education.

Paralleling the national conception of humanistic education was the continuing growth and understanding of behaviorism and its possible applications in education. Operant conditioning, behavior modification, and use of behavioral objectives became common in the context of the accountability movement of the early 1970's.

Now ASCD publishes its 1977 Yearbook: *Feeling, Valuing, and the Art of Growing: Insights into the Affective.* Once again, we have a book that can make a difference in American education.

Here we find a synthesis of the learning activities of the past fifteen years. Although some may have feared that behaviorism and humanistic education were on a collision course, thoughtful educational leadership has been working for more rewarding directions of these forces toward mutually acceptable goals. This book brilliantly lights the way for such leadership. It clarifies the value of both forces in our schools and educational programs. It helps the reader understand the principles and meanings underlying humanistic education as well as the thinking of fourth and fifth generation behaviorists. It sharpens our perceptions and aids our becoming.

In my view, the authors speak well for ASCD and its position. This book may even be seen as a position paper for ASCD and American education throughout the remaining years of the twentieth century. Some may reject the position. Many may not understand it. But let no one *misunderstand* one aspect. Nowhere in the position defined in this Yearbook does one find advocacy for a "retreat from the basics." Rather, one first finds a firm insistence on a broader goal of knowledge, attitudes, and skills. Competencies required for life functions are part of that broad goal, but they *are* only a part. Other aspects are just as important and just as deserving of time, support, and intelligent evaluation efforts. Second, one finds authentic insistence that the processes used to achieve a goal can sometimes be more important than the goal achievement itself. Hence, many processes become goals in themselves, just as the activity of play is its own goal.

I am proud to have the opportunity to introduce this book to the American education scene. It has the potential to make a lasting difference there.

PHILIP L. HOSFORD, *President 1976-77*
Association for Supervision
and Curriculum Development

Introduction

"... Now We See Through A Glass Darkly...." [1]

❧

How rich, varied, and marvelous is the person! Endowed with a miraculous ability to make sense out of the richness of perceptions, impressions, and experiences, the person has infinite possibilities. Such infinite versatility and complexity can both enhance and deteriorate a human being's personhood.

The individual can simultaneously probe deeply into innermost thoughts while reaching expansively into the world. The ability to turn inward allows one to live a life that is personally satisfying. The opportunity to encounter the richness of the outer world permits one to live in community with others. Qualities of being alone and being in communion must combine in the same person to assure a rich, full life.

If the person were not so versatile and complex, ideal environments might be constructed which would encourage the person to move toward some idealized standard in a planned manner. But

[1] 1 Cor. 13:12, King James Version.

1

such is not the case. Consider a few contradictory qualities of persons.

The person can, because of an innate curiosity, search diligently for answers to a problem, yet can sometimes drive teachers and parents to distraction because of laziness. The person can sometimes develop unique inventions and at other times be content to rely solely on the inventions of others. The person can sometimes reach out to others in gestures of caring and at other times behave as though the wellsprings of affection were utterly drained.

The person may sometimes climb tirelessly to new heights and at other times be dragged down by petty annoyances, irritabilities, and hurts. The person may sometimes search diligently for new understandings and yet give up when feeling lack of support in the search. The person may be thoughtful about the rightness and wrongness of situations and yet be bewildered by shades of gray often found in ethical and moral dilemmas. The person often wants to be part of a group, but simultaneously may cherish solitude. The person may be humble in some situations, proud in others; sometimes inspiring but frequently wanting to be inspired. The person is a delight, a puzzle, a maze, a living but, simultaneously, a dying being.

In trying to satisfy the thirst for more penetrating insights into the person, poets, anthropologists, physical and social scientists, theologians, and lay persons have submerged themselves in gathering data, developing theories, and considering images. But still we know so little.

Among those who should be concerned about the problem of the person's heritage, present capabilities, and future potentials are educators. Yet, how frequently only partial, even inaccurate, and miniscule images of the person are taken into account in planning school curricula. Curricular theories vacillate, sometimes describing the human being as a doer or a behaver. In such theories only what is observed is taken into account in curriculum planning. Other theories focus upon the person as an enquirer, but frequently these theories so carefully spell out the how and what of inquiry that the areas into which the student is interested in inquiring are ignored. Again theories may focus upon the acquisition of facts, principles, or generalizations. Or, at the other extreme, we find theories which call for educators to abdicate professional responsibility as the child unfolds.

We all know the story too well. We all know about the wealth of how-to-do-it books that flood the market, but how many of them are built on solid and thoughtful images of the person? We all know about the excessive emphasis given to performance on standardized achievement tests which evaluate only low-level cognitive skills. Current curricular patterns frequently ignore, repress, deny, or negate those aspects of the person that add richness, color, and texture to human living. We do indeed see through a glass darkly.

The Plan of the Book

Initially when we were asked to write a book about the affective domain, we had some reservations, for even as much of the literature dealing with cognition deals with lower level processes, so much of the literature on the affective deals with lower level feeling behavior. Therefore, we sought to take the affective beyond the realm of pure pleasure, delight, or feeling. We felt that the affective basically is concerned with maturing, growing, and becoming more complete persons. Thus the title of the book: *Feeling, Valuing, and the Art of Growing: Insights into the Affective*.

For help in our striving to see persons more clearly we asked individuals representing a variety of walks of life to contribute chapters. Insights into human development and social foundations are found in Part One. Chapter 1 broadly outlines images of humankind. Chapter 2 deals with the problem of settings as they relate to the affective. Part Two includes insights from a number of fields which we felt might shed light on our understanding of the affective. Persons with expertise in writing, in art, in the physical sciences, in philosophy, in the psychology of groups, and in human behavior shared ideas that might help us understand more fully what we mean by the affective. The similarities and differences of these writers are interesting to note. Part Three is a discussion of schooling which attempts to give consideration to the person as a feeling, valuing, growing being. Attention is given to means of describing what the schools are currently doing in the affective domain. Included in Chapter 9 is "The Involvement Instrument" which is one way of considering a process possessing many affective components. Chapter 10 then projects what the school might look like if attention were given to the affective. Finally, the curriculum worker is presented as a key person in shifting the emphasis toward the whole person. This book is designed to help us see the affective a little more clearly and also to give major attention to higher level affective processes.

Why the Book

Recent years have seen some frightening developments in education. First, across the country one finds evidence of undue censorship of educational materials. Although certain kinds of caution should be exercised in deciding what is appropriate for the young, on the other hand, the attempts to prevent children from dealing with and thinking about the moral dilemmas of our times encourage a safe but bland curriculum. Thus, one reason for the book is to present some perspectives on the affective which call for the individual to deal with areas of life which may be controversial but meaningful.

Related to this issue are other conditions which make educators reluctant to deal in any area in which questions might be raised by parents, pressure groups, or administrators who have the power to cause teachers to lose their jobs. The result again is a program which may lack the vitality to be of major interest to those involved in it.

A third development which seems to preclude attention to the affective is a growing attention to achievement in reading as measured by standardized tests. Basically neglecting the why of reading, persons place untoward emphasis on narrowly defined programs which develop a limited range of skills but which may not evoke strong feelings on the part of the student.

Lastly and perhaps most basically, as a group of professional persons we have not been concerned enough that our students find delight in learning, develop interests which are absorbing, exercise judgment in discriminating among alternatives, and become committed to the worthwhile. This book sheds light on images of the person and school experiences that make sense when wholeness, maturity, and commitment to ideals are seen as the goals of the school.

Suggestions for Reading This Book

Although many readers will read through the book chapter by chapter, others may look only at parts that particularly interest them. Still others will place the book on the shelf, perhaps for future reference.

For those who choose to look at the book fairly carefully we would like to suggest one way of examining it. We have selected some broad topics: definitions of the affective, views of the person, settings and the affective, and school programs which enhance the affective. For each of these topics we have suggested some places to look or ideas for extension or follow-up of themes of this work. For the reader's convenience we have set up a series of If . . . Then . . . statements in columnar form.

Definitions of Affect

If you want . . .	**Then . . .**
To see the different levels at which affect may be present and get some idea of the complexity of the process	Study the framework for analyzing affective behavior developed by Phenix. Consider the wholeness of the process (Beittel). Think about basic human processes such as decision making, valuing, loving, etc., as they relate to the affective (Hedges-Martinello). Consider play as a source of insight about affect (Yamamoto and Berman). Consider "all-rightness" and its relation to affect (L'Engle). Consider involvement as a means of drawing together various components of affect (Roderick). Consider the moral and its relation to affect (Simpson).

Views of the Person

If you want . . .	**Then . . .**
To contemplate richer, fuller views of the person *To see the human being as an amazing culture-making, culture-maintaining person*	Develop explicit alternatives to the behavioral model (Patterson). Build upon the fuller images of humankind shared by Yamamoto, Berman, Hedges-Martinello, Roderick.

To find support for helping children and youth learn wholes instead of discrete parts

See how a potter goes about working (Beittel).
See the problem of children being faced with an endless array of seeming dichotomies (Webb).
See the necessity of dealing with wholes in the involvement process (Roderick).
See the work of Fair.

To understand recent trends in the physical sciences as they relate to the affective

Settings and the Affective

If you want ...

Then ...

To think about the relationship of friendly and unfriendly environments to affective development

See Webb's chapter.

To study settings which seem to induce wholeness in behavior

Study the potter's setting described by Beittel and qualities of settings conducive to involvement (L'Engle).

To understand time in relation to the affective domain

Consider the difference between *kairos* (inner lived time) and *chronos* (physical or clock time) referred to by L'Engle, Beittel, and Phenix.

School Programs and the Affective

If you want ...

Then ...

To ensure student interest

Try an integrated approach to learning (Hedges-Martinello).

To ensure that schools remain a part of society

Go beyond the intellectual into personal and social development. Much of intellectual development can be accomplished via computers.

To ensure that the child can live wisely in a given culture

Plan the program so that the content of the student's conscience is developed (Simpson).

To plan programs that provide opportunities for students to develop many aspects of personhood

Make sure the activities of the school are real (L'Engle) and firsthand (Hedges-Martinello and Roderick).

To establish a school setting that provides opportunity for the learner to acquire the most valuable contribution the school can make

Provide opportunities for children to learn to make sense out of life (Hedges-Martinello).

To explore the tension between mastery of an area and mystery inherent in human living

See how a potter deals with this dichotomy (Beittel).

To get a grasp of the personal and the mythical as it relates to the affective

See the attention given to myth by Beittel and L'Engle.

To look at a person's needs as an individual and as a member of a group

Read and compare the insights provided by Simpson and Patterson.

To understand how relevance can influence the affective

Knowingly plan programs which possess varying degrees of relevance to specific learners (Hedges-Martinello).

To find evaluation procedures compatible with the affective domain

Try describing what a person says and does through diary-fashion recordings or the use of observational systems (Roderick). Concentrate on growth from benchline data rather than idiographic comparisons (Hedges-Martinello).

Use the Phenix typology.

To help students examine concepts from the affective domain in a systematic manner

To assist curriculum workers to be instrumental in developing programs with a heavy emphasis on the affective

Examine ideas in the Berman chapter.

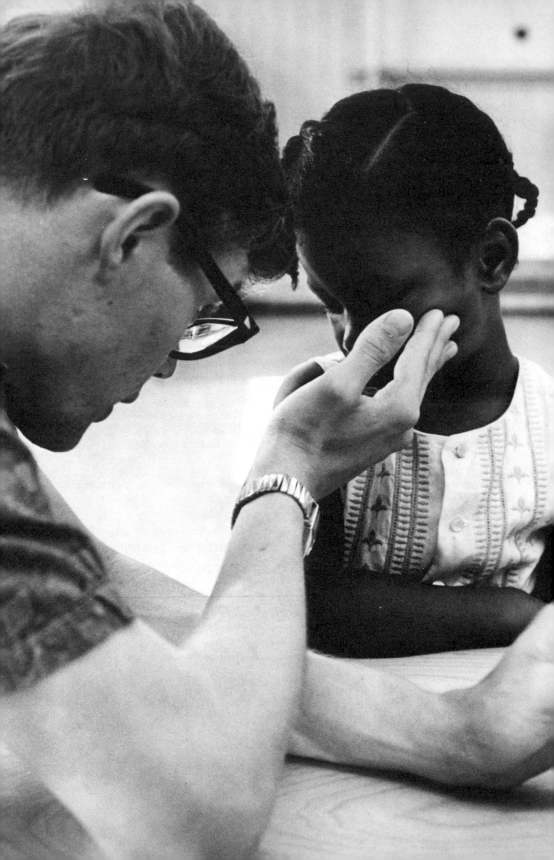

Part One

Humankind in Settings: A Case for the Affective

*H*umankind is alone and yet part of a larger setting. Every person can think, feel, and value, yet simultaneously be trapped within settings which tend to cut off basic human qualities. The person is a reflecting, pondering being who can consider his or her place in the universe. Each of us has a highly specialized mind, the depths of which have not begun to be probed.

Each can, at least to some degree, create the conditions which satisfy the self. At the same time, we all at times feel ourselves to be in a state of disequilibrium or in an environment which appears to be unfriendly or out of our control. The tension between persons and settings is an old story—ever so poignant, ever so real, ever so demanding of attention.

In the two chapters which follow we have the unresolved riddle of human existence. Yamamoto, with his unusual ability for probing the depths of humankind, depicts the glory and the responsibility of the person. He uses the concept of play to tease out some provocative ideas about persons. Persons at play are most perfectly human, for in play we have the opportunity to be in control, to create new vistas, to integrate insights into new wholes (also a quality of meditation), and to apply the discipline and structure necessary to most successful endeavors.

9

Having observed the rebellions and revolts of the past several years, Webb describes settings which are in many ways hostile to the person. In his observation, the person finds himself or herself acquiescing to the demands of the setting or breaking out in rebel fashion from the shackles which prevent living fully and positively. Only the creative person, according to Webb, is apt to survive the "dehumanizing nature of bureaucratic institutions." "The combination of commitment to truth, inquiry, and activism, as well as concern for the impact of action on the social world, helps the creative individual to keep whole in a pluralistic society." [1]

Within recent years much attention has been given to the interaction of persons and settings. One has only to review the work of Rudolf Moos, Roger Barker, and Edwin P. Willems to realize that neither an existentialist viewpoint nor an environmentalist viewpoint alone is adequate to explain human behavior. We need some blend of the two. Yamamoto and Webb start our thinking about persons as feeling, valuing, and growing within complex and sometimes unfriendly settings.

[1] For a compilation of certain of the literature on the creative person, see: Louis J. Rubin, editor. *Life Skills in School and Society.* 1969 Yearbook. Washington, D.C.: Association for Supervision and Curriculum Development, 1969.

1

Humankind: Shadows and Images

Kaoru Yamamoto

"**M**an is a conscious reed," said Blaise Pascal. A being as weak as a wind-swept reed, a being so fragile that it takes little more than a drop of water to destroy it. Human, nevertheless, is a special kind of reed, a reed aware of its own finitude and capable of self-reflection. Throughout its existence, the reed has pondered things within, things without, and its place in the total scheme of the immense universe.

Homo sapiens is indeed a peculiar creature, not merely because it has stood erect to free its hands for purposive development and uses of tools, not only because it has evolved a highly specialized brain to facilitate the adaptation process necessary for its survival, but also and primarily because of the virtual impossibility of its recreation.

Life, even cellular life, may exist out yonder in the dark. But high or low in nature, it will not wear the shape of man. That shape is the evolutionary product of a strange, long wandering through the attics of the forest roof, and so great are the chances of failure, that nothing precisely and identically human is likely ever to come that way again.[1]

[1] Loren Eiseley. *The Immense Journey*. New York: Random House, Inc., 1957. pp. 160-61.

11

Human beings are different and alone. They are the only ones who may understand, as well as misunderstand, themselves, and who can bestow dignity, as well as indignity, upon each other. They have essentially no one else with whom to share their experiences of splendor and depravity, grandeur and pettiness, ecstasy and agony. If schooling is to have anything to do with education and education with humanization, schools must strive to nurture in their students a full awareness of this solitary nature of mankind, and of the inevitable oneness of human fate beyond the realms of immediate historical and geographical concern. That humans possess an immense potential for both good and bad no one would deny but, without continuous search for self-knowledge, they can readily turn against themselves to ring a death knell for all the family of humankind.

The Perennial Enigma

Human beings have long puzzled over who they are and what their life is about. The questions have remained the same but the proposed answers have varied across time, space, and people. Successive epochs have seen different ideas and sentiments about our relationships with nature (including life forms other than human), artifacts, fellow human beings, and oneself. In other words, each age built a model of a person and acted accordingly toward the self, others, things, and events. Life was described, explained, and regulated in terms of the dominant image of humankind, and all the models and the attendant elaborations have made up the human cultural heritage.

Stars Above

One marvels at the stars in the firmament, wonders about unfathomable depths of an ocean, stands in awe of lofty peaks, and trembles in the face of quakes and winds. Who, or what, gives rise to all these, and how? Where do we belong? Whence do we come, and where do we go? These queries have led to diverse interpretations of man vis-à-vis nature. In some instances, nothing but chaos and cataclysm is seen for the universe, and our existence is as meaningless an accident as anything else. "Vanity of vanities, says the Preacher, vanity of vanities! All is vanity. What does man gain by all the toil at which he toils under the sun?" [2]

[2] Eccles. 1:2-3.

Kaoru Yamamoto * *is currently Professor of Education at Arizona State University. He has been interested in the exploration of developmental processes, mental health in education, and humane inquiry into human affairs. His publications include* College Student and His Culture *(1968),* Teaching *(1969),* The Child and His Image *(1972),* Individuality *(1975), and* Death in the Life of Children *(1977). He is a Fellow of the American Psychological Association, and the immediate past editor of the* American Educational Research Journal.

Equally pessimistic, so far as humankind's potential influence on its own fate is concerned, is the view that it resides in a universe totally designed and controlled by a benign divine scheme.[3] Unlike the tumultuous picture seen above, lawfulness and regularity are restored to the universe. Nevertheless, things here proceed inexorably toward their prearranged state of perfection with or without human beings. In other words, humankind is not at the center of this cosmos characterized by order and harmony.

Different images may be drawn, however, once humans affirm the possibility of changing the course of history through their own will and action. In some instances, the primal force, be it identified as gods, spirits, or whatever, may be perceived as basically benevolent. Here, humans can potentially affect their destiny either passively through prayer or actively through work. In the familiar Western theological terms, a person may be saved either by grace or by merit. The second coming of Christ epitomizes the desired result in this context. It should also be noted that the juxtaposition

* In keeping with the emphasis on persons in this book, each author was requested to write his/her brief autobiographical statement.

[3] These contrasting interpretations are neatly summarized by Fred Polak by using the two dimensions of *Sein* (essence) and *Willen* (influence), each of which is dichotomized into optimism and pessimism. In: *The Images of the Future*. San Francisco: Jossey-Bass, Inc., Publishers, 1973.

of unconditional with conditional modes of acceptance and love is abundantly clear in many child rearing, as well as schooling, practices.

Others, particularly of non-Western traditions, have often expressed their feelings of basic trust, or of being one and at ease with the whole creation, in poetic words of wisdom such as the following:

> Now this is what we believe.
> The mother of us all is earth.
> The Father is the sun.
> The Grandfather is the Creator
> Who bathed us with his mind
> And gave life to all things. -
> The Brother is the beasts and trees.
> The Sister is that with wings.
> We are the Children of Earth
> And do it no harm in any way.
> Nor do we offend the sun
> By not greeting it at dawn.
> We praise our Grandfather for his creation.
> We share the same breath together—
> The beasts, the trees, the birds, the man.[4]

If, on the other hand, the primal force is regarded as less than benevolent, not to say downright malevolent, passive strategies of human beings would go beyond prayers, as commonly understood, to seek appeasement and reconciliation. Various forms of sacrifice-making and bargaining may be resorted to here, a well-known example being one's handling of approaching death.[5]

In contrast, active efforts may hinge upon the uses of rationality and technology. We subdue, conquer, and exploit nature to our (alleged) advantage. The spirit of classic science has neutralized and mechanized external powers, and humans have conceived their own utopias that are probably unlivable but at least logical.[6] In all this, the importance attached to artifacts is undeniable and, alas, one's

[4] Nancy Wood. *Many Winters*. Garden City, New York: Doubleday & Company, Inc., 1974. p. 18. Copyright © 1974 by Nancy Wood. Illustrations copyright by Frank Howell. Reprinted by permission.

[5] Elisabeth Kübler-Ross. *On Death and Dying*. New York: Macmillan Publishing Co., Inc., 1969.

[6] Familiar examples of recent origin include: Aldous Huxley. *Brave New World*. New York: Bantam Books, Inc., 1958; George Orwell. *1984*. New York: The New American Library, Inc., 1949; and B. F. Skinner. *Walden Two*. New York: Macmillan Publishing Co., Inc., 1948.

relationship with others has come to resemble that between a man and his cherished possessions and products.[7] It is indeed a part of the human irony that the original affirmation of one's autonomy and power has led to one's self being reduced to the material sphere of things!

Man Within

The dominant interpretation of the universe as the Great Machine has found its counterpart in the image of *Homo ex Machina*.[8] Throughout the nineteenth century and much of the twentieth, ostensibly differing views of human beings have been presented in the forms of, for example, the biological being determined by hereditary givens (Darwin), psychological being under the control of life and death instincts (Freud), or sociological being caught up in the economic system (Marx). On scrutiny, however, most of them reveal some fundamental similarities to betray their common origin.

One of these parallel features is the perception of individuals as fundamentally inert entities that are manipulated by some alien agents. These forces may be located within the person (instincts, drives, needs, etc.) or outside the person (stimuli, rewards, incentives, etc.). The essence of the story is the same in both cases: "The devil made me do it!" The person as an actor vanishes and, in place of the person, an object is found, being under the control of one or any combination of these determinants. It merely adds to the irony to see this "object" referred to as "the subject" in *scholarly* reports on studies of social-behavioral sciences.[9]

In typical theories of human behaviors today, an individual is activated by certain drives to make responses to particular stimuli, and the so-called drive reduction or gratification reinforces these responses to bring about an altered likelihood for their recurrence. The person, as depicted here, does not act, but merely reacts until a balance has been restored among the various forces at work. Needless to say, the same mechanism applies to all sorts of inanimate objects, ranging from heavenly bodies to elemental particles. If we learn the directions and magnitudes of the operative forces, the behavior of humankind should become as predictable and con-

[7] Erich Fromm. *The Sane Society*. New York: Holt, Rinehart & Winston, Inc., 1955.

[8] Floyd W. Matson. *The Broken Image*. Garden City, New York: Doubleday & Company, Inc., 1966.

[9] Kaoru Yamamoto. *Individuality: The Unique Learner*. Columbus, Ohio: Charles E. Merrill Publishing Company, 1975.

trollable as that of any physical object. To that end, we observe, describe, forecast, and manipulate.

Unfortunately, the traditional, homeostatic model is closed in nature, and it is largely past-oriented. A good example is that diagrammed in Figure 1, a system suitable in closed computer designs

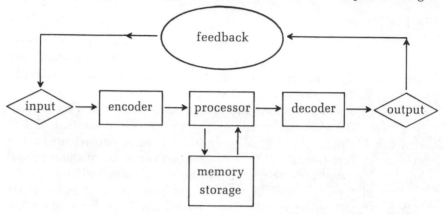

Figure 1. An example of a closed system model.

but applied by some to open human functions.[10] When so adapted to living organisms, however, this neat scheme fails to account for the fact that organisms opt for growth rather than stability, for change rather than immutability, and for active becoming rather than passive being.[11]

Even at the cost of considerable disruption and discomfort, human beings seek to go beyond their present equilibrium or steady state for further individuation.[12] All kinds of exploratory and mastery activities, which are playful, spontaneous, curious, and creative, cannot be subsumed under merely utilitarian, balance-maintaining views of humankind. Without these challenge-seeking and discontinuity-producing actions a person, as well as an institution, misses the vital instrument for innovation and self-renewal.[13] Another way of saying this is to characterize humans as forward-looking, purposive beings. Their eyes are firmly fixed on the future, on what

[10] A case in point is: James C. Chalfant and Margaret A. Scheffelin. *Central Processing Dysfunctions in Children: A Review of Research.* Washington, D.C.: U.S. Government Printing Office, 1969.

[11] Gordon W. Allport. "The Open System in Personality Theory." In: *Personality and Social Encounter.* Boston: Beacon Press, 1960. pp. 39-54.

[12] Ludwig von Bertalanffy. *General System Theory.* New York: George Braziller, Inc., 1968.

[13] John W. Gardner. *Self-Renewal.* New York: Harper and Row, Publishers, 1965.

is possible and potential, and they are not powerless captives of the present and past.[14]

Paradoxically, man is much more than who he is. The "dilemma may lie in the fact that, while trying to be what he is, he cannot help attempting to become what he is not."[15] Throughout life, the individual searches for meaning in an ever-larger frame of reference, and is concerned with ever-expanding realms, from a small ego-centric sphere first to wider social theaters, then to humankind as a whole, and finally to the total cosmic scene.[16] This is indeed a striking facet of the mystery and wonder of the feeble reed.

The Reservoir

In any case, the human enigma must be individually puzzled over by every person for full appreciation of its complexity and significance. In his or her own way, each has to, and does, form an image of what a person is, no matter how crude or limited it might be. After all, no one can grow for someone else, and no one can live a borrowed life. The person's autonomy and dignity surely hinge upon this effort to build one's own unique model, because a human being is only "free to the extent that he makes choices, that he consciously strives to design his life, that he accepts personal responsibility for his behavior."[17]

In the choice-making process, informed decisions can only be made when based upon an untrammeled consideration of all possible alternatives and their consequences. The challenge for education as a freeing and enhancing endeavor is to provide people, young and old alike, with an uncurtailed view of the rich legacy of humankind, and to encourage them, in their personal unravelling of the common enigma, to choose wisely from the full spectrum of our cultural heritage. If anyone or anything thwarts them of the opportunity to reach, and draw freely and liberally from, the rich reservoir of human experience, the individual is truly deprived—

[14] Charlotte Bühler and Melanie Allen. *Introduction to Humanistic Psychology.* Belmont, California: Brooks/Cole, 1972.

[15] Kaoru Yamamoto. "Man in Urban America." In: Edwin L. Herr, editor. *Vocational Guidance and Human Development.* Boston: Houghton Mifflin Company, 1974. p. 83.

[16] Ernest Becker. *The Structure of Evil.* New York: George Braziller, Inc., 1968; Viktor Frankl. *Man's Search for Meaning.* New York: Washington Square Press, 1963.

[17] Chris Argyris. "Essay Review of B. F. Skinner, *Beyond Freedom and Dignity." Harvard Educational Review* 41:561; November 1971. Copyright © 1971 by President and Fellows of Harvard College.

deprived, most profoundly, of his or her own roots, because that is where the cumulative record is found of all previous human efforts for self-understanding and where all the varied images are seen of humankind at the height of glory as well as in the depth of misery. That is what makes any *cultural deprivation* so seriously handicapping: not the absence of myriad amenities as such, not the immediate lack of socially useful means and skills, and certainly not the alleged differences in the styles of life. Without an awareness of, and a ready access to, this vast reservoir of culture, we are ignorant and easily fall prey to arrogance, bigotry, and despair. We fail, in other words, to become fully human under such circumstances.

Some might spurn the concept of human roots and reject the past as irrelevant or even undesirable. Change is the only reality, they would argue, and progress is their catchword. However, locomotion is inconceivable in the absence of certain fixed loci to reference its direction, level, distance, or speed. Likewise, change must be predicated upon permanence if it is to be purposeful. A rudderless ship may move endlessly, but its navigation is utterly random. Newness only for the sake of newness, change merely for change's sake, is chaotic. Without a basic sense of stability and strength of tradition as the secure springboard for considered action in the present and future, all the frantic activities of humankind are doomed by their blindness. "Tradition is the cement of continuity. . . . It preserves the pride of the past for the education of the future. It gives the significance of time to the actions of the present and the meaning of a defined place in history to the everyday behavior of the individual." [18]

How, then, should we lead our charges to a touching encounter with the precious legacy of the multitude who have gone before them? How would we help them in their exploration into this immense heritage, and in their examination of numerous models, alternatives, and opportunities? How do we facilitate formulation and revision of their own, hopefully more considered and more humane, images of human beings that serve as a tentative guide in their ongoing quest for identity and meaning? These are but a few of the urgent queries before us educators. First, however, are we ourselves fully aware of what is in that reservoir, and how our school curriculum draws from it? That is the question posed for this particular Yearbook.

[18] Leontine Young. *Wednesday's Children.* New York: McGraw-Hill Book Company, 1964. p. 108. Copyright © by Leontine Young. Reprinted by permission.

Needless to say, it would be futile to attempt, in a single slim tome, to duplicate voluminous encyclopedias. We shall, instead, try to give a glimpse of diverse perspectives on humankind's understanding of its place vis-à-vis nature, artifacts, other beings, and itself. To begin, in Chapter 2, Webb explores the nature of this cultural reservoir with all its currents, pools, shoals, and backwaters.

In Part Two, six authors share some new insights gleaned from their respective areas of endeavor. The treatise ranges from examination of the biological roots of humankind (Fair in Chapter 6) to that of its moral knowledge (Phenix in Chapter 3). An exposition on arting is presented in Chapter 5 (Beittel). *Homo sapiens* is described as a being that dreams (L'Engle in Chapter 4), plays (the rest of this chapter), interacts (Simpson in Chapter 8), and contemplates itself (Patterson in Chapter 7). The reservoir is indeed deep and the water is wide.

Finally, in Part Three, the focus is turned to the familiar ground of the school, and the challenge for educators is delineated. The possible contribution of formal education is viewed both in the present (Roderick in Chapter 9) and for the future (Martinello and Hedges in Chapter 10). In the concluding chapter, Berman studies the implications of all these discussions for curriculum workers of today and tomorrow. The Yearbook Committee's hope is that this volume succeeds in throwing further light upon the uniqueness of the human being as both a creator and a creature of culture.

The Child at Play

If we take a fresh look, the enigmatic character of human life, repeatedly mentioned in the preceding section, is observable everywhere. As an example, take such a seemingly simple matter as children's play. "Man is perfectly human," said the German poet, Friedrich von Schiller, "only when he plays." This is perhaps so because play epitomizes the unique juxtaposition of opposites in humankind. Through the means of play, a person is transformed from a powerless pawn in the world to its ruler. Play represents "the human ability to deal with experience by creating model situations and to master reality by experiment and planning." [19] Nurturance of such ability is obviously critical for the development of the sense of competence and self-confidence. The child believes in, and practices, control over various facets of life within the play

[19] Erik H. Erikson. *Childhood and Society*. Second edition. New York: W. W. Norton & Company, Inc., 1963. p. 222.

sphere. Thus the child is a living invitation for exploration, integration, and transcendence.

To Be the Master

"Fantasy is an exploration of living reality, and play a rehearsal of living reality, and we use them both as tools of growth that will help us first understand our reality, and then help us shape it with awareness and competence." [20]   The child at play is removed far enough from exigencies of actuality to engage safely in reformulation of experience so as to relive, digest, and absorb it into his expanding life space. He is doing this on his own accord in his own time at his own pace—here, *he* is in charge of things and people, not the other way around. The ego rules, and the process of assimilation (after Piaget) predominates.[21]

In play, the child is the master of the situation and the actor in command of his fate, rather than a passive object at the mercy of alien forces. Here, in contrast with commonly held views, the child is a self-directing being in control, developing and savoring the precious outlook of competence and autonomy.

He is tasting and re-tasting life in his own terms and finding it full of delight and interest. He projects his own pattern of the world into the play and in so doing, brings the real world closer to himself. He is building the feeling that the world is his, to understand, to interpret, to puzzle about, to make over. For the future, we need citizens in whom these attitudes are deeply ingrained.[22]

Openness is one of the basic elements in play. Exploration of different possibilities in a secure environment without any premature judgments and screening of feelings—that is what nurtures and heals. The experience serves not merely as release of tension but also as confirmation of one's deeper resources and as reintegration of one's total being. While these principles are most dramatically demonstrated in therapeutic uses of play,[23] and in some instances

[20] Leila Berg. *Look at Kids.* Baltimore: Penguin Books, Inc., 1972. p. 120. Copyright © 1972 by Leila Berg.

[21] Jean Piaget. *Play, Dreams, and Imitation in Childhood.* New York: W. W. Norton & Company, Inc., 1962.

[22] Barbara Biber. "The Role of Play." *Vassar Alumnae Magazine* 37(2): 1951. Reissued 1959, 1963, and 1965. Reprinted by permission.

[23] Three readable descriptions of play therapy may be found in the following: Virginia M. Axline. *Dibs in Search of Self.* New York: Ballantine Books, Inc., 1964; Dorothy W. Baruch. *One Little Boy.* New York: Dell Publishing Co., 1964; Richard D'Ambrosio. *No Language but a Cry.* New York: Dell Publishing Co., Inc., 1970.

of remedial education,[24] the same dynamics would apply to all play activities. Unfortunately, we adults close off many potential avenues of exploration with our hasty acts of intervention, thus dampening the child's curiosity and curtailing his or her autonomy. Berg gives a good example as follows:

> A friend told me recently that she was watching a child build a sandcastle and not succeeding, and found herself very surprised the child didn't lose her temper; almost she decided to help the child. Much later, still thinking about the child's surprising self-control, she suddenly realized the child wasn't building a sandcastle at all—but that she, the adult, assumed that was what she was doing, and therefore that she was failing. If we look at children from the height of the little hill we have captured, they are bound to seem unsuccessful adults. Unfortunately we have the power to act on our arrogant and mistaken assessment of the situation, and generally do so. So we hurry on, desperately trying to organize the chaos that is building up in our own untranquil mind, listening only to what the child would mean if he were adult and not to what the child is saying.[25]

So, but Not So

Aldous Huxley once characterized the human being as "a multiple amphibian," [26] existing simultaneously in many dissimilar universes: both a visceral being of reflexes, sensations, and emotions, and a cerebral being of cognition, memory, and thought. Part of the world of the concrete, the human being yet builds and lives largely in a world of the abstract or symbolic; a self-centered creature, yet also a member of a rather gregarious species. Rational in consciousness the human being is, at the same time, bound to a nonrational subconscious. Play is a medium by which the human may probe and expand the self to fulfill his potential as the inhabitant of all these seemingly incompatible universes.

Of particular relevance here is the sense of unrealness that underlies play. According to Marett, this element of make-believe is found in all so-called "primitive" religions and child's play. Both the believers and playing children are good actors in that they can get quite absorbed in their roles. They are serious, and that also makes them good spectators.[27] They can be scared stiff by the

[24] Sara Smilansky. *The Effects of Sociodramatic Play on Disadvantaged Preschool Children.* New York: John Wiley & Sons, Inc., 1968.

[25] Berg, *op. cit.*, p. 22.

[26] Aldous Huxley. "Education on the Nonverbal Level." *Daedalus* 91: 279-93; Spring 1962.

[27] R. R. Marett. In: Johan Huizinga. *Homo Ludens.* Boston: Beacon Press, 1955.

roaring of something that they are well aware to be no lion; they can be moved to panic by the dying of something that they know fully well to be no tree.

Recognized also by such astute observers of children as Chukovsky and Piaget, this awareness of the *so, but not so* state of affairs carries some far-reaching implications. It is to be recalled that much confusion has been caused by the Aristotelian way of thinking that says, "*A* is *A*," or "If *A*, never not-*A*." This is the familiar either/or orientation, in which a clear dichotomy is postulated to give polarized judgments.[28] Thus, anyone who has been convicted of a violent crime is all evil and cannot possibly have any tender feelings toward others. Children classified as slow can hardly be expected to learn much about anything. There are only two kinds of men (the courageous and the weak), women (the pure and the bad), or races (the superior and the inferior). There is only one right way to do anything, and a single correct answer to every question. Sanctions are thus given categorically, and various forms of prejudice are sustained on this kind of argument. As a result, the world is deprived of much human richness and depth in the name of precision and logic.

Fortunately, humankind is both *A and* non-*A*, a devil *and* an angel, a sinner *and* a saint, and a coward *and* a hero: a being so complex as to defy any pigeonholing in a simple niche, or two or ten. In playing, children can and do jump freely across many categorical boundaries to remind us that all these classifications were originally intended to help clarify our experience, never to bind us and blind our vision. Life is "variegated and flexible, allowing a limitless number of variations. . . . In truth, at times, the child does not so much adapt himself to the truth as he adapts the truth to himself, for the sake of an imaginary play situation." [29]

Life cannot be stopped and resumed at will, but play can. It is remarkable to see how effortlessly children step in and out of the play sphere, thus protecting both the so-called fantasy and reality. They can freely experience and examine many taboo feelings or thoughts in the world of make-believe. Moreover, they can safely leave them there until ready to recognize and accept them in

[28] S. I. Hayakawa. *Language in Thought and Action.* Third edition. New York: Harcourt Brace Jovanovich, Inc., 1972.

[29] Kornei Chukovsky. *From Two to Five.* Berkeley, California: University of California Press, 1963. p. 27. Copyright © 1963 by Miriam Morton. Reprinted by permission.

the other world. The fact that they can move from one to the other with ease serves as an essential safeguard for growth.

The paradox here is, of course, that play itself is a part of life. Perhaps, a more apt expression may have been that "life *can* be stopped and resumed at will," at least in play. In the same way, time cannot be readily compressed and expanded—but it can! Indeed, the child at play is an amphibian across multiple spheres of time; the physical time, psychological time, cultural time, and Great Time (over against the passing time).[30] A playing child can get free of the grip of linearity. A moment's reflection will show how completely dependent we are upon this notion of linear progression; it is found in the way we organize, for example, our daily schedule and calendar, schooling, career, and language. Most adults are so caught up in the serial structure (one thing at a time, leading to the next) as to take it for granted, never even wondering about diverse paths of development, different ways of grouping students and arranging curriculum, or alternative modes of communication. The child, however, does still wonder and wander.

New Vistas

Among the many boundaries freely crossed or straddled by the child are those within the play sphere itself. These realms have been described variously, but mostly in developmental terms. Thus, for example, Erikson has children moving from autocosmic sphere (playing with one's own body) to microsphere (the small world of manageable toys) to macrosphere (the world shared with others).[31] Piaget applies a tripartite scheme to activities beyond the nascent stage of the first two years: practice games (exercise for the pleasure of exercise or of being the cause), symbolic games (involving make-believe representation of absent elements), and games with group-sanctioned rules.[32] Moore and Anderson differentiate four perspectives to be cultivated in play: the agent perspective (through puzzles that fit together with certainty), patient perspective (through games of chance with much uncertainty), reciprocal perspective (through games of strategy, in which assumption of others' viewpoints

---

[30] Our discussion here cannot do justice to this important subject of time. For further study, see such sources as: Jean Piaget. *The Child's Conception of Time.* New York: Ballantine Books, 1971; J. B. Priestley, *Man and Time.* New York: Dell Publishing Co., Inc., 1968; and Henri Yaker, Humphry Osmond, and Frances Cheek, editors. *The Future of Time.* Garden City, New York: Doubleday & Company, Inc., 1972.

[31] Erikson, *op. cit.*

[32] Piaget, *op. cit.*

becomes indispensable), and referee's perspective (through an overall judgment of aesthetic qualities in games).[33]

In all these formulations, the critical feature seems that children try out many different roles in increasingly varied and expanding social cosmos. Every role is a possibility to be explored and, out of the resultant repertoire, two better-focused images will emerge, those of self and humankind.

By being themselves in other circumstances, by being other people in either familiar or new and different circumstances, children and young people develop, first at the intuitive and unconscious level and then at a fully conscious level, a sympathy and understanding and compassion for others which is rooted in the emotional and physical and spiritual self as well as in mere intellectual knowledge. . . . But at the same time another development also takes place—that of discovering fully and truly about oneself.[34]

By assuming all sorts of roles, the child comes to command various ways of thought, feeling, and action at his or her disposal. Alternatives may then be examined, preferences clarified, choices made, and tentative integration attempted. Valuing, in other words, is continuous, and the synthesis dynamic. Answers are not known beforehand, and do not stay closed. Any decision is originative and not passive calculation. "We do not know what choices will be made in the future. This unknowledge gives freedom for conceiving many, perhaps indefinitely many, sequels to any present actions."[35]

The diverse realms (or kinds) of play also familiarize the child with various forms of cooperation and conflict resolution. Different contexts require interactions with oneself (intraindividual), with peers within one's own group (intragroup, interindividual), or with other groups (intergroup), further adding to his or her repertoire. In view of the typical focus of American formal education on the second type of competition, and of the preferability of the other two types in many situations,[36] such function of play can hardly

[33] Omar K. Moore and Alan R. Anderson. "Some Principles for the Design of Clarifying Educational Environments." In: David A. Goslin, editor. *Handbook of Socialization Theory and Research.* Chicago: Rand McNally & Company, 1969. pp. 571-613.

[34] Brian Way. *Development Through Drama.* London: Longman, Green and Co., 1967. p. 176. Reprinted by permission of Longman Group, Ltd.

[35] G. L. S. Shackle. "Decision: The Human Predicament." *Annals of the American Academy of Political and Social Science* 412: 4; March 1974.

[36] Urie Bronfenbrenner. *Two Worlds of Childhood, U.S. and U.S.S.R.* New York: Russell Sage Foundation, 1970; James S. Coleman. *The Adolescent Society.* New York: The Free Press, 1961; Muzafer Sherif. *In Common Predicament.* Boston: Houghton Mifflin Company, 1966.

be minimized. It has been said that the English word, "school," or Latin "schola," derives from Greek "skholē," which means leisure, leisure devoted to learning. Indeed, in leisure and play, we school ourselves in numerous ways for life. "Is it surprising that people who live least effectively, creatively and absorbedly are those who have been allowed least play, least fantasy, self-expression, exploration?" [37] Observations on severely neglecting or abusive parents and their hapless children bear witness to the sad truth of this statement. "Few of them knew how to play. . . . They sought escape rather than recreation." [38]

Harnessing

The human potential that is dormant beneath the level of consciousness has often been commented upon.[39] Various channels, including meditation or receptive awareness, have been suggested for tapping the precious source for insight and integration. One of these is found "in all forms of imaginative activity—day-dreaming, spontaneous elaboration of fantasy, creative expression in colour, line, sounds and words." [40] Certainly, play is another case in point.

The challenge, in the first instance, is to reach such potential so as to free it. Personal involvement and release must be there, and play amply provides for the needed curiosity and exploration. Yet, this "stage of romance" must be complemented by two others, those of "precision" and "generalization." [41] Whether one agrees with Whitehead's terminology or not, the gist of the story is that the unleashed potential ought to be modulated and harnessed for artistic refinement and creative cultivation. A carefree release of one's energy is not enough—the complete picture requires structure, discipline, and yes, a certain degree of detachment. A delicate balance must be struck between *disinterested* (not uninterested) engagement and enduring devotion, between aesthetic propriety and passionate immersion, between deliberate deferral and immediate

---

[37] Berg, *op. cit.*, p. 120.

[38] Young, *op. cit.*, p. 32.

[39] Examples include: Erich Fromm. *The Forgotten Language.* New York: Holt, Rinehart & Winston, Inc., 1951; William James. "Talks to Students." In: *Talks to Teachers.* New York: W. W. Norton & Company, Inc., 1958. pp. 132-91; Lawrence S. Kubie. *Neurotic Distortion of the Creative Process.* Lawrence, Kansas: University of Kansas Press, 1958.

[40] Herbert Read. *Education Through Art.* New York: Pantheon Books, 1958. p. 191.

[41] Alfred North Whitehead. *The Aims of Education and Other Essays.* New York: The Free Press, 1967.

involvement, or between unreserved autonomy and considered conformity. Interestingly, these paradoxical requirements are not only the distinguishing characteristics of play [42] but also the necessary conditions for general creative processes.[43]

Play activities serve to encourage imaginative predisposition in children and develop an *as if* orientation as a constructive skill for both personal and social functions.[44] The make-believe or fantasy tendencies are not a mere mechanism for escape. Rather, these are an indispensable part of the readiness for creativity. Here, one must be fully *in* the experience, but must at the same time be *out* of it. One must feel deeply, and value authentically, within a given context; yet, one should also keep alive a fresh, naïve perspective to stand outside the context. Always, therefore, one ought to go beyond the current, familiar, and prevalent. "The art which creates things both great and small is not the capacity for solving problems. That may seem a curious statement, but the real art of life consists in finding out what is the question to be solved, and the person who can find out what the problem is to be solved is the man who really makes the contributions to life." [45]

Solving problems after they have been identified, and after the situation has been defined, is one thing; seeing possibilities where none has been seen before is another and more profound challenge. To ask an *as if* question of the world demands a playful and daring spirit. To ask a *just suppose* question of oneself requires openness and courage. In both instances, it entails raising an unsettling query of one's comfortable position in a familiar environment. It induces us to take another look at ourselves. To let go of the familiar and secure is difficult. To face the unknown within oneself, to choose to believe in the ultimate positive potential of humankind, and to value such learning in the struggle for maturity—all these experiences are the disturbing but necessary antecedents, as well as concomitants, of increased awareness, humility, and integrity. Again, play offers an invitation.

[42] Huizinga, *op. cit.*

[43] Frank Barron. *Creative Person and Creative Process.* New York: Holt, Rinehart and Winston, Inc., 1969; Howard E. Gruber, Glenn Terrell, and Michael Wertheimer, editors. *Contemporary Approaches to Creative Thinking.* New York: Atherton Press, 1962.

[44] Jerome L. Singer. *The Child's World of Make-Believe.* New York: Academic Press, 1973.

[45] Hughes Mearns. *Creative Power.* Second revised edition. New York: Dover Publications, 1958. p. 239.

From the position of secular man (*Homo sapiens*), then, we are to enter the play sphere of the festival, acquiescing in a game of belief, where fun, joy, and rapture rule in ascending series. The laws of life in time and space . . . will dissolve. Whereafter, . . . we are to carry the point of view and spirit of man the player (*Homo ludens*) back into life: as in the play of children, where, undaunted by the banal actualities of life's meager possibilities, the spontaneous impulse of the spirit to identify itself with something other than itself, for the sheer delight of play, transubstantiates the world—in which, after all, things are not quite as real or permanent, terrible, important, or logical as they seem.[46]

The Quest

The child at play is a constant reminder that, no matter how convincing the argument might appear for the moment, an interpretation of education in manufacturing terms misses something of import, something of human significance. A child is not raw material to be treated in the school factory to meet someone else's specifications. The yields of production, and the efficiency of operation, are not the only, and certainly not the most suitable, measures to judge the fruits of educational encounters.[47] The *process* of such meetings of minds and souls is in itself more worthwhile than any by-products. "The value of teaching and of learning, in this view, is like the value of play; it is intrinsic and immediate. . . . In play, the object of an activity is the activity itself."[48]

Although the motif of this culture may continue to be the narrow intellect, radical reductionism, excessive specialization, and utilitarian preoccupation, humankind itself remains the best evidence to argue for a broader and deeper interpretation of what it means to be human. It is revealing in this connection to read a recent article on the dead-end character of the highly technical line of research on artificial intelligence. By relying on sophisticated digital computers, these studies have reported some initial progress in the simulation of *ideal* languages and abstract logical operations merely to run into an impasse in attempting to handle more *mundane* functions of perception, problem solving, thinking, and the like. It appears that the multi-valued world of man resists the inroad of the two-valued (binary) computer programs. The human capability of becoming cognizant, first of all, of the total constellation of an

---

[46] Joseph Campbell. "The Historical Development of Mythology." In: Henry A. Murray, editor. *Myth and Mythmaking.* New York: George Braziller, Inc., 1960. p. 44. Originally published in *Daedalus.*

[47] Yamamoto, *Individuality, op. cit.*

[48] Thomas F. Green. *Work, Leisure, and the American Schools.* New York: Random House, Inc., 1968. pp. 157-58.

experience frustrates the mechanistic effort to reduce the fundamental gestalt into elementary components which are readily ame-
nable to serial (linear) operations for confirmation. The embodied
capacities of the human being defy any "detached, disembodied,
objective" approaches to gain full comprehension of the world.[49]

Unlike machines built upon the rule of one-to-one correspondence between specific stimuli and particular responses, humans
size up the whole situation to offer a flexible, general set of solutions
that may be utilized in myriad different ways under varied circumstances. The indeterminacy allows freedom of thought, feeling, and
action. That is what opens up new vistas and invites original
explorations.

Life is such a precious gift that it would be a shame if it were
not cherished thoroughly and expanded beyond the confines of the
known and obvious. Life is a mystery, and humankind is an enigma.
Much is to remain indescribable and unpredictable, but merely to be
valued and appreciated. Ironically, these matters may have been
hidden from our learned, but not from our babes. Thus, we read of
transcendence in the Plowden report, where the place of expressive
movement (whether as dance or drama) is discussed in primary
education:

> . . . the aim is . . . to develop each child's resources as fully as
> possible through exploratory stages and actions which will not be the
> same for any two children. When these ends are pursued successfully,
> the children are able to bring much more to any situation than that which
> is specifically asked of them; the results transcend the limits of what can
> be prescribed or "produced", and lead to a greater realisation of the high
> potential of young children.[50]

As Isaacs argued, "those who have watched the play of children have long looked upon it as Nature's means of individual
education. Play is indeed the child's work, and the means whereby
he grows and develops."[51] The spirit of play, and the world of
make-believe, must be restored in learning and teaching, if our
education is to help raise future generations that *care, share, and
dare.*

[49] Hubert L. Dreyfus. "Artificial Intelligence." *Annals of the American
Academy of Political and Social Science* 412: 21-33; March 1974.

[50] Central Advisory Council for Education (England). *Children and Their
Primary Schools.* Volume 1. London: Her Majesty's Stationery Office, 1967.
p. 257.

[51] Susan Isaacs. *The Nursery Years.* New York: Schocken Books, Inc.,
1968. p. 9. Reprinted by permission.

2

Youth Life-Worlds and the American Culture

Rodman B. Webb

*T*he task of this chapter is to explore the relationship that exists between individuals and society in the American culture. A special emphasis will be placed on the experience of growing up American and attention will be given to those portions of everyday life that help create the varying images of self and humankind that young people accept as real. Within this context we will look briefly at this nation's recent youth movements in an effort to determine their relationship to the culture at large.

We will neither attempt to describe nor apply the myriad models of humankind provided us by science and philosophy. Our task will rather be to confront the everyday life-world of typical citizens as they lead their typical lives. We will try to expose and begin at least to explore the ways individuals greet and define the modern world they live in. Space considerations will limit our exploration and we will not do justice to the complexity of the topic. Our attempt will be to sketch its general dimensions by setting out some of the more significant aspects of the everyday life-world of the modern individual.

Social Moorings in Pluralistic Society

"He who marries the spirit of an age," W. R. Inge has said, "soon finds himself a widower."[1] Events of this century have accelerated to the point where it is now at least conceivable that today's *Zeitgeist* could become next week's nostalgia craze. The barrage of shocking events which we experience via the media (assassinations, civil strife, Vietnam, violent crime, Watergate, CIA and FBI corruption, ecological chaos, terrorist bombings, inflation, recession, unemployment, the killings at Kent and Jackson State, epidemic drug addiction, to name but a few of the past decade's horrors) consumes our attention and saps our hope and strength. Because such issues are necessarily compelling and perhaps because we can endure only one catastrophe at a time, these events tend to hide as well as aggravate (the two are not contradictory) a fundamental disequilibrium within the life-world of individuals. Part of this disequilibrium is revealed by the fact that we have become perplexed by our own actions and being.

"At no time in history," Max Scheller remarked half a century ago, "has man been so much of a problem to himself."[2] In greater numbers and to a greater degree than our ancestors, the modern individual is unclear as to how to fit into the social world. Our identity has lost its social moorings and society seems less capable of providing stable objects for our allegiance. "It would be difficult," wrote John Dewey, "to find an epoch as lacking in solid and assured objects of belief and approved ends of action as is the present."[3]

It was Dewey's belief that the self "is both formed and brought into consciousness through interaction with environment."[4] Thus, the development of self depends, in large part, on the stability of the environment in which it exists. This is especially true during the period of primary socialization when a child discovers the self through the discovery of the culture.

[1] W. R. Inge. Quoted by Peter Berger. In: "The Liberal as the Fall Guy." *The Center Magazine* 5(4): 38; July/August 1972. Reprinted by permission of *The Center Magazine*, a publication of the Center for the Study of Democratic Institutions, Santa Barbara, California.

[2] Max Scheller. *Man's Place in Nature.* Hans Meyerhoff, translator. New York: The Noonday Press, 1969. p. 6.

[3] John Dewey. *Individualism Old and New.* New York: Capricorn Books, 1962. p. 52. Copyright © 1929, 1930 by John Dewey; renewed. Reprinted by permission of G. P. Putnam's Sons.

[4] John Dewey. *Art as Experience.* New York: Capricorn Books, 1958. p. 282.

Rodman B. Webb *is Assistant Professor of Education at the University of Florida, Gainesville, where he teaches courses in the Sociology of Education. He has written* The Presence of the Past, *a Study of the Philosophies of Alfred Schutz and John Dewey, has edited* Education in the American Culture: Toward a Sociological Consciousness, *and has served on the advisory board of* Annual Editions: Readings in Education. *He has worked with the Florida model of the national Follow Through project, has done research in teacher belief systems and pursues an interest in phenomenological sociology.*

Identity formation becomes problematic when a society loses its cohesion and becomes a mere collection of competing environments. Such is the case today. Modern culture has become pluralistic due to such interacting events as the acceleration of change, the influx of large immigrant populations, the segmentation of work into narrow specializations and the attendant social distribution of knowledge, as well as the increased technocratization and bureaucratization of human life.

Within the context of these events it is becoming increasingly difficult to coordinate the psychological and the social aspects of human existence. The pluralistic nature of our culture offers unprecedented opportunities to individuals but it is unlikely that we will capitalize upon such opportunities if we lack the habits of awareness, reason, and intelligent action. Yet it is just these habits which are most endangered by the vagaries of pluralistic culture. ‚As Dewey has pointed out,

Today there are no patterns sufficiently enduring to provide anything stable in which to acquiesce, and there is no material out of which to form final and all-inclusive ends. There is, on the other hand, such constant change that acquiescence is but a series of interrupted spasms, and the outcome is mere drifting.[5]

[5] John Dewey, *Individualism Old and New, op. cit.*, p. 150.

The problem Dewey identifies leads us around a disheartening circle. The development of mind, intelligence, and self are social processes. As the social structure becomes ever more segmented it simultaneously becomes less able to produce in individuals the habits necessary to meet the problems at hand.

Americans have struggled in the twentieth century to free themselves from the more stifling aspects of rural society. In doing so, however, they seem to have also lost a wholeness provided by small *Gemeinschaft* settings. It is not very helpful to yearn nostalgically for an irretrievable (and probably romanticized) past; nevertheless, the comparison of certain features of past and present can be instructive. W. I. Thomas wrote in the first quarter of this century, "In . . . the American rural community of fifty years ago nothing was left vague, all was defined. But in the general world movement to which I have referred . . . not only the particular situations but the most general situations have become vague." In the small matters of everyday life and in the larger systems of belief to which we adhere, we are left without clear definitions for the situations in which we find ourselves. "There are," as Thomas pointed out, "rival definitions [for every situation] and none of them is binding." [6]

Yeats capsulized this state of affairs poetically:

Things fall apart; the center cannot hold.
Mere anarchy is loosed upon the world.
The blood-dimmed tide is loosed, and everywhere
The ceremony of innocence is drowned.
The best lack all convictions while the worst
Are full of passionate intensity. [7]

Dewey saw education as a viable means for dealing with the vague and pluralistic nature of modern society. The development of mind and self could no longer be left to the hapless interactions of children and the multiple environments of the modern world. "The only way in which adults consciously control the kind of education which the immature get is by controlling the environment in which they act, and hence think and feel." [8] Schools would have to provide a "simplified environment" to counter the chaotic pluralism typical of everyday life. The school would function to coor-

[6] W. I. Thomas. *The Unadjusted Girl.* New York: Harper Torchbooks, 1967. pp. 81-82.

[7] William Butler Yeats. "The Second Coming." *Collected Poems.* New York: Macmillan Publishing Co., Inc., 1950.

[8] John Dewey. *Democracy in Education.* New York: The Free Press, 1944. pp. 18-19.

dinate "within the disposition of each individual the diverse influences of the various social environments into which he enters." Schools would mediate "the antagonistic poles" of competing realities which put individuals in danger of "being split into beings having different standards of judgment and emotions for different occasions." [9]

Clearly education has failed to accomplish what Dewey hoped for it. Rather than decreasing the pluralistic impulse of modern society, schooling may have accelerated it. For all the educational rhetoric about integrated curricula and teaching for rational thought, schools have built into their very structure the pluralistic characteristics of modern society. Rather than attempting to present a unified environment, schools celebrate and extend the fragmentation of modern life. In this activity they are not countering the pluralistic tendencies of modern consciousness but making them an objectified force in the schools. Our schools have become an institutional training ground for what the Dutch sociologist, Anton Zijderveld, has labeled "Intellectual Tailorism." This term refers to the tendency of the modern mind to conform "to the pluralization of the world through specialization which cuts reality into little pieces, each piece being the domain of a relatively small group of experts." [10]

Schooling and Technological Consciousness

Schools are where our children are systematically introduced to the pluralistic nature of modern reality. We are not simply referring here to the tendency of education to organize knowledge into separate subject matters, though this is a reflection of the pluralization we are referring to. We are also interested in the cognitive style that must be adopted by students in order to adequately handle the schooling experience. We are similarly interested in the high correlation which exists between the cognitive style appropriate to educational institutions and that style which dominates life in a technological, bureaucratic society. It is our contention that the life-world of the "adjusted" student is, on the surface at least, similar to the life-world of the "adjusted" adult.

[9] *Ibid.*, p. 22.

[10] Anton Zijderveld. *The Abstract Society: A Cultural Analysis of Our Time.* Garden City, New York: Anchor Books, 1970. p. 76. Copyright © 1970 by Anton C. Zijderveld. Reprinted by permission of Doubleday & Company, Inc. I am indebted to Zijderveld together with the works of Peter Berger for much of the following discussion of Modernity.

For our purposes we will not be so much interested in the specific stock of knowledge which children and adults have at hand as we will be in the presuppositions upon which such knowledge is based. These presuppositions are deeply sedimented in the consciousness of individuals and may be so taken for granted that they seldom, if ever, are subjects of reflection. In order to understand either the culture of the school or the culture at large, it is necessary to clarify the pre-reflective assumptions which fund human intentions. "The things which we take for granted without inquiry or reflection," Dewey has said, "are just the things which determine our conscious thinking and decide our conclusions." [11]

Most school children, like most adults in the "real world," come to assume that knowledge can be categorized into specialties. They further assume that knowledge is socially distributed among experts in specialized areas and that a hierarchy exists among the experts within a field of study. Despite this hierarchy, however, it is assumed that persons within a certain range of expertise are essentially interchangeable. It should not matter to individuals, in principle at least, what telephone operator they get, what mechanic is on duty, what teacher they have for ninth-grade English, or what doctor treats their illness. Everyone holding a specific position is expected to have a grasp of specified knowledge and to act in a manner typical of the position held (that is, competently). We assume that both knowledge and the possessors of knowledge are organized into systems which minimize the importance of personality and maximize functional efficiency.

The dissection of knowledge into specialties is paralleled by the assumption that human actions, especially within a technological or a bureaucratic setting, can be divided into the component parts which make them up. Thus, both knowledge and action can be segmented and ordered sequentially according to some institutional scheme.

The "componentiality" of knowledge and action is carried over into the cognitive style of individuals. Reality itself becomes segregated into areas of specialization which have no necessary connection with one another. Work within a specialization is further dissected into its constituent components which are, as Berger has observed, "apprehended and manipulated as atomistic units." [12]

---

[11] John Dewey, *Democracy in Education, op. cit.*, p. 18.

[12] Peter Berger, Brigitte Berger, and Hansfried Kellner. *The Homeless Mind: Modernization and Consciousness.* New York: Vintage Books, Random House, 1974. p. 27.

American education epitomizes the segmentation mentality we have been speaking of. Behavioral objectives and teaching machines are but current examples of the "cult of efficiency" which rules education. While it is true that children may no longer need to memorize endless unrelated facts, they are still, in large numbers, engaged in the even more fruitless task of memorizing abstract, disembodied, and woefully meaningless "concepts."

The abstract nature of school knowledge parallels the nature of life and knowledge in culture as a whole. As Zijdervelt has described it,

Modern society is an essentially abstract society which is increasingly unable to provide man with a clear awareness of his identity and a concrete experience of meaning, reality and freedom. This abstract nature of society is caused primarily by its *pluralism,* i.e., by its segmentation of its institutional structure. Compared to tribal societies and their overarching kinship systems, or to medieval society with its rather uniform, namely, Christian, structure of meaning, modern society appears to be chaotically pluralistic. As a result of this pluralism society has lost . . . much of its existential concreteness. The abstract nature of modern society is sufficiently illustrated by such modern cultural expressions as abstract painting and sculpture and electronic music. On the level of interpersonal relationships the abstract nature of contemporary society is illustrated by the fact that a large number of the personal face to face relations of pre-modern society have been replaced by the relations of official functionaries who practice the roles of their social positions.[13]

Zijdervelt is speaking to the fact that "modern society has become abstract in the experience and consciousness of man."[14] Similarly, it is on the level of consciousness that we are trying to examine the phenomenon of schooling in America.

Faced with a proliferation of possibilities and a seemingly endless array of disconnected concepts, it becomes difficult for many children to hold their world together in any meaningful totality. If a child, however, fails to keep control of the concepts he is dealing with or does not behave within the bounds of institutionally defined normalcy, the chances are getting ever greater that he will be sent to institutional personnel, expert in dealing with children of "that type." Here a child may begin to get the message (if it has not been received already) that he too is an abstraction, an interchangeable component who is not defined by unique characteristics but rather according to some abstract or universal principle accorded to all people of his type.

[13] Anton Zijderveld, *The Abstract Society, op. cit.,* pp. 48-49.
[14] *Ibid.*

While the school vocabulary in these circumstances tends to be highly humanistic, the diagnosis and treatment a child is likely to undergo is borrowed from the infinitely abstract theories of the social sciences. Whatever the merits of these theories or the work of school specialists who wield them, the child's treatment experience may further reify (objectify abstract concepts into seemingly real things over which individuals have little control) the abstractions the child faces. The experience can heighten an awareness that "modern man . . . does not 'live society,' he faces it as an often strange phenomenon." [15]

The school acquaints children with the fact that people can interact impersonally on a role to role, or more accurately, a function to function, basis. Such interaction patterns are not found in the typical family setting most children are accustomed to. Family life is characterized by the attempt to accept each family member in their human totality. Individual functions are not clearly delineated and family members are expected to act in ways which reflect a group rather than a personal interest. Institutions, on the other hand, run according to a different emotional calculus, as well as different rules and values.

School is a child's first long-term experience with bureaucracy. Upon entering its walls a child is introduced to a world where functions are narrowly defined and power grows not from the personality of the individual who wields it, but from the role he or she plays within the institution. The military phrase, "You don't salute the man, you salute the uniform" describes institutionalized power. Willard Waller explains "in institutionalized leadership personalities are forced to conform to the pre-existing pattern; they are pumped up or deflated to make them fit their situation." [16]

The transition from family to school is not always easy. Because children are less likely than adults to accept such transitions unquestioningly, it is necessary for the institution to provide explicit legitimizations for the institutional order. If schools are to operate smoothly (and it is presupposed that this is desirable) students must come to accept the schooling experience as a legitimate part of

[15] *Ibid.*

[16] Willard Waller. *The Sociology of Teaching.* New York: John Wiley & Sons, Inc., 1939. pp. 189-90.

growing up. It is particularly helpful, as school officials never tire of reminding parents, if the home is "supportive" of the school operation.

Frederick Wiseman's now classic documentary film,* *High School*, gives us a dramatic example of the kind of legitimizations school functionaries are likely to give for institutionalizing leadership. In one sequence in the film a student has been assigned to detention study hall by a teacher for an offense the student insists he did not commit. The teacher has sent him to the official disciplinarian for processing. Standing before the disciplinarian's desk the student is told, "First of all, you showed poor judgment. When you're being addressed by someone older than you or in a seat of authority, it's your job to respect and listen . . . We are out to establish that you can be a man and that you can take orders." The student protests, claiming that, by his lights, being a man entails doing what he thinks is right. "You have to stand for something," the student says meekly. The disciplinarian does not respond to the substance of the student's argument but rather redefines the situation. "I think your principles aren't involved here. I think it's a question now of proving yourself to be a man. It's a question here of how do we follow rules and regulations." The student is defeated, accepts the punishment "under protest," and retreats.

Schooling gives the child the experience of being processed; being treated not as a unique being but rather as one among many. Students can't help but get the sense that "by his nature the bureaucratic functionary is," as Harvey Wheeler has described him, a person "who must perform each of his allotted roles with impersonal detachment. His concern is not substance but process, not matter but form, not essential justice but legal authority!" [17]

Thus, it becomes accepted as official doctrine that all students are to be afforded equal treatment, judged by standardized rules and, when necessary, issued standardized punishments. While such predictability may make it easier to navigate one's way through the bureaucratic institutions of society, the sterile sameness which bureaucracies offer makes it difficult to build or maintain an identity within bureaucratic structures.

---

* *High School* (1968) directed and edited by Frederick Wiseman. Courtesy of Zipporah Films, Inc.

[17] Harvey Wheeler. *Democracy in a Revolutionary Era: The Political Order Today*. Santa Barbara, California: The Center for the Study of Democratic Institutions, 1968. p. 89. Reprinted with permission.

Bureaucracies are characterized by their orderliness, predictability, and a presumption of competence. Knowledge, activity,
and authority are segmented and hierarchically arranged within the
bureaucratic structure. Interactions are depersonalized and regulated by a carefully defined code of justice. All of these characteristics are alive in typical school settings. They form the
undergirding assumptions upon which the educational system is
erected. Whatever the merits of such conditions for technological
production they do not form a conducive atmosphere for educating
the young or developing a clear sense of identity in our children.
These activities demand a high degree of involvement while bureaucracies demand a passive clientele.

Multiple Life-Worlds and Modern Identity

The modern individual lives life in a wide assortment of
institutions, each demanding its own stock of knowledge, structure
of relevance and, in some cases, mode of being. Our trafficking
among the many life-worlds of family, business, church, professional
organizations, political parties, recreational groups, and the rest
necessitates a frequent shifting of our cognitive and emotional gears.
We must step in and out of roles with the facility of a summer stock
actor. Like the actor we dare not let ourselves become so committed to one role that it will hamper our performance of the next
role we will have to play. Modern role playing has a migratory and
temporary character and can make only limited claims upon individuals. A youngster must be the teacher's student, the parent's
child, and "one of the gang." Each role must be filled, but cannot
be played to the exclusion of any other.

The segmented character of modern life has many dimensions.
At one level we rarely obtain a clear vision of the totality of an
institution we function in. We lack what corporate executives call
"the big picture." At another level, beyond the horizon of any
particular institution, it is unlikely that we have even a mythical
notion of a totality or ultimate meaning our several institutions may
serve. There is no encompassing order available from religions,
economic theories, political ideologies, science or other portions of
our "cultural reservoir" capable of tying modern life into a meaningful totality. We share no common transcendent assumptions.
The German social scientist, Benita Luckmann, has stated, "Con-

temporary man no longer 'naturally' sees himself as a useful and necessary member of a social whole geared into a meaningful plan of existence within the totality of the cosmic or divine order." [18]

Identity formation is particularly difficult in the context of contemporary life. The segmentation of the institutional world demands an equivalent segmentation of personality. Just as the world at large defies coordination into a meaningful totality, so, too, do our several roles resist coordination into a single identity. This is not to deny George Herbert Mead's point that "a multiple personality is in a certain sense normal." [19] The human being has always played several roles and thus we have, as James has said, "as many social selves as there are individuals who recognize [them]." [20] The modern problem does not grow simply out of the fact that we play several roles, but rather out of the difficulty we have in building these roles into a subjective unity.

"There is usually an organization of the whole self with reference to the community to which we belong" wrote Mead. "The unity and structure of the complete self reflects the unity and structure of the social process as a whole." [21] Modern society, as we have seen, does not supply the meaningful unity and structure to which Mead refers. There is no comprehensive interpretation of reality from which to gain our bearings. Thus, as Berger has stated, "Modern man is afflicted with a permanent identity crisis." [22]

Without a central unity we experience our several selves as disconnected, a state Erikson calls "identity diffusion." [23] Lines of cleavage [24] separate one role from another and we may experience

---

[18] Benita Luckmann. "The Small Life-Worlds of Modern Man." *Social Research* 37(4): 584; Winter 1970. Published by the Graduate Faculty of the New School for Social Research. For a useful description of the existence of pre-modern man see: Eric Voegelin. *Order and History.* Volume 1. *Israel and Revelation.* Baton Rouge: Louisiana State University Press, 1956.

[19] George Herbert Mead. *On Social Psychology.* Anselm Strauss, editor. Chicago: The University of Chicago Press, 1956. p. 207. Copyright © 1966 by the University of Chicago.

[20] William James. *The Principles of Psychology.* Volume 1. New York: Dover Publications, Inc., 1950. p. 294.

[21] George Herbert Mead, *On Social Psychology, op. cit.*

[22] Peter Berger, *et al., The Homeless Mind, op. cit.,* p. 78.

[23] Erik Erikson. *Identity: Youth and Crisis.* New York: W. W. Norton & Co., Inc., 1969. p. 212.

[24] George Herbert Mead, *On Social Psychology, op. cit.*

our playing of a role as superficial or, to use Holden Caulfield's epithet, as "phony." [25]

In situations such as we have been describing individuals may move in one of at least two directions. The first direction may be called the "institutional option" wherein individuals reject their subjective experience of isolation and seek meaning and unity within their institutional roles. Going in another direction, what we can call the "personal option," individuals may detach themselves from their institutionalized roles by either passively enduring them or rejecting them altogether. In such cases individuals may carve out for themselves what German sociologists have called "a private sphere" where human interactions are personalistic, concrete, and emotionally charged.

The Institutional Option

Erving Goffman describes what transpires when an individual takes the "institutional option" as a means to identity formation. In such cases, Goffman states, "the self . . . can be seen as something that resides in the arrangements prevailing in the social system for its members. The self in this sense is not the property of the person to whom it is attributed, but dwells rather in the pattern of social control that is exerted in connection with the person by himself and those around him. This special kind of institutional arrangement does not so much support the self as constitute it." [26]

There are, of course, degrees to which we can divest ourselves of individuality and draw an identity from the institutional order. In its milder forms we may find the ideal type Riesman called "the other directed man." [27] In more extreme cases, such as Goffman describes, we discover rather lifeless role players who are without personal qualities.[28]

[25] J. D. Salinger. *The Catcher in the Rye.* New York: Bantam Books, 1945. The sociological term "role" and the phrase "playing the role" have popularly come to mean, especially in the vocabulary of the young, severe insincerity.

[26] Erving Goffman. *Asylums.* Garden City, New York: Anchor Books, 1961. p. 168. Reprinted by permission of Doubleday & Company, Inc.

[27] David Riesman, Nathan Glazer, and Reuel Denney. *The Lonely Crowd: A Study of the Changing American Character.* Garden City, New York: Anchor Books, 1950.

[28] For a fascinating exploration of the implications of Goffman's model of man, see: John Helmer. "The Face of the Man Without Qualities." *Social Research* 37(4): 547-79; Winter 1970. For a literary investigation along a similar theme, see: Robert Musil. *The Man Without Qualities.* Eithne Wilkins and Ernest Kaiser, translators. New York: Capricorn Books, 1965.

The multitude of institutions we moderns must inhabit makes extreme identification with any one institution difficult. Public proclamations of institutional loyalty seem slightly absurd today.[29]

The Personal Option

The more common method for dealing with identity diffusion is not to quest for an institutionally supplied "wholeness" but rather to beat a strategic retreat into the private sphere. There, with a little help from carefully selected friends, the attempt is made to manufacture an ordered existence, identify a "natural" or "real self" and construct a subjective sense of purpose. Identity formation, Luckmann tells us, has become a do-it-yourself operation in the modern world:

> In comparison to traditional social orders, the primary public institutions no longer significantly contribute to the formation of individual consciousness and personality, despite the massive performance control exerted by their functional rational "mechanisms." Personal identity becomes, essentially, a private phenomenon. This is, perhaps, the most revolutionary trait of modern society. Institutional segmentation left wide areas in the life of the individual unstructured and the over-arching biographical context of significance undermined. From the interstices of the social structure that resulted from institutional segmentation emerged what may be called a "private sphere." The "liberation" of individual consciousness from the social structure and the "freedom" in the "private sphere" provide the basis for a somewhat illusory sense of autonomy which characterizes the typical person in modern society.[30]

Within the domain of the private sphere full expression can be given to the affective dimensions of life which must be carefully controlled (or in Freudian terminology, suppressed) in the public sector. Emotionality may come to be defined as more "real" and

[29] The following excerpts from Watergate testimony are examples of the loyalist mentality referred to above: John Caulfield: "I felt very strongly about the President, extremely strongly about the President. I was very loyal to his people that I work for. I place a high value on loyalty." Bernard Barker: "Sure. I am not—I was not there to think. I was there to follow orders, not to think." H. R. Haldeman: "Those who served with me at the White House had complete dedication to the service of this country. They had great pride in the President they served and a great pride in the accomplishments of the Nixon administration in the first four years." John Ehrlichman: "I do not apologize for my loyalty to the President any more than I apologize for my love of this country." John Mitchell: "And I was not about to countenance anything that would stand in the way of that reelection." U.S. Congress Senate Select Committee on Presidential Campaign Activities. *Presidential Campaign Activities of 1972.* Washington, D.C.: U.S. Government Printing Office, 1973.

[30] Thomas Luckmann. *The Invisible Religion.* New York: Macmillan Publishing Co., Inc., 1967. p. 97. Copyright © by Macmillan Publishing Co., Inc.

essentially more legitimate than the cool detachment which characterizes bureaucratic role playing. The family and romantic love
take on a deep significance as the main curators of reality maintenance. Uninhibited friendship, personalistic religion, myriad do-
it-yourself activities, and other voluntary affiliations contribute to
the life-world of the private sphere.

Arnold Gehlen has pointed out that the private sphere, because
of its subjective foundations, has little in the way of objective
support. It is, to use Gehlen's term, "under-institutionalized" and
therefore is easily disrupted.[31] Although the private sphere offers
"unparalleled liberty" to individuals, it lacks institutional support
and as a result is highly fragile, leaving individuals vulnerable to
sudden attacks of anxiety and anomie. It is especially vulnerable to
intrusions from the public realm, for as Tocqueville noted, "As the
public sphere expands the private sphere contracts." [32]

Youth and Discontent

It is getting increasingly difficult for adults to understand what
their children are thinking and feeling. Often we fail totally to grasp
what the young are saying. The phrase, "When I was young . . ."
is ridiculed by our children, not only because it so often serves as
an introduction to a condescending message, but also because the
past bears so little resemblance to the present. The world is experienced by children in a different manner than it is now or ever was
experienced by adults.

There are structural explanations for this phenomenon. Children go to school at an earlier age and stay in school for longer
periods than they ever have before. Many children enter day-care
centers or preschool before the age of three. Seventy-six percent
of five year olds are enrolled in primary education programs. The
same percentage (76 percent) of all seventeen year olds graduate
from high school and 58 percent of all recent high school graduates
enter a degree-credit program in a college or university.[33] Children
today are exposed to significantly more adults trained in the super-

[31] Gehlen's work, to my knowledge, has been translated into English.
For a discussion of his theory see: Peter Berger and Hansfried Keller. "Arnold
Gehlen and the Theory of Institutions." *Social Research* 32(1): Fall 1965.

[32] Alexis de Tocqueville. *Democracy in America.* Volume 2. H. Reeve,
translator. New York: Schocken Books, Inc., 1961. pp. 256-58.

[33] W. Vance Grant and C. George Lind. *Digest of Educational Statistics.*
Washington, D.C.: U.S. Department of Health, Education and Welfare, 1973.
pp. 44, 55, 13.

vision of the young. Children spend more time being supervised by these adults than they will spend with any other grown-ups including, perhaps, their parents.

Parent-child contact has been drastically reduced. This is due not only to television and organized extracurricular activities (such as summer camp, scouting, and Little League) but also to the increased incidence of working mothers. More than half of mothers with children from six to seventeen years of age are presently in the labor force. Thirty-seven percent of mothers with children under six are engaged in full-time work.[34] Divorce is also a factor in the lessening of parent-child contact. If present rates continue it is estimated that one child in six will lose a parent to divorce before he or she reaches eighteen years of age.[35]

Children are cut off from contact with young people of different ages. Schools are organized to encourage this age segregation. The number of multi-generational homes is diminishing. And there is little opportunity for valuable work experience which can provide a sense of accomplishment and expose young people to adults in non-school settings.[36] These differences between the world of the young today and the world which existed for previous generations have implications for identity; that is, they have implications for how young people see themselves in relation to the adult world.

We have already alluded to the fact that adults seek identity either by attaching themselves to institutions in the public sphere (the institutional option) or retreating to a private sector usually centered around family life (the personal option). The family, no doubt, serves a similar function for some children. As they grow to adolescence, however, it is not unusual for a child's perceptions of the family to change dramatically. Whereas, parents may see the family as a center of creativity, identity formation, and essential freedom, the child may begin to experience the family as an external reality, coercive, inhibiting, and stifling of identity. For many children, though certainly not all, the family loses its modern function

[34] Women's Bureau. *Highlights of Women's Employment and Education.* Washington, D.C.: U.S. Department of Labor, 1974. p. 1.

[35] Urie Bronfenbrenner. "The Roots of Alienation." In: *American Families: Trends and Pressures, 1973.* Washington, D.C.: U.S. Government Printing Office, 1974. p. 148. For further discussion of problems in the American family, see: Hattie Bessent and Rodman Webb. "The Role of the Parent." In: Ira Gordon and William Breivogel, editors. *Building Effective Home-School Relationships.* Boston: Allyn & Bacon, Inc., 1976. pp. 94-102.

[36] James Coleman et al. *Youth: Transition to Adulthood.* Chicago: The University of Chicago Press, 1974.

as a private sector where individuals are free to create and maintain identity.

In an earlier day when the family was more intimately connected with the community at large, an adolescent's changing perceptions of family life did not necessarily constitute a problem. The child was free to draw closer to significant others outside the family, take on an apprenticeship or begin to build a family of his or her own. There were escape routes, none of which were particularly threatening to the family unit.

Today, in contrast, these escape routes have been largely closed. The young stay in school. They must learn to "make do" in the home either repressing their new perceptions of family life and thereby extending their childhood, or expressing their frustration, thereby disrupting family harmony.

The young cannot easily take the "institutional option" open to their parents. They have no institutions available to attach themselves to. The school is too impersonal, temporary, and pluralistic for the student to identify closely with. School personnel want children to be happy in the school environment and hope they will take their education seriously. They grow suspicious, however, when students internalize the rules and bureaucratic procedures of the school and begin to see the institution in the same way as the adults who run it. Students are neither expected to be disruptive nor are they expected to identify totally with the institution. A modest degree of detachment from school rules is encouraged. The well-rounded student is able to hold the institution at some distance, being neither a tattletale nor an apple polisher and giving more attention to peers than to the school. Role distance is an institutional expectation and the school's equivalent of the "organization man" is seen as abnormal. Schools encourage and perhaps necessitate role distance but young people often experience it as a form of insincerity. They must adopt a stance which Huckleberry Finn called "playing double." For example, students often find themselves having to play simultaneously to the contradictory expectations of separate groups.[37] Teachers demand one set of behaviors and meanings while fellow students expect another. To alleviate this institutionalized tension students develop a kind of double consciousness; one for dealing with their peers and another for dealing with school officials.

[37] For a discussion of role distance by Erving Goffman, see: *Encounters: Two Studies in the Sociology of Interaction.* New York: Bobbs-Merrill Company, 1971. pp. 85-152.

When the demands of one group collide with the expectations of another, students may have to create a space between what they do and what they believe themselves to be. This kind of role distance is exemplified by a student obediently carrying out directions of a teacher while secretly divulging the insincerity of these actions to peers through a stance, expression, or gesture. This activity, along with myriad others such as "working the system" and "impression management," encourages what Erving Goffman has called "a certain bureaucratization of the spirit . . ." which allows a student's several selves to exist in near atomistic isolation.[38] When this occurs there is not only a separation between the various roles a student must play but there can also be a deep division between these roles and what the student subjectively senses herself or himself to be.

In order to bind together this divided sense of self a young person may retreat into youth itself, into what Coleman called the "adolescent society." Small cliques of friends are the closest thing to a private sphere the young can muster. These groups tend to have little connection with the adult world and have few, if any, institutional supports. Differences of opinion can quickly slip out of hand and a child can be set adrift by the peer group. The reality formed in the peer group is often consuming and supportive but it is also quick to change, inherently precarious, and potentially volatile.

Being a part of adolescent society makes it easier to neutralize the perceived coercive power of both the family and the school. It is not usually the case that peer relationships totally replace the meanings supplied by the home and the school (the child must learn to live in all three spheres simultaneously), but the realities supplied by the peer group tend to expand during adolescence as other realities contract. There is a minimum of conflict as long as the peer group reality does not overly challenge realities of other spheres.

One of the ways the peer groups can help neutralize the power of the school is through the process of redefining institutional meaning structures. Students learn to deal with what are seen as unreasonable demands and unnecessary affronts to selfhood by defining these situations away. Waller discovered this activity in the schools he studied in 1930. "Whatever the rules that the teacher lays down, the tendency of the pupils is to empty them of meaning. By mechanization of conformity, by 'laughing off' the teacher or hating him out of all existence as a person, by taking refuge in self-initiated

[38] Erving Goffman. *The Presentation of Self in Everyday Life.* Garden City, New York: Anchor Books, 1959. p. 56.

activities that are always just beyond the teacher's reach, students attempt to neutralize teacher control." [39]

When such activity transpires on a small scale it can help students to deal with the day to day aggravations of school life. When they transpire on a larger scale they can challenge the legitimacy of the institution. When the coercive power of the school cannot be held in abeyance, defined away, or given positive meaning by students, there is likely to be rebellion in some form. Such rebellion may fuse with other dissatisfactions and the school may be perceived as just one part of a larger system of oppression. Mario Savio defined the University of California at Berkeley in just such terms.

> Last summer I went to Mississippi to join the struggle there for Civil Rights. This fall I am engaged in another phase of the same struggle, this time in Berkeley. The two battle fields may seem quite different to some observers, but this is not the case. The same rights are at stake in both places—the right to participate as citizens in democratic society and to struggle against the same enemy. In Mississippi an autocratic and powerful minority rules, through organized violence, to suppress the vast, virtually powerless, majority. In California, the privileged minority manipulates the University bureaucracy to suppress the students' political expression. That "respectable" bureaucracy masks the financial plutocrats: the impersonal bureaucracy is the efficient enemy in a "brave new world."
> In our free speech fight at the University of California, we have come up against what may emerge as the greatest problem of our nation—depersonalized, unresponsive bureaucracy.[40]

We badly underestimate the discontent of young people if we see political activism as its only expression. There are other expressions that deserve the attention of educators. Among these I would include: (a) the growing number of young people availing themselves of counseling services; (b) the legions devoting themselves to holistic religious movements of every conceivable stripe; (c) the swelling ranks of conservative political organizations on campus; (d) young people running away from home at a present rate of more than a million a year; (e) the attitude swings of non-college youth toward agreement with attitudes held by their opposite numbers on the college campuses [41]; (f) the skyrocketing rates of vandalism in the

[39] Willard Waller. *The Sociology of Teaching.* New York: John Wiley & Sons, 1939. p. 196.

[40] Mitchell Cohen and Dennis Hale, editors. *The New Student Left.* Boston: Beacon Press, 1966. p. 254.

[41] Daniel Yankelovich. *The New Morality: A Profile of American Youth in the Seventies.* New York: McGraw-Hill Book Company, 1974.

schools making them, perhaps, our most vandalized institutions; (g) the growing crime rates among young people [42]; (h) the growing suicide rate among young people; (i) the increased use of drugs by the young; and lastly, (j) the new silence that pervades schools today which seems to me less a sign of contentment than an indication of mild depression.

We tend not to regard these activities as part of "student movements." This may be because such behaviors are not seen as having a direct connection with schools, they are seen as personal rather than public problems. It may be because many of the groups referred to are not articulate and do not tend to tie their behaviors into an analysis of larger systems. Or it may be that we simply do not listen to what is being said. We must recognize, however, that there are many styles of protest and begin to analyze them not only in terms of the issues of the day but also in terms of the conditions of modernity which promises their continuation in the future.

Styles of Adaptation and Rebellion

Individuals can be characterized by the way they relate to the world around them. W. I. Thomas identifies three ideal types of individuals in modern society. He calls them the philistine, the bohemian, and the creative man.

[42] A Senate Sub-committee To Investigate Juvenile Delinquency sent questionnaires to the superintendents of the 757 school districts and received 516 replies. Preliminary findings showed the following increases in school crime between 1970 and 1973: (a) homicides increased by 18.5 percent; (b) rapes and attempted rapes increased by 41.1 percent; (c) robberies increased by 36.7 percent; (d) assaults on students increased by 85.3 percent; (e) assaults on teachers increased by 77.4 percent; (f) burglaries of school buildings increased by 11.8 percent; (g) drug and alcohol offenses on school property increased by 37.5 percent; (h) dropouts increased by 11.7 percent; and (i) the number of weapons confiscated by school authorities had risen by 54.4 percent.

School vandalism had also increased. Working from sub-committee figures I have estimated that windows of school buildings are being broken in New York City at the rate of one every two minutes around the clock and throughout the year.

The same sub-committee has estimated that violent juvenile crime has increased by 246.5 percent in the last 13 years. Over the same period youthful offenses against property have increased by 104.6 percent. "Today persons under 25 years old are committing 50 percent of all violent crimes and 80 percent of all property crimes." Committee on the Judiciary, United States Senate. *Our Nation's Schools—A Report Card: 'A' in School Violence and Vandalism.* Washington, D.C.: U.S. Government Printing Office, April 1975.

The Philistine

The philistine is a conformist. Thomas describes him as adapting "his activities completely to the prevailing definitions and norms; he chooses security at the cost of new experience and individuality." [43] Conformity is, in itself, not an evil. It is always necessary to some degree. The questions for educators are, "What kind of a world do schools offer children?" and "What do we give them to conform to?" I have tried to show that schools socialize students into a "technological consciousness." This style of thought accepts without question the pluralization of the world, expects orderliness and predictability, adjusts to the abstract nature of modern life, and can accept individuals as interchangeable functionaries.

There is some philistine in us all. We simply could not exist in modern society without accepting these presuppositions to some degree. My argument is not so much against technological consciousness as it is against the fact that we impose it on children at such an early age and we give them so little opportunity to view the world from a different perspective.

As we have already seen, it is difficult to maintain a concrete and unified sense of identity in an abstract and pluralistic world. In order to achieve autonomy in adulthood a positive sense of self should be acquired in early life. Most often this is accomplished by working with others in mutually fulfilling enterprises to achieve shared goals. The opportunity for this kind of activity is diminishing in modern society. It constitutes a disturbingly small part of school life. It is more characteristic of the underlife of the school than it is of its formal activities.

Paul Goodman often stated that no one escapes socialization. He believed, however, that some parts of socialization can be delayed so individuals can develop a sense of who they are and what they are about.[44] We should certainly delay socialization into technological consciousness. Youngsters must learn to know and understand people before they are taught to categorize them and accept them as functionaries. They should be introduced to the essential connectedness of knowledge before it becomes compartmentalized, packaged, and programmed for efficient consumption. They must deal with concrete objects before they can learn to manipulate abstractions. To do otherwise is to produce philistines

[43] W. I. Thomas. *On Social Organization and Social Personality.* Morris Janowitz, editor. Chicago: The University of Chicago Press, 1966. p. 172. Copyright © 1966 by The University of Chicago.

[44] Paul Goodman. *New Reformation.* New York: Random House, 1969.

totally dependent on societal definitions of reality and incapable of striking out on their own. The irony here is that modern society changes so quickly that philistines soon lose sight of what it is they are trying to conform to. The fact is that modern society makes meaningful conformity exceedingly difficult.

The Bohemian

Thomas used the term bohemian to describe the individual who "is unable to fit into any frame, social or personal, because his life is spent in trying to escape definitions and avoid suppressions instead of building up a positive organization of ends and attitudes. . . ." [45] More and more young people are falling into this category. They are unable to accept a society they experience as coercive, phony, and contradictory. They are also unable to connect with others to develop more preferable meanings for the world.

The actions of the bohemian can take many forms, as we have seen in the past decade. Some young people have thrown off society's definitions of reality only to wander aimlessly from one movement to another in search of meaning and themselves. There is an implicit faith on the part of such renouncers that behind the masks and roles society imposes upon them there dwells a more real and likeable self, Emerson's "aboriginal self," Rousseau's "noble savage." This "true being" is thought to be in fundamental harmony with nature and with other "true beings" in the world.

This was the hippie quest but it was shared by a multitude of religious crusaders, drifters, delinquents, cultists, astrologers, charisma chasers, and guru followers. Even portions of the sensitivity movement can be analyzed under the bohemian heading. The ideology of these groups is often that a better self can be liberated from within us if group members are willing to cast off their pretensions and reveal their true feelings. The results promised are a deeper, more meaningful union between people. Ironically, this sense of belonging is best achieved (according to some experts) among people we hardly know. Like Blanche in *A Street Car Named Desire*, increasing numbers of people are learning to depend on "the kindness of strangers."

The problem shared by bohemians is how to most efficiently reject society. Nonconformity is only a first step. Beyond it lie more complete rejections of society as bohemians disassociate them-

---

[45] W. I. Thomas, *On Social Organization and Social Personality, op. cit.,* p. 172.

selves from societal structures wherever they are found. Many bohemians find these structures woven deeply into their own thought processes. The challenge then is to "raise consciousness" above the society's definition of reality. Not surprisingly we find renouncers discrediting rationality as an appropriate response to societal problems. For example, a student wrote George F. Keenan to insist: "To calmly speak the language of sterile rationality while all about us people die absurdly is criminal. It is time for those who place their faith in the order of the rational mind to heed the call of the heart." [46]

Some bohemians go even further and discredit sanity as "false consciousness" and embrace insanity as an ultimate liberation. Insanity, according to R. D. Laing and others, is the only rational response to an irrational world.[47] Bohemians unable to achieve insanity through the normal course of events are able to induce it chemically via drugs. By "turning on" the drug user is able to "drop out" of society, to desocialize himself/herself and thereby "tune in" to an extra-social reality. Here, it is claimed, an individual can find unity with the world. This description of a hallucinogenic drug experience is not untypical:

My first psychedelic experience was triggered by 400 milligrams of Mescaline Sulphate. It did indeed induce a flight, but instead of fleeing from reality, I flew more deeply into it. I have never before seen, touched, tasted, heard, smelled and felt so profound a personal unity and involvement with the concrete material world. . . . My exponentially heightened awareness saw through the static, one-dimensional, ego-constructed, false front which is the consciousness-constructed reality of the everyday world.[48]

Much more can be said about recent bohemian activities than we have space for here. Suffice it to say that the hippie movement of the last decade has a unique position among American social movements. As Louis Yablonsky has pointed out, the hippie phenomenon, however powerless, was one of the first American social movements to totally reject the American social system.[49] The hippie's non-bohemian counterparts in the new student left have the distinction of being America's first political movement not directed by adults.

[46] Quoted by Robert R. Sherman. In: *Democracy, Stoicism and Education: An Essay in the History of Freedom and Reason.* Gainesville: University of Florida Press, 1963. p. 2.

[47] R. D. Laing. *The Divided Self.* New York: Pantheon Books, Inc., 1969.

[48] Anton Zijderveld, *The Abstract Society, op. cit.,* pp. 100-101.

[49] Louis Yablonsky. *The Hippie Trip.* New York: Pegasus, 1968. p. 320.

Bohemians are likely to create problems for schools. Teachers cry for help in dealing with their behavior. Disciplinary hierarchies are formed, counselors are put on the case, police are assigned to the schools, new disciplinary techniques are developed. Nothing seems to work largely because we fail to address the structures of school and society which create these behaviors. Some free schools accepted the counterculture demand for total freedom and refused to impose any restrictions. They reduced discipline problems but often failed to alleviate the bohemian sense of normlessness.

Creative Man

Thomas identified another kind of individual who avoids the extreme privatization of the bohemian but simultaneously escapes the Babbitry of the philistine. Thomas calls this alternative ideal type the "creative man."

Basic to the makeup of such a being is a willingness to resist the dehumanizing nature of bureaucratic institutions, even while recognizing the need of institutional order. Ever the pragmatist, creative man holds open the possibilities of being wrong even while fighting vigorously for what he believes to be right. Neither compulsively nonconformist nor miserly in the acceptance of change, the creative person sees individualistic acts as only "an intermediary stage between one system of values and another. . . ." A violator of norms, the creative individual creates and endures disorderliness but such nonconformity is always "expressed in the setting and solution of problems, in the creation of new values. . . ." [50]

While creative man is sometimes a disrupter, he is never without feeling for the problems such disruptions may cause. He is a "temperamental rebel" with a respect for conformity when conformity is justified. Thomas offers Charles Darwin as an example of creative man:

Darwin was not a rebellious person; he was simply engrossed in a pursuit, and was very timorous about it. In common with his naturalist friends he had long realized that something terrible was about to happen to the Old Testament, but when he finally had the proofs that species were not immutable he wrote to his friends that it was "like confessing murder," and in spite of the appreciation of the scientific world he felt deeply to the end of his life the censure of the religious-primary group which accused him of a determination to "hunt God out of the world." [51]

[50] W. I. Thomas, *On Social Organization and Social Personality, op. cit.,* pp. 172-73.

[51] *Ibid.,* p. 173.

The creative person has a good deal to contribute to society. The combination of commitment to truth, inquiry, and activism, as well as concern for the impact of action on the social world, helps the creative individual to keep whole in a pluralistic society. In the language of the young, "He has his head together." The creative person is the one most likely to "make do" in modern society, to contribute to it, and maintain an identity within it. Thomas wondered in 1917 when he constructed these ideal types if it would be possible for schools to consciously educate for the creation of creative man. That question is still open today and forms the basis for this book's inquiries into education.

Part Two

Persons From Various Fields Speak: Insights into the Affective

*I*n order to help clarify and to explore more extensively the affective or feeling, valuing, and the art of growing, we asked individuals concerned about human nature, but from different stances, to write about the affective. From the following chapters we hope to learn more about: (a) the facets of the affective inherent in each perspective; (b) those themes or ideas common to the several insights; and (c) the meaning of the first two points for curriculum development and supervision.

In reviewing the affective from the perspective of an ethicist, Phenix proposes five levels or modes of affect and their ethical correlates. For each mode he also discusses implications for schooling. In essence, Phenix provides the reader with a tool for clarifying issues pertinent to the affective and for achieving, in his words, the understanding that "affect is not a single simple phenomenon such as emotion, but a complex of interrelated types and levels of experience that should be integrated according to principles of harmonization and mutual reinforcement."

Madeleine L'Engle, in, "Ousia and MTII: A Writer Speaks" discusses her approach to discovering the realness of life. An individual's Memory Treasure House (MTH) is built by reaching into the past and in turn looking to the future. The creative use of these

memories L'Engle calls *anamnesis* which leads the way to *ousia*—
"the realness of things." The search for *ousia* constitutes the motivation to write, paint, or compose a song, and from the writer's
perspective a facility with words moves us from anamnesis to *ousia*
to what L'Engle calls a hope or belief in the "all-rightness" of the
universe.

Having viewed the affective from the perspectives of an ethicist and a writer, we move to a discussion of affect by an artist. In
Beittel's exquisite description of the potter in the process of arting,
we experience vicariously the commitment, grace, unity, and fullness of being Beittel ascribes to that process. We experience the
artist's "Yes" to life and action.

Fair's chapter title, "The Reluctant Student," signals his concern with the relation between motivation and emotion. He reminds
us that no one discipline or any one institution can in and of itself
change the direction humankind appears to be taking, a direction
toward "amorphousness—the lack of warmth of conviction or of an
essentially idealistic concern with the Other." The school and
society must unite in examining this trend from a broad perspective
that includes our past. In discussing the individual, Patterson presents an overview of man from behavioristic, psychoanalytic, and
humanistic perspectives. From the humanistic viewpoint, Patterson
moves to a definition of affective education and suggestions for
focusing our efforts in that direction.

The final chapter in Part Two is directed toward viewing the
person as a member of a community. That humankind's uniqueness
loses its significance when it cannot be expressed within "a specific
shared world" is but one perspective from which Simpson views
the concept of unity. For those concerned with the future and with
change, Simpson also posits critical questions about the nature of
socialization into groups.

From the several perspectives on the affective presented in this
Part we might try to derive definitions of the affective. A range
definition would probably be most appropriate. However, instead
of attempting this, we have identified some of the threads which
run through several or all of the chapters.

The descriptions of human nature clarify the affective and confirm, in some instances document, the complexity of it. Pervading
the perspectives is the theme of the unity of life or humankind as a
whole being. This unity is exemplified by the expressed interdependence of the affective and the cognitive. Although fragmentation
characterizes some realities of present-day living, humankind desires

and can better achieve unity given the appropriate environment and necessary understanding of self and others. Among the more specific ideas related to the larger concept of unity espoused by the authors are the following:

The Person. The person participates wholeheartedly in life. The involvement is total in that it includes the person's body, feelings, images, and interactions with others. The individual acts upon the environment and is in at least partial control of it and of the self. The person whose life is characterized by a unity of experience moves beyond what is and searches for new perspectives and possibilities. The person is not only aware of his or her values but holds them and assumes responsibility for his or her actions.

Knowledge. In order to decrease the confusion and increase our knowledge about affect we need new, more complete theories and techniques appropriate to understanding the total human being. To that end we must examine our assumptions and become more explicit and precise. Intuitive as well as rational sources of knowledge must be honored and sought, and we must study the person interacting, focusing on the process and not just completed products.

Time. When there is a wholeness to life, personal interactions indicate certain perspectives on time. Several of the writers speak of a time sense that is not quantitative but qualitative in that the learner in the act of creating is beyond clock time of minutes and hours. Time is also viewed from the perspective of gaining a sense of history of oneself and of projecting one's future. Life is seen as continuous in time. Tradition, where one comes from, one's memories, projections, and ability to embrace a sense of time not meted out mechanically all contribute to the unity of life.

Context. Permeating the chapters and giving support to the concept of unity is a recognition of the importance of one's environment or context. A human being is seen as both creature and creator of the environment. A facilitative environment characterized by trust and creative love is necessary for the development of attitudes such as respect, concern, and care for self and others. Educators who plan for and with learners need to understand that an environment teaches more than stipulated learnings and that in order to effect change we must be attuned to factors in the context that facilitate a learner's finding out about self and others.

Community. The importance of significant others in the life of an individual is the basis for a sense of community that seems to envelop and support the rest of the ideas related to the broader concept of unity. Individuals are "co-creators" in the process of generating knowledge and in discovering new learnings. Any significant changes must be accomplished cooperatively. It is imperative that humans be empathic persons who can, in Patterson's words, feel what others feel and who treat others as living beings and not things. We need to work to preserve the dignity of the individual as a member of a community—a community that respects and is respected by each member. Warmth, conviction, and respect must permeate personal interactions that cross all age lines. The interdependence of human beings is sharply brought to focus in a study of the affective.

Additional examples of unity may be found in the chapters which follow. Other themes and sub-themes may be identified that shed new light on classroom practices designed to enhance the person as a feeling, valuing, and growing being.

3

Perceptions of an Ethicist About the Affective

Philip H. Phenix

*C*oncern about the affective dimension in human experience has always been a central feature of ethical reflection. In ethics, such concern takes the form of defining and refining such basic concepts as "good," "right," and "responsibility" in relation to human action and of exhibiting the grounds for preferring one form of action over another. Obviously, such matters are of central importance to the educator, whose essential task is to help learners to do the right, fulfill the good, and live responsibly.

It is not surprising, then, that many observers view the contemporary crises of education—indeed, of culture and civilization generally—as primarily ethical in nature. The rapid changes in the conditions of modern life, due largely to the accelerated rate of technological development, have resulted in profound dislocations of traditional values and in the undermining of confidence in accepted moral standards. Knowledge in every field has grown exponentially, while the wisdom to use that knowledge responsibly has seemed if anything to decline. Accordingly, a clamor has arisen for greater attention to moral education and to the development of character, in order to close the gap between power and virtue and to reestablish a sense of direction and purpose in the human enterprise.

Unfortunately, the problems of ethics are not of easy resolution, and it cannot be said that ethicists are at all of one mind regarding the problems of the affective domain. Ethical concepts have perennially been, and still remain, exceedingly elusive of precise and universally accepted definition and justification. In particular, they suffer by comparison with concepts and conclusions in the strictly cognitive domains, especially the natural sciences, by virtue of the difficulty they present of arriving at universally warrantable assertions. Hence the charge commonly made that ethical standards are "purely subjective," or simply symptomatic of one's private feelings and therefore not subject to public verification nor rational defense. Under the circumstances, it is understandable that proposals for moral education and for more attention to values in the curriculum are often met with skepticism or resigned indifference.

In spite of these uncertainties, there are promising suggestions in ethical philosophy that may assist substantially in the clarification of issues in the affective domain in education. These suggestions may be viewed in two aspects, namely, in terms of analytical distinctions and in terms of synthetic coordination of these analytic elements. On this basis it is possible to construct an intelligible theory of the affective domain, by displaying the structure of affective dimensions as reflected in ethical thought. From such a theory useful conclusions can be drawn for educational practice in relation to affective experience. (See Table 1 for the analytical schema in summary form.)

Levels of Affect

The required analysis depends upon drawing a distinction between at least five different but interrelated levels of affect. From the standpoint of value theory, affect does not name a simple quality, but is a complex concept embracing a range of interdependent meanings. To some extent these distinctions have already been made in previous essays in this volume, in differentiating between "feeling," "valuing," and "the art of growing."

Organic Needs — Ethics of Survival

The most elemental aspect of affect is rooted in the biological cravings of the human organism. A person is also an animal, with organic drives and impulses, with needs for food, clothing, shelter, sexual gratification, and the like. The human being has inborn

Philip H. Phenix *is Arthur I. Gates Professor of Philosophy and Education at Teachers College, Columbia University. A graduate in mathematical physics at Princeton, in theology at Union Theological Seminary, and in philosophy at Columbia, he served as professor and later as Dean at Carleton College, before joining the Teachers College faculty. His special interests are the theory of knowledge, ethics, and hispanic culture and education. Among his publications, which include works on education and religion, values, human nature, and epistemology, he is best known for his book,* Realms of Meaning: A Philosophy of the Curriculum for General Education.

demands that must be met by resources in the environment. The basic wants of every person are connected with survival in and adaptation to the natural world. In this sense, organic adjustment is the fundamental law of life.

In ethical terms, this elemental type of affect is reflected in the idea of self-preservation as the first and most fundamental law of life. The right of survival is taken as virtually axiomatic in all ethical systems and underlies most of the other "higher" concepts such as the worth of each person, the right of self-defense, and property rights. Without the minimal basis of biological survival, no other values are realizable. In this sense one is justified in affirming a radical (in the literal meaning of "root") materialism: the natural and organic sources of all personal existence are primordial and quintessential.

It follows that these basic ground-values deserve a place of honor in the educative experience. It is appropriate that the young learn to appreciate and respect the primal impulses on which life depends. It is one of the great contributions of Freud and his followers to have understood the crucial nature of organic desires in the subsequent development of the healthy person; to deny their existence or to curb them arbitrarily as though they were inimical

	1.	2.	3.	4.	5.
Levels of affect	Organic needs	Feelings	Interests	Judgments	Idealizations
Types of ethics	Survival	Hedonic	Self-realization	Critical	Progressive-normative
Functions of the person	Bodily (Homeostasis)	Sensitive (Passion)	Conative (Action)	Rational (Thought)	Self-transcending (Vision)
Stages of moral development [Adapted from Kohlberg]	Preconventional	Interpersonal concordance	Law and order	Social contract	Universal principle
Evolutionary stages	Matter	Life	Personality	Society	Beloved community
Social functions [Adapted from Arendt]	Labor	Work	Action	Contemplation	Transformation
Learning goals	Adaptive skill	Creative construction	Communal collaboration	Critical inquiry	Comprehensive commitment
Key disciplines	Of survival: Skill and technique	Of celebration: The arts	Of decision: Policy studies	Of logical reason: The sciences	Of transcendence: Philosophy and religion
Key social agencies	Homes, farms, shops	Studios, museums, media	Communities	Schools and research institutes	Religious and quasi-religious fellowships

Table 1. Schema for an Ethical Analysis of Affective Dimensions in Education

forces is to prepare the way for no end of personal frustration and failure.

The wise pedagogy of the early years is necessarily based on an ethic of organic survival and adaptation. The young must be instructed from the start in what must be done to avoid physical danger and to ensure satisfaction of basic needs. All of the habit-forming routines of infancy and early childhood are dedicated to these ends. Upon the successful inculcation of viable patterns of habitual response through rewards and punishment, guided by the best available knowledge of psychological conditioning processes, depends the possibility of the good life for the person at all stages of his or her subsequent life career.

Feelings — Hedonic Ethics

The second meaning of affect embraces the idea of subjective response expressed in feelings of delight or pleasure. These feelings are generally associated with organic satisfactions, but are not identical with them and go beyond them. The pleasures one receives in seeing beautiful sights or hearing harmonious sounds transcend the satisfaction of organic drives. The delights of the senses are a superadded affective stratum, dependent on the functioning organism but not simply an expression of its adaptive achievements. The values of feeling affect comprise a relatively autonomous emergent domain rooted in the organic but flowering out into new and distinct qualities of experience.

Corresponding to this second type of affect is a type of ethic—hedonism—in which pleasure is taken as a measure of the good. On this view, the desirable life is one that maximizes pleasure and minimizes its opposite, pain. On the social scale it yields the ethics of utilitarianism, according to which the good consists in maximizing pleasure and minimizing pain for the greatest number of people.

Feeling values constitute the basis for the sense of immediate worth in existence. They express present enjoyment of quality. One does not need to interrogate their meaning nor demand justification for them, since they simply present themselves as experienced consummations. They are what they are; they raise no questions; they fulfill themselves. As with organic cravings, it is important that the young learn to accept and enjoy their own feelings and to trust the messages they convey. To do so is the only basis for fostering a life with direct and unquestioned satisfactions. One need not elaborate on the predominance of ugliness and pain in the world to understand how much in need it is of persons who can appreciate and promote simple love and joy in things perceived. From an early age children need the time and occasion simply to sense their own bodies and the world around them, and to discriminate the varieties of qualitative experiences of which they are capable. They need opportunities to observe and respond to the manifold wonders of their surroundings in an atmosphere of quiet hospitality to fresh and interesting sense perceptions.

A hedonic ethic thus has an important role to play in modern education. Sensitivity, capacity for discrimination, tenderness, gentleness, consideration, listening, appreciative awareness: these are all modes of behavior that require nurture if the goal of a humane life for humankind is to be realized. For such nurture to occur, learning situations must be provided in which the value of the experience in itself is acknowledged, instead of being regarded as preparation for something else. Young people of the "now" generation increasingly recognize and reject the "receding horizon" view of life and learning, according to which consummations are postponed until some future date, at which time they are to be fully enjoyed because adequately secured and prepared for. In a rapidly shifting and essentially unpredictable existence the young rightly demand a type of learning experience in which affective fulfillments are immediately practiced and achieved and not only anticipated in the future.

Affect in both of the first two modes is essentially in the nature of a "passion," that is, a reactive response to presented stimuli. They differ in respect to the degree of incorporation and identification. Organic cravings are integral to the organism's physical existence, and their satisfaction is achieved through incorporative transactions with the environment. Feelings, on the other hand, are responses in which there is a separation or "distance" between the objects perceived and the enjoying subject. The flower or the song enjoyed, for example, maintains its distinct identity, while the food desired by the hungry person is incorporated in the act of organic satisfaction.

Interests — Ethics of Self-Realization

The third type of affect substitutes the active for the passive mode. Values of this type may be described as a person's interest or intention. They express some determination of an active nature rather than a passive response to a want or to a presented sense object. The goal of such activity is to attain some power over things or persons by controlling the environment, both natural and social, in accordance with certain purposes or ends in view.

These conative values correspond to the ethic that identifies the good with self-realization. They underlie the classic forms of ethical egoism, according to which the good is measured by the degree to which the demands of the will are satisfied. Hobbes and Nietzsche in different ways saw the human being as essentially in search of power and the various forms of social organization as ways of minimizing the conflicts of competing wills. Perhaps those who have most clearly articulated the conative element of affect in modern times are the existentialists. They see human beings as defined by their active intentions. They hold that a person has no fixed nature given by inheritance, but that a being creates the self by free decisions. Being is a projection of self into the future by deliberate acts of decision. A person does not absorb independent values from outside the self, but posits them by free self-determination.

In both of the first two types of affect, the person as passive respondent is, as it were, a captive of the environing world. Response is in obedience to the imperious demands of impulses or to the allurements of the world of sensory forms. In the third type the person is free. The individual does not depend upon forces or structures either outside or within, but independently acts as a creative force that structures existence according to the self's own interests and purposes.

Modern education has given a prominent place to the nurture of this kind of affect. All curricula concerned with activity rather than passive reaction to presented stimuli emphasize it. Students who are preparing to assume responsible roles in society must clearly learn to practice the arts of creative decision. In a world in continuous transformation they must learn by practice how to formulate and carry through novel and unprecedented patterns of behavior. More and more young people are refusing to repeat the formulas inherited from the past and are claiming their right and duty to create their own appropriate futures. They accordingly require a form of educative experience that breaks sharply with the traditional assimilative-transmissive mode and that emphasizes instead the inventive-constructive type that will fit them for the world of the future.

Furthermore, the self-realization ethic in education throws into high relief the need for individualization or personalization in the educative process. The person is regarded as a unique creative agent and not as a more or less standardized copy of an assumed ideal prototype. To "educate" in these terms means something quite distinct from the common notion of forming the person according to a preexistent model. It requires the setting up of conditions in which the learner may freely exercise a capacity for active decision making in accordance with his or her own self-image and own distinctive purposes. Such cultivation of conative affect presupposes a learning environment rich in alternative possibilities and in resources for their fulfillment. It depends on a high degree of flexibility in the organization of learning experiences and generous hospitality by personally secure teachers to a wide variety of initiatives on the part of their students.

These concepts of education based on the self-realization ethic have long been recognized, as in the emphasis on individual differences, in the project approach to teaching, and in the contemporary open school movement. Within this frame of reference the teacher is essentially a helper rather than a master or director. The teacher's task is to be sensitive to the student's developing interests and abiding purposes and to assist in exploring and realizing them.

The three types of affect considered to this point may be conveniently categorized by reference to the time dimension, as follows: Organic impulse affects refer to the past. They arise from causal factors that influence the organism in the direction of more satisfactory biological adjustment to inherited environmental conditions. Feeling affects refer to the present. They represent the person's awareness of immediate qualities in patterns of sensory response. Conative affects, finally, refer to the future. They reflect the projection of the person's being into intended future states. From such an analysis in terms of time, the first three kinds of affect may be summarized briefly as pressures, presences, and promises.

Judgments — Critical Ethics

The fourth type of affect introduces an important new element, namely, that of critical reflection, appraisal, or judgment and a corresponding critical ethic. The first three types simply are what they are; there is no question of justifying them or evaluating them. A want is a pressure from an antecedent state of the organism that asserts itself. A pleasure enjoyed in the perception of some harmonious presence simply declares itself in experience, admitting no correction and requiring no defense. Similarly, a purpose is an existential project of being that neither seeks nor expects justification beyond its own positing. But this is not the end of the matter. For affects are not single isolable elements of experience. They are manifold, and they enter into competition and conflict with each other. Hence the need for reflection and criticism.

The deliberative reflection of critical ethics produces what may be termed rational affect. This term will seem to entail a contradiction for those to whom reason and affect are regarded as opposites. A stronger case can be made for holding that in fact reason is the best ally of affect, through its office of coordination and ordering to reduce destructive conflicts. The function of reason is to consider relationships among affects, enabling the person to organize them in such a way as to maximize their compatibility.

John Dewey's critical ethics deals with rational affect in making the basic distinction between the desired (whether in the form of a want, an object of pleasure, or an intention) and the desirable. The desired becomes the desirable only through the process of reflective evaluation. A rational affect is experienced when impulses, pleasures, and intentions have been subjected to critical reflection in which alternatives, compatibilities, and mutual reinforcements of personal realization are explored and decided upon.

There is a dimension of rationality, however, that goes beyond the personal harmonizing functions already referred to. Impulse, feeling, and purpose are all oriented essentially to the individual person and make no reference to the wider social context, except as environment for the person's activity. The essential function of reason is to establish ever wider circles of relation, aiming at common agreement. Reason is the tool by which persons are able to transcend their subjectivity and enter imaginatively into the experience of others. In this quality of imaginative self-transcendence that is the aim of rationality one can see a deeper reason why rationality and affect are not disjunctive and why the claims of intelligence may be so persistent and affectively powerful in human experience. For, if the consequence of reflective thought is to extend relationships toward universal consensus, then its fruit is the affective reinforcement that stems from all personal mutuality. Through reason one senses a participation in experience that is more significant than one's own private subjectivity of impulse, feeling, or purpose.

Hence the development of critical intelligence is of basic importance for affective education. Through it the person gains the means not only for making discriminating judgments among competing affective claims in one's own personality, but also for relating these claims to those of other persons so as to achieve a progressively higher harmony between the needs, feelings, and intentions of the self and of others. Such intelligence is the ground both for effective communication and for the growth in the sense of community by which the richness of affect in the interpenetration of experiences of distinct and varied persons is achieved. Such community building is the goal to which Dewey referred in his advocacy of democratic education through the nurture of critical intelligence. The goal of Dewey's method of intelligence, with his emphasis on the scientific outlook, was not rational understanding for its own sake, but the cultivation of a deep and secure affective life in a community of shareable experience.

Idealizations — Ethics of Progressive Norms

Finally, a fifth aspect of affect needs to be distinguished. It is not enough that desires, feelings, and interests be rationally appraised so as to afford defensible judgments of desirability. For there is always the possibility—indeed, the effective certainty—that what is judged as worthy of approval is so only in a partial and limited way or even that the judgment is altogether mistaken. Since reason itself is subject to limitations of fallibility and finiteness, it may mislead, even at its best.

It therefore appears necessary to presuppose an overarching affective principle that may be called the commitment to idealization, to ensure the continuation of the drive toward ever fuller value realization. The principle is evident in a variety of human domains: in the commitment of scientists to the continuous reconstruction of models, laws, and theories; in the search of artists for the continual refreshment of the aesthetic vision; in the efforts of social reformers to fashion a progressively more just social order. It is what Plato termed the Idea of the Good, that forever indefinable source of particular goods of which the latter are but dim reflections, that central Sun of reason that gives whatever measure of intelligibility any particular objects of knowledge possess.

The platonic reference might suggest the term ideal affect for this fifth type. However, care is necessary to avoid the notion of the ideal as a fixed absolute system of values, since such would be the very negation of what is here intended. That is why the term idealization may be preferable. The essence of the matter is precisely the principle of criticism of fixed absolutes, in favor of unending creative revision. The scientist's devotion to truth is based on the conviction that there is more and deeper understanding to be attained beyond the present stage of knowledge and beyond any

conceivable future stage. The moralist's dedication to social reconstruction presupposes an order of goodness higher than any now
attained and finer than any utopia that may be envisioned. Commitment to idealization is a kind of affect of affects—an affective
principle that guides the flowering of affect on all of its other levels.

The ethic of progressive idealization constitutes the ground for
all education that aims at continuous creative growth. Without it
the commitment to reconstruction is lacking and the way is opened
to static conceptions of truth and justice. The commitment to
idealization is the necessary presupposition of really serious inquiry,
in the absence of which there is no basis for challenging given
impulses, feelings, purposes, and critical judgments. Genuine inquiry
rests upon the acknowledgment of structures of value that are
preferable to any already realized or realizable. It presumes the
possibility of progress beyond every degree of attained excellence.
Education involving such an ethic is particularly imperative in the
present stage of civilization, when the rapidity and profundity of
change make the acceptance of fresh perspectives necessary, when
the consequences of destructive conflicts are so disastrous that
readiness for creative reconciling of alternatives is essential, and
when the magnitude of cultural complications and frustrations make
faith and hope in renewing possibilities prerequisite for taking heart
to build a better future.

Synthesis of the Levels

Recapitulating, our analysis has distinguished five aspects or
types of affect: organic impulse, feeling, intention, rational appraisal,
and progressive idealization, and for each a corresponding ethic
has been identified: survival, hedonic, self-realization, critical, and
progressive-idealist. In each case the importance of cultivating that
element of affect in teaching and learning has been pointed out.

Making analytic distinctions, however, does not suffice for the
curriculum maker, who needs to know how these several elements
relate to one another within the whole educative process. Hence
the need for a synthetic view. As already indicated, a strong case
can be made for the educator making provision for each of the five
types of affect in the curriculum. It is not surprising, then, that one
finds advocates for each type among educators concerned with
affective education. For some, affective education means giving due
attention to organic needs. Others emphasize the cultivation of
sensitivity to feelings. Still others are concerned with individual

purposes. Some are most interested in rational insight as a value and others in the development of continuous growth possibilities. The harm comes from treating these several types of affect as independent and separable, when in fact they are intimately interconnected. One of the main sources of confusion in affective education is a segmental view of affect and the absence of the necessary coordinating outlook.

For example, modern depth psychology has shown the mischief that results from compartmentalizing reason and feeling, and has indicated the road to healing as a reintegration of the two through recognition of the role of the passions in the processes of reasoning and the role of reason in the wise ordering of the passions. Similarly, contemporary psychology has made clear the importance of satisfying basic bodily needs if the person is to develop realizable personal goals and properly functioning rational capacities. Social scientists have demonstrated the role that group affiliation plays in the formation of purposes and how necessary the critical consideration of alternatives is to expose the idols of class and culture.

This problem of the order and integration of affect has been one of the classic themes of ethical theory. Plato's dialogues were largely concerned with effecting a synthesis that would do justice to all of the various aspects of personality within a comprehensive framework. He did not deny the needs of the body, but he believed that they had to be subordinated to higher sensibilities. He recognized the place of purpose and intention in the growth of a forceful personality, but he believed these goals should be pursued under the guidance of reason. He acknowledged the value of logical processes, but held that reason itself had to proceed under the inspiration of a transcendent ideal beyond finite comprehension or actualization.

A genuinely normative ethics is comprehensive enough to make due provision for impulse, pleasure, ego assertion, critical judgment, and idealization. None of the aspects of affect is denied, but each is placed in proper relation to the others according to a basic principle of value maximization. Perhaps the most important contribution of the ethical perspective to the theory and practice of education is this understanding that affect is not a single simple phenomenon such as emotion, but a complex of interrelated types and levels of experience that should be integrated according to principles of harmonization and mutual reinforcement. The central aim of education may be formulated as just such integration of affect.

Affect and the Nature of the Person

This picture of affect levels and their integration on the basis of a comprehensive normative ethic is made even more convincing by considerations drawn from a number of independent domains of inquiry. To begin with, the distinctions noted accord well with classic conceptions of the nature of the human being. The familiar trilogy of thought, will, and feeling as aspects of personality are other names for rational affect, conative affect, and hedonic affect as discussed above. Idealizing affect can be translated into what has traditionally been called spirit, or the power of self-transcendence in the activity of striving toward perfection, while the first of the levels of affect, the impulsive, can be interpreted as the somatic dimensions of human life.

Modern functionalism represents the human being not as a collection of separate parts, as, for example, in the concept of body and soul as distinct entities, but rather as an integrated organic whole with different functions. The person functions as an adaptive biological organism in respect to certain of its environmental relationships, as a sensitive perceiver in others, as an active projector of purposes in still others, as a rational evaluator in some, and as an idealizer in others. In each of these types of activities it is the same total entity behaving, but in functionally distinguishable ways.

In this classic picture of human nature the several functions are evidently related to one another in a hierarchy of interdependence. Each functional level depends on and presupposes the preceding ones. Thus, all forms of affective experience depend on the basic functions of nutrition, reproduction, organic growth, and self-maintenance that keep the person in homeostatic continuity within the shifting environment. Building on this base, it is possible for the person to have perceptions, enjoyments, and emotions in response to variegated surroundings. At the next level, the person is prepared to undertake executive functions, mounting initiatives that effect changes in the world in accordance with imagined ends-in-view. Only on the basis of these three initial functional capacities is the person in a position to move to the level of symbolization and intellection, in which alternative possible intentions, emotions, and wants may be conceived and coordinated. Finally, the function of idealization comes into operation only on the basis of the four preceding functions, which supply the essential materials for its quest toward excellence.

The educator with such an understanding of human nature sees the task as helping to provide conditions in which all of the five levels of personal functioning may be given the opportunity for exercise, and in which they are related in the proper order of subordination. From the standpoint of normative ethics, the proper subordination entails the preeminence of rational affect, energized by the commitment to idealization, as the basis for making the desirable choices among the wants, feelings, and purposes of the lower levels.

The aim of education is, then, the growth of persons in the power of making wise rational choices among alternative goals, perceptions, and drives, within a framework of faith in continuous growth possibilities. This aim cannot, however, be realized through the teaching of abstract moral principles, cut off from the concrete intentions, desires, and drives of the more primordial affective levels. The vision of ideality and the harmonizing power of reason are properly the controllers of human learning, but only in intimate and unseverable relation to the prior levels of affect which alone provide the substance that reason and vision can meaningfully organize.

Developmental Psychology and Levels of Affect

The description of human nature in terms of a series of interconnected levels of affect with ethical valences is further supported by the findings of modern developmental psychology. Particularly significant in this regard are the studies of Erik Erikson, with his concept of the eight developmental stages of life, of Jean Piaget, with his principles of genetic epistemology, and most recently of Lawrence Kohlberg, with his analysis of the stages in moral development.

These developmental investigations are of great importance to the educator, for they suggest that the hierarchy of affective levels is not merely an analytic tool for making functional distinctions, but also a clue to the chronological sequence followed by the person growing toward maturity. A brief summary of Kohlberg's scheme will permit us to relate his analysis of developmental sequence to the affect levels previously distinguished, together with their ethical correlates.

Kohlberg identifies six stages of moral development, on the basis of empirical inquiries into the actual processes of moral reasoning employed by subjects asked to make judgments in a series of hypothetical decision situations. The first stage is marked by orientation to punishment and obedience. The person acts on the basis of threats and promises to the self's own security and survival. In the second stage, of instrumental relativist orientation, decisions are made so as to maximize satisfaction in particular situations and to solve problems in order to yield the greatest adaptive harmony in the given environment. Kohlberg calls these two stages preconventional, since they refer to judgments made independently of social awareness. They correspond roughly to the first two levels of affect identified above as impulse and desire since punishment and obedience govern when conduct is concerned with securing organic needs and the hedonic standard applies when the person has developed some detachment from biological imperatives and seeks the intensification of sensory delights.

Kohlberg's stages three and four constitute the conventional level, the former being that of interpersonal concordance and the latter that of law and order. At this level the person is aware of the self's own interests and purposes and of the corresponding ego demands of other persons, and seeks means to realize desired goals by coordinating them with those of others so as to minimize destructive conflict. This social adaptation is, however, without benefit of critical deliberation and thus is called conventional. At this level the ego adjusts its demands for social survival and satisfaction just as the person at the somatic and sensory levels adapts to the environment of forces and perceptual stimuli.

Kohlberg's stages five and six constitute what he terms the post-conventional, autonomous, or principled level. They correspond respectively to what have been referred to above as rational affect and the commitment to idealization. Stage five in Kohlberg's terminology is characterized by a social contract, legalistic orientation, in which deliberate procedures for the harmonizing of interests are worked out and encoded in principles of rationally justified positive law rather than reflecting the purely customary constraints of the law and order orientation in the fourth stage. In the sixth stage the orientation is that of universal ethical principle, in which the person justifies conduct on the basis of a presumed ideal of universal justice that transcends particular cultures, private or group interests, or even the decisions of critical jurisprudence.

Kohlberg claims that cross-cultural developmental studies provide a secure basis for an empirical ethics by disclosing a definite series of sequential levels of moral development culminating in a stage of universal ethical principle, including respect for persons and equal rights for all, that accords with the highest visions of philosophic ethics. Though it may be questioned whether it is logically possible to derive ethical norms from empirical observations, such developmental inquiries clearly provide valuable suggestions for the curriculum maker regarding the ordering of affective learning experiences.

Affective readiness. Developmental sequence has three distinct aspects that the educator should not confuse. The first has to do with stages of physiological and psychological readiness, to which an average age chronology can be attached. Piaget has particularly emphasized this aspect in his studies of the cognitive and moral development of the child. It is found that very young children are generally not prepared to understand the rules of social convention, let alone the abstract principles of rational ethics. At the beginning they are ready only for learning through experiences that reflect immediate organic needs or direct sensory perceptions of the environment. At older ages they are successively ready to formulate longer-range goals, to engage in rational reflection about alternatives, and to commit themselves to the search for universal norms. It is manifestly the responsibility of the teacher to adjust the teaching in the affective domain to the readiness level of the students and not to expect them to be able to comprehend or practice kinds of moral behavior of which they are not capable at a given age level.

Affective prerequisites. The second aspect of developmental sequence concerns the matter of affective prerequisites. Here it is not primarily a question of chronological age, but of structural elaboration. Generalizations and abstractions presuppose a basis in prior concrete particulars. Direct organic satisfactions are a prerequisite to the more detached pleasures of sensory contemplation, and these in turn provide content for the projection of purposes, the consideration of alternatives, and the formulation of ideals. The lower levels of affective development are related to the later ones as the data of individual observations are to the laws and theories derived from them in the process of inductive reasoning.

The distinction between age level and stages of elaboration is an important one for two reasons. First, since persons may advance in their affective development at widely differing rates, chronological age is no more than a rough measure of learning readiness. Second, people of any age may manifest affective responses at levels lower than the highest of which they are capable. Thus, adults who are capable of principled behavior based on intelligent consideration of consequences may in fact be governed by organic impulse, by hedonic considerations, or by ego demands. The educator needs to be ready to deal at any age with every level of affective development and to assess each student's needs in accordance with the degree of logical sophistication manifested in his or her moral conduct so as to lead the student by an inductive process to the highest level he or she is prepared to attain.

Affective norms. The third aspect of developmental sequence is the strictly normative one. Here it is a question of moral maturity according to a hierarchy of preference. The stage of universal ethical principle is presumed to be the highest and not merely the most advanced, elaborate, or latest in time. From this standpoint, an ethic of universal ideals is regarded as a better ethic than hedonism or egoism. In the normative scale, persons do not just develop through the successive moral stages, but they improve or advance as they pass from level to level in such a hierarchy as that described by Kohlberg. The educator is thus provided with goals toward which to direct the teaching effort and with standards by which to evaluate the degree of moral maturity attained by the learner.

This matter of a normative hierarchy of stages is of importance in discussions on the issue of moral education. Many students of the subject, impressed by the diversity of moral standards in different cultures and by the apparent impossibility of arriving at a stable consensus on norms of conduct, adopt a position of ethical relativism, denying that there are any universal ethical principles and holding that the notion of progressive improvement through continuous idealization is illusory. They advocate a nonjudgmental stance in value education, seeking only that each learner realize his own values without reference to any general standards of preference.

An example of this nonjudgmental approach to the affective domain in education is the value clarification strategies put forward by Louis Raths, Merrill Harmin, and Sidney Simon. These strategies are based on the conviction that what is important in value education is not the inculcation of given values but the development of skills for identifying and practicing what the learner freely chooses and most highly prizes. It is assumed that a value is not really clarified until one has made a choice after thoughtfully examining the consequences of alternatives. When such critical examination has been made, and when the learner has affirmed the choices, publicly declared a commitment to them, acted on them, and developed patterns of repeated action around these beliefs, he or she can be said to have realized the goals of value inquiry.

The value clarification approach corresponds to what was earlier referred to as the fourth affective level, namely, that of rational affect. What it appears to reject is the fifth level, that is, the commitment to progressive idealization, since an important assumption of the value clarification approach is that there are no objective goods in the value domain and that the sole aim is for each person to discover what the self really believes.

Useful as the practice of value clarification is, a normative ethical position requires that one ask not merely what a person regards as desirable but what really is desirable, and such a question leads to the search for universal ethical norms. The case is clearest in science, where few would consider it enough to clarify one's own beliefs about the world. The important commitment is to what is true objectively, and this presupposition is equivalent to a principle of progressive reconstruction of scientific understanding based on a process of continuous projection of ideal possibilities. Normative ethicists take the same position in regard to other affective domains. For them, it is not enough that each person clarify what to believe concerning justice, for example. The really important commitment is to justice itself, as a universally obligatory moral principle. This is not to claim that the ethicist or anyone else knows or can identify with certainty what that universal principle is. It is only to assert that one ought not remain satisfied with the clarification of individual beliefs as though they were exempt from a higher and more universal judgment.

A normatively oriented educator considers that judgments of higher and lower, better and worse, are essential. Such orientation assumes that the task is to help the learner toward a better life and toward the development of improved character. In making these judgments the educator necessarily presupposes some such hierarchical scale as that of the five levels of affect earlier described or that of Kohlberg's stages in moral development. Not content with things as they are and with simply recognizing and accepting the affects that learners presently exhibit, a person so oriented considers a commitment to betterment and progress the mainspring of educative endeavor and the only justification for dedication to it.

On the other hand, the ethically well-grounded educator is aware of the pitfalls of a moralistic and legalistic outlook in which it is presumed that the absolute values toward which the educative process ought to be aimed and the ideal character traits that learners ought to attain are known. This educator recognizes the contribution that the nonjudgmentalists have made in calling into question the presumptiveness of this position, but does not cut the nerve of continued value inquiry and commitment to a universal ideal by adopting the stance of nonjudgment. The commitment is rather to making the best value judgments possible, and to helping others to improve their own values (not just to accept them, however sincerely held), recognizing that we all stand under the higher judgment of a universal ideal that transcends all finite realizations.

Evolution and the Levels of Affect

The types and levels of affect identified above can be seen in still wider perspective by considering the process of organic and cultural evolution. By doing so it is possible to establish a foundation for affective development in the cosmic process itself and thus to suggest a source for values in the very nature of the evolving universe. It seems reasonable to draw a parallel between the developmental levels identified in the maturation of individual persons and the successive stages in the emergence of new levels of coordination in the evolutionary scheme, thus recalling the biological principle that "ontogeny recapitulates phylogeny," that is, that individual organisms develop in stages that are analogues of the stages of species emergence.

An obvious parallel exists between the main levels of evolution and the five affective levels identified above. The primary evolutionary level is that on which matter appears as the organization of elemental particles into configurations of energy in the form of atoms and molecules. This level of basic physical forces corresponds to the impulse level of affect. The second stage of evolution is defined by the emergence of life as more complex energy configurations with novel principles of coordination, including the power of self-perpetuation, that are not shared by inorganic systems. This second level corresponds to the hedonic type of affect, concerned as it is with sensitive responses that transcend impulsive drives. On the third level of evolution human life emerges, with the novel power of conscious self-identification and free projection of purposes. This stage parallels the conative level in the affective hierarchy. At the fourth evolutionary level society and culture emerge, based on the organization of human beings with shared principles of coordination for common ends. This level corresponds to that of rational affect. Finally, the entire evolutionary process may be viewed as having an inner principle of progressive organization leading through mutation and selection to successively higher levels both of individuality and of mutual coordination. This cosmic principle of orthogenesis, or of qualitative directional selectivity, may be taken as the evolutionary counterpart of the fifth affective level, of commitment to continuous idealization.

Through such an analysis of material, biological, personal, and cultural evolution a number of leading process philosophers, most notably Alfred North Whitehead, have suggested a cosmic basis for ethics and a foundation in the natural world for the processes of human growth and development toward ideal ends. What is most significant for present concerns about these formulations is the prominence they give both to affect and to the process of education. For the emergent evolutionist, affect is not an epiphenomenon—a mere concomitant of more basic experience. Rather, it is the very stuff of reality. According to Whitehead, the basic units of reality are constituted by subjective feelings of value or importance. The world of objective phenomena, even that of the inorganic realm, has an inner core of qualitative prehension, creative construction, and striving for consummation, the nature of which can be appreciated by examining one's own states of consciousness.

If affect is so universal and so fundamental to the nature of things, it should be possible to derive standards of preference and ethical norms for selection among competing affects from the study of cosmic evolution. With such an orientation, the educator may find guidance for the formulation of educational aims, both for the individual person and for the cultural scene as an organized structure giving maximum freedom and initiative within a context of mutual cooperation and respect.

Social Institutions and Affective Education

In order to translate such a scheme of cosmic priorities into practical curricular terms the educator needs to return to the particulars of social institutions and the disciplined studies through which learning takes place. In this regard, there are valuable suggestions in the analysis of levels of human activity made by Hannah Arendt in her book, *The Human Condition*. She draws distinctions among the following: labor, as the form of activity required for the sustenance of life in the endless cycle of production, consumption, and reproduction; work, as the activity of the individual creating nonconsumable objects that yield lasting enjoyment; action, as the activity of decision for the creation of the enduring human community with a history and purposes that transcend individual interests; and contemplation, as the pursuit of a rational vision of the unchanging order of things. Her thesis is that while all these elements are necessary for human life, modern industrial civilization has reversed the classical priorities and elevated labor to the highest place, to which work and action are subordinated, with contemplation eliminated altogether. This amounts to a radical reversal of values, that is, in the hierarchy of types of affect, with ominous consequences for the future of humankind and civilization.

Learning Goals and Key Disciplines

The educator concerned with making a contribution to the right ordering of human life in accordance with the basic requirements of the human condition can view the task as the normative one of reaffirming the great priorities, in which survival labor, creative work, and communal action are all honored and accorded their due place within a contemplative vision of progressive emergence. Labor requires the learning of adaptive skills through what may be termed the disciplines of survival. These include the whole range of skill subjects and technical studies designed to yield maximum control over the environment and fullest satisfaction of organic needs.

Work values are developed through activities of individual creative construction guided by principles of aesthetic selection. These are within the province of the arts, which may be termed the disciplines of celebration or of consummatory experience. Action is the goal of the policy disciplines, in which the learner gains experience in projecting purposes and in coordinating his or her purposes with those of others within a context of communal organization and collaboration in the making of decisions and covenants. Contemplation is the aim of the scientific disciplines, aimed at the progressive refinement of reason and the development of an intelligent vision of human possibilities. All of these disciplines are subject to coordination and infusion by the insights of the disciplines of transcendence, concerned with the search for wholeness, comprehensive commitment, fully normative ethical judgment, and cosmic process, as exemplified in such studies as metaphysics ontology, theology, and cosmology.

Key Social Agencies

Each of the types of affect has certain social institutions to which it is peculiarly related and to which learning is especially relevant. Families, industrial organizations, and agricultural facilities are particularly concerned with survival processes and with the satisfaction of organic wants. Studios, museums, and media of communication are especially relevant to the presentation of objects for the delight of the senses. The various voluntary associations of the community, including clubs, peer groups, political parties, and the like, are the most relevant agencies for the expression of interests and purposes. Laboratories, libraries, and research institutes are the institutions in which rational affect is most basic. Finally, the various types of communities of faith, both religious and secular, are devoted to the celebration of the commitment to progressive idealization.

The educator needs to be aware of this variety of institutional channels through which the affective life is characteristically developed and expressed. Some have interpreted this to mean that schools should be abandoned, believing they have outlived their effectiveness, largely as a result of ignoring or mishandling the affective (that is, significant, valuable, important, relevant, deeply felt, etc.) elements in human experience. Some of these critics of the schools would charge the several types of institutions referred to in the preceding paragraph with the nurture of the corresponding types of affective development.

On behalf of schools it can be argued, on the other hand, that with a properly conceived curriculum they afford a viable and effective institutional structure for affective learning to take place. Such schools must manifestly be organized in such a way as to act in close interaction with all of the institutions of society mentioned above and with due awareness of the affective elements represented by each. The central task of the school is to serve as a distinguisher of the sources and kinds of affect and as a coordinator of these types according to defensible and productive principles of precedence and priority. The foregoing analysis of affective aspects and their synthesis into a normative hierarchy of progressive development suggests an approach to such principles from the standpoint of an ethicist.

References

Kurt Baier and Nicholas Rescher. *Values and the Future*. New York: The Free Press, 1969.

C. M. Beck, B. S. Crittenden, and E. V. Sullivan, editors. *Moral Education: Interdisciplinary Approaches*. Toronto: University of Toronto Press, 1971.

Barry I. Chazan and Jonas F. Soltis, editors. *Moral Education*. New York: Teachers College Press, 1973.

Erik H. Erikson. *Childhood and Society*. New York: Norton & Company, Inc., 1963.

Lawrence Kohlberg. *Stages in the Development of Moral Thought and Action*. New York: Holt, Rinehart and Winston, 1970.

Lawrence E. Metcalf, editor. *Values Education: Rationale, Strategies, and Procedures*. 41st Yearbook. Washington, D.C.: National Council for the Social Studies, 1971.

C. Ellis Nelson, editor. *Conscience: Theological and Psychological Perspectives*. New York: Newman Press, 1973.

Philip H. Phenix. *Education and the Common Good*. New York: Harper & Row, 1961.

Jean Piaget. *The Moral Development of the Child*. New York: Collier Books, 1962.

Louis Raths, Merrill Harmin, and Sidney B. Simon. *Values and Teaching*. Columbus, Ohio: Charles E. Merrill Publishing Co., 1966.

John Martin Rich. *Education and Human Values*. Reading, Massachusetts: Addison-Wesley Publishing Co., 1968.

4

*Ousia and MTH: A Writer Speaks**

Madeleine L'Engle

When our youngest child was a very small boy, he said to me one evening at bedtime, "We're human animals, aren't we, Mother? But we're made differently, without tails, or barks, or meows. Only with talks."

I learn from my children. We are the only talking beast, using words, used by words, seeing by the word. Recently the same son, then a sophomore at college, said that in one of his courses he'd been told of an operation which is being performed on certain violent mental patients who have failed to respond to all other treatment. A small incision is made in the brain, and violence is brought under control, but the patient has a memory span of no longer than ten minutes. Think about this. Who would you be if you could remember no further back than ten minutes ago? WHAT would you be?

I am concerned by a deliberate fostering of memory loss for all of us, not only the dangerously insane. It is part of the rampant anti-intellectualism which is spreading across our country. Our educational system is self-admittedly foundering; but if we are not educated, if we don't read, if we don't remember, we're more easy to manipulate.

We have become a generation of amnesiacs. Young people tell me, "I can't talk to my parents because they don't remember what it was like to be my age."

Memory Banks

Without memory not of only our own doings, but our backgrounds, our country's background, we would be someone else. We would not be ourselves. We are learning a great deal about our genetical banks, about DNA and RNA. We also need to learn about our memory banks. If I didn't have the memory of my parents and grandparents, if I didn't share in this heritage, I would not only be a different person, I would definitely be less. If we didn't, all of us, share in the memory of our ancestors, every generation would have to invent the wheel and the needle all over again. We are different from animals not only because of our talks, but because of the extraordinary but little-appreciated fact that we can look back to our past, and we can look forward to our future. Our genetic storehouse is DNA; alongside this I would put what I call M-T-H, Memory Treasure House. Our MTH is of inestimable value, and is an essential part of our brain's complicated electronic system. Without MTH we would have no stories, plays, poetry, no fairy tales, fantasy, myth. Children would play no games of Make Believe.

My husband, who is in a television soap opera, has many lines to learn nearly every night, and must be what, in the theater, is called a *quick study*. But once each day's show is over, he is free to forget the lines. It's different for me. A story teller may not forget anything which might conceivably be of some use in a story; I have no memory whatsoever for anything else, including numbers. I can look numbers up when they are needed; but anything which is possible story gets filed away in my memory treasure house, my MTH.

Most of my story material comes from life, from my own experience, even fantasies like *A Wrinkle in Time* and *A Wind in the Door*, or stories set back in the past, such as *The Love Letters* and *The Other Side of the Sun*. But part of my personal experience comes to me from my reading throughout the years, from the books which are our civilization's recorded MTH, and from conversations with all kinds of people who have been willing to share their own MTH with me.

The greater and deeper our memory of the past, the wider our vision of the future. The more full our MTH, the more integrated we

Madeleine L'Engle: *Born New York City; educated here and abroad; AB Honors, Smith. Married to actor Hugh Franklin; three children. Twenty-three published books. Short stories, articles, poetry. Lecturer at large; part-time teacher, actress, dog walker, piano player, full-time cook, people-lover, wife, friend, writer, human being.*

are as human beings, and the more free. This takes structure, enormous, disciplined structure, in a day when structure is unfashionable. But if you want to climb to the roof of a house, you need a ladder; you can't just float up. If you want to be free to dance and make love, you have to have the structure of your skeleton; without this structure you'd be an amorphous blob. There is a structure which is rigid and imprisoning; but there is also the structure which liberates, which sets us free.

It's a great pity that memorizing has gone out in the grade schools. The discipline of memorizing is a salutary one, and it can also be great fun. My young English agent was brought up in this tradition, which has lasted longer in England than in the States. He drove Hugh, my husband, and me, one beautiful English summer's day, to Stoke Poges, to the graveyard where Thomas Grey wrote his famous elegy. I turned to John and commanded, half joking, "All right, declaim." To my admiration, John put his foot up on a tombstone and recited the entire elegy.

Another time John and I took a long drive together. We passed the time most pleasantly in reciting poetry antiphonally. I started with *'Twas brillig and the slythy toves.* John went on to declaim long passages of Macaulay and Tennyson. I spieled off some Chaucer; we moved on to Shakespeare and the Psalms. And I realized to my chagrin that I remembered not nearly as much as I used to. I am busy rectifying this error.

Vocabulary and the Creative Use of Memory

Of what use is all this memory? For one thing, it is a constant vocabulary conditioner for us; we are losing words rapidly out of the rich and glorious English language; the bits and pieces of poetry and plays which I remember keep many words alive for me, and this is no small thing. The less my vocabulary, the less my ability to think, and the more easily I can be manipulated and controlled; the less a person I become. And the less free. One of the first things a dictator does is to limit education, cut down vocabulary, so as to have more control over the people. When Hugh and I went on a literary pilgrimage to Russia, to visit Tchekhov's house, Dostoevsky's house, Tolstoi's house, I almost did not get a visa because I am a writer; writers keep enlarging their vocabulary; they think; they can cause trouble.

Against the creeping amnesia of our culture I would put anamnesis: anamnesis; against amnesia; against forgetting. Anamnesis, the creative use of memory. I am, both theologically and politically, neither a conservative nor a liberal, but a radical, radical in its base meaning: radix: root. I would go back to my roots, would exercise anamnesis. This is essential to me as a writer, but this does not mean dwelling in the past; anamnesis is the key to the future; without memory the future does not exist. My stories have to have meaning in the world of today if what I write is to have any verisimilitude—that almost forgotten word, that very good word.

If what I write isn't believable, then I have failed. While I was in college I wrote a story, a true story, and I wrote it exactly as it happened. My professor said, "It's a well-written story, but I don't believe it." "But it's true!" I cried defensively. "That's exactly the way it was! It's true!" He replied calmly, "If I don't believe it, it isn't true."

I learned an extremely difficult and important lesson about writing at that moment. If I don't make a story true for the reader, then it isn't true.

But what is truth? For an artist of any discipline it is verisimilitude, a likeness to what is real. A likeness to what is real is as close as the human being can come to reality, and we must be open to those moments when we are given our own glimpses of verisimilitude, that likeness to what is real, to what is beyond the finite world of provable fact, to that which transcends the limited world of limited memory.

I search for verisimilitude, for my glimpses of reality, in my stories, particularly in the fantasies, like *A Wrinkle in Time* and *A Wind in the Door*. Now that these books are out of my hands, published, and out in the wide world, I am beginning to learn what they are really about, and where they have taught me more about reality than I knew before—because my books know far more than I do.

The nature of reality has baffled philosophers and theologians for many thousands of years, and I'm certainly not brash enough to try to offer a new definition. I only want to point out that reality is far more than meets the human eye—or ear—or mind. John Stuart Mill says that although we can know things to some extent, we cannot know them exhaustively.

For instance, what is a frog? What is the *reality* of a frog? I was fascinated by a scientific article which showed pictures of a frog as seen by a human eye, by a bird's eye, by a snake's eye. Each saw a very different creature. Which frog was more real? And why are frogs so often in fairy tales?

The Greeks have a word for the realness of things, the essence of frog, of stone, of bread and wine, of you and me: *ousia*.

We move from anamnesis to ousia, for the creative use of memory can help teach us the essence of things. It is a search for ousia, for realness, in a world that depends more and more on the unreal, which impels the human animal to stretch both backwards and forwards in memory, to paint a picture, or sing a song, or write a story.

Freedom and Authority

In the current sense of the word I was probably less free when I was twelve, thirteen, and fourteen, than at any time before or since, because I was in an English boarding school. In those days, the life of an English schoolgirl was completely and arbitrarily structured. In our dormitories we were permitted only one article on our chests of drawers or beds—this meant one picture of mother and father, or one stuffed animal, or one book. We did everything to bells, woke, dressed, worked, played, changed, ate, slept, and even bathed to bells; we had a 15-minute bath "hour" once a week; the water wasn't very hot, and we had no central heating; so this wasn't as great a deprivation as it might seem. At night we used to sit in bed rubbing mentholatum into hands which were chapped raw, with the tears running down our cheeks.

I was the only American in the school, so everything I did which broke even the smallest rule was an international incident. The English children could do all kinds of horrendous things without smirching the Union Jack. Anything I did was a reflection on all—at the time—48 states. "Do you want us to think that every American girl is like this?"

I had to write out Milton's *Il Penseroso* at least a hundred times, and it took me years before I could read Milton with any pleasure whatsoever. And yet I learned more about freedom—and authority—during those years than in any period I can remember, not the authority of bells and gym tunics and restrictions on what I could do and where I could do it, but that strange, unknowable, definite authority which ordered and liberated my real self.

In the spring, when our chapped hands finally healed, and we moved from heavy woolen underwear and scratchy serge uniforms to Liberty cottons, we were given small garden plots to cultivate. We were assigned partners; I was number 97 in the school, 97 on my uniforms, on my desk, my napkin cubbyhole, my shelf in the classroom, my locker in the common room—and my partner was 96. Already the process of unnaming had begun. We were allowed to bring in the produce of our gardens for tea, so most of the kids planted tomatoes and lettuces and cress and radishes. Ninety-six and I planted poppies. Nothing but poppies.

It was permissible and possible when I was twelve to be considerably more naïve and innocent on such subjects than it is today. So we ate poppy seed sandwiches, poppy flower sandwiches, poppy leaf sandwiches, and went to bed every night with our dream books and a flashlight under our pillows.

My dream book has been lost somewhere, but I still remember many of those dreams, some of which were truly fabulous—though I doubt if they came from the poppy sandwiches: I've had even more fabulous dreams without any such assistance.

Perhaps if we had been allowed more time for daytime dreaming, for excursions into the world of imagination, myth, fantasy, for what George Macdonald called "holy idleness," we would not have had to depend on our nighttime dreams. But idleness of any kind, holy or no, would not have been tolerated in that school.

Even back then during the Punic Wars we were rebelling against the circumscribed world of provable fact in which the English schoolchild was imprisoned. Our civilization was rushing toward the devastation of the Second World War, and yet we were being taught to live in a climate where it was still assumed that human beings are capable of understanding and solving all problems by their own effort and will, that we are capable of providing the authority which can free humankind.

What we children were doing with our dream books was instinctively rejecting this false illusion, and refusing to equate the whole of ourselves with that very small fragment of ourselves which we can know, control, and manipulate, that very small fragment of ourselves over which we, personally, have authority.

The old iceberg analogy has been used so often that we tend to forget that it's really valid. It's just become part of the jargon. But it's true that the part of ourselves over which we have control is only that tiny part of ourselves which is surfaced above the water. And the largest part of ourselves is in that strange, underwater, unknown, as yet very much undiscovered self.

It takes a certain humility to admit that this largest part of ourselves is that part of the iceberg which is below the water, that part of ourselves over which we have very little control, but wherein lies an extraordinary freedom.

The frightening results of limiting ourselves to that fragment of ourselves over which we have personal dictatorship are all around us. It's often faster to walk than to take a taxi in midtown New York. Our telephones work part-time at best. There's some kind of an unwritten law which decrees that each time we have a price raise in postal service, that service is going to deteriorate. A cable from England recently took two weeks to arrive. When one boards a plane, one is not at all certain, despite the cursory searching of bags and person, that the plane will arrive at its destination without being hijacked. My dishwasher breaks down whenever I'm giving a dinner party, and the washing machine blows up whenever a baby in diapers is around.

The machines which were to set us free are enslaving us. The death toll from highway accidents mounts daily. Prices at the super-market skyrocket. There's botulism in the soup, mercury in the fish, and strontium 90 in the milk.

And yet far too often parents and teachers today, just as they did when I was a child, are trying to bring up children as though we live in a world in which we can make everything all right if we'll only try a little harder, a world in which we can, and ought, of our own effort, be good. This is part of our inheritance from our Puritan ancestors, and it is not in itself a bad thing to want to be good. Far from it. But when I try to make myself virtuous, the me I can manipulate and coerce, the me over which I have authority, is only the small part of me of which I am conscious. It is the dangerous assumption that this fragment of me is the whole of me which causes me to blunder over and over again. What my finite, conscious, authoritarian mind tells me I ought to do, and what the untamed, unknown, submerged part of me actually makes me do, are often in direct conflict.

Nor is this only my problem; it is part of the human condition, and has been for many thousands of centuries. Two thousand years ago Paul of Tarsus had the rueful honesty to admit that the very things he wanted to do were the things he did not do, and the things he didn't want to do were the things that he did.

This is something about ourselves which many people do not have the courage to accept. Growing into maturity ought to be a journey into integration, our conscious and super- and subconscious selves opening to each other; but far too often growing up is a process of fragmentation, one reason our mental hospitals are daily more overcrowded, one reason the suicide rate is mounting.

There is a frightening story of the now almost unknown pianist, Ethel Lijinska. I have a few old, superb recordings of her playing, and she was a great pianist. But she was so imprisoned by stage fright that one time, when she was in a taxi on her way to Carnegie Hall to give a major concert, she said suddenly to the taxi driver, "Take me to Grand Central Station," and she got on a train and fled. And that was the end of her career.

The conscious and nonconscious minds are not quite that alienated for most of us; nevertheless a reminder of this story always gives me pause. And Alfred North Whitehead writes quite bluntly that he has no idea why he does the things which he does, or why he does not do the things which he does not do. If Alfred North Whitehead, that eminently reasonable, rational man can say this, what about the rest of us?

For me, the great mediator between the conscious and the unconscious mind is art; to write a story, play the piano, look at a picture, is to bind broken-ness together. But it takes courage to dive down into the unknown waters of the unconscious, and when I draw back from doing so, I remind myself of the caterpillar who looked disapprovingly at a butterfly and remarked, "You'll never catch me going up on one of those things."

How do we find the freedom to move from the restricted world of the caterpillar to the world of the butterfly? I think we do have to go through death and resurrection, and this is not easy.

C. S. Lewis tells about the death of Charles Williams. Not expecting his death, Lewis had gone to the hospital to see him, taking an article he wanted to discuss. He also expected to take home messages to their mutual friends. Upon arriving at the hospital he learned instead that Charles Williams was dead. He walked home through the familiar streets of Oxford—they seemed to be new streets; the same thing was true of his friends; the whole world seemed altered.

I was in early adolescence when my maternal grandmother died. Her death, too, was unexpected. We were spending the summer with her at the beach, and after she died we had to drive into town. I remember my sense of shock as we drove through the crowded streets of midtown that everything wasn't actually physically different, that everybody didn't know that my beloved grandmother had died. The world was different: nobody we passed on the streets knew it, and this seemed to me outrageous.

This was more than a selfish, childish reaction. Perhaps we are supposed to walk more often through the streets of that different world, where all our awareness is more acute—not our awareness of ourselves, or our own subjective reactions, but an awareness that we *are* part of each other, that no man is an island, and that separation is not freedom, but death.

For me the meeting of these two worlds, the world in which we move and do our daily chores, and the strange world of ultra-awareness that the shock of death can show us, ever is found in art. I must confess that it is difficult for me to separate art and religion, in that art is often the most authentic expression of religion possible to the human being. Confusion arises because some of the worst art, and some of the worst religion, are found in so-called religious paintings or music. Pictures of Jesus as a pale consumptive wandering along the shore of the Galilean Sea, clutching his bleeding heart as he looks sorry for himself, have done only harm to both religion and art.

Sometimes—and this is a hard pill for many of us to swallow—the atheist is better qualified to paint or compose or write for the church than the believer, not because he is an atheist, but because he has not been trapped by a man-made image of God. Therefore it is easier for the Spirit to speak through him than through someone who sees God in his own image, safe in a box, controlled and unthreatening.

If I deliberately try to write a "religious" poem or story, it will be bad religion. Such a story has to decide to be written and then, despite me, use me as the matter through which it can be spoken.

Great religious art in all fields is, for me, the results of all kinds of human beings, some believers, some "heretics," some agnostics, some atheists, some saints. It doesn't matter *who* made

The Bach B Minor Mass
Blake's poems

Poulenc's Organ Concerto
Shakespeare's plays
Rouault's clowns
Dostoevsky's novels
Picasso's Harlequins
Donne's poems
Kafka's apocalyptic stories
Alice in Wonderland
The Odyssey and the Iliad
The Wind in the Willows
The Greek myths
Plato's dialogues
Kandinsky's abstractions
Van Gogh's suns and moons and stars.

All that matters is that they have been made incarnate. For the underwater area of the artist's mind, no matter how atheist the surface, is religious. To paint a picture, or make music, or tell a story, is a religious activity. A great painting, a great symphony, a great play, share in divine transfiguration, whether or not the artist believes in God. An artist of integrity will be the servant of the work. Whether or not an artist recognizes the glory of the master doesn't really matter as much as the willingness to serve. Father Timothy Kallistos Ware once remarked that we may rest confident that at the last judgment the angels will produce such works of art as testimony on behalf of the artists.

A professor from whom I learned a great deal once told us that we do not judge great art; it judges us. *It judges us.* And the judgment of the work of art is quite apart from the merit, or lack of merit, of the artist.

But when we limit ourselves to the above-the-eyebrows world over which we have authority, we tend to judge. And in doing so, we often forget that a work of art is, in fact, a work. Serkin did not sit down at the piano and play Beethoven's Appassionata Sonata without doing his finger exercises. Guernica did not spring full blown from the canvas. *The Brothers Karamazov* wasn't tossed off in a week; it encourages me to remember that Dostoevsky did version after version of his novels.

To turn closer to home for an analogy, when I got out of college I lived for a while in Greenwich Village in New York with three other girls. One of them has gone on to be a concert pianist. No matter what the rest of us were doing she practiced eight hours a day, finger exercises, one tiny phrase over and over again for what seemed forever. She was working for her first New York concert, and I'll never forget Handel's *Harmonious Blacksmith Variations,* or the *Brahms Second Piano Concerto,* or the *Bach Chromatic Fantasy and Fugue* as they slowly moved to life as she grew with them. If she diligently practiced the music, it also practiced her.

Montaigne says "the work of its own force and fortune can second the workman and surpass him, beyond his own invention and knowledge." I witnessed the truth of this as I saw the great compositions pushing the young pianist. When a work of art does this, then more of the archetypical iceberg is freed to come out of the dark waters and into the light of the sun.

I learned something of this myself during that same period when I went through my first shattering experience of falling in love and having the love turn to ashes. I not only survived but did a considerable amount of growing up through the writing of my first full-length novel.

I had cause, then, to be grateful for the English boarding school which taught me to concentrate on a story or poem in any amount of noise and confusion. I concentrated on that first novel because it was what saved me.

The concentration of the small child at play is analogous to the concentration of the artist of any discipline. In real play, which is real concentration, the child is not only outside time, but outside the *self*—in the real sense of ecstasy—*ex stasis.* He has thrown himself completely into whatever it is that he is doing. A child playing a game, building a sand castle, painting a picture, is completely IN that activity. Any self-consciousness is wholly focused outside himself. The self is *free*—not because a child doesn't have any responsibilities and has escaped, for the brief moments of play from the authority of the parents—but because—to use Einstein's beautiful phrase, he has "cast off the shackles of selfish desire."

When I was working on that first novel I was genuinely and painfully unhappy. But during the actual writing I was at play; like the small child I was completely thrown into the activity so that what might have been a totally destructive experience became instead a creative one, and a freeing one.

I was freed by that time of writing as my book wrote me, not as I wrote it. The same thing is true when I read a book; the books which matter to me are those which read me. The music I play, or listen to, is that which actively participates with me in harmony or counterpoint. The same thing is true in graphic art. There has got to be an amorous interaction between the work of art and the person who is opening to it. Any actor will tell you that the audience can make or break an evening in the theater; the audience collaborates, quite literally, with the actor, to make something which is greater than either alone. Such is true not only in actual performances of plays, or concerts, but also in our response to a statue by Praxiteles, or a painting by Rouault, or a poem by Blake.

But: Is art true? Is a story true? Is the story of Peter Rabbit true? Is *The Tempest* true?

In limiting ourselves to the world over which we have authority—we can't control Macbeth or Huck Finn or Jonah—we're losing those things which are above, below, beyond, past, through, over, that small area encompassed by our conscious, authoritarian minds.

To turn again to a personal analogy, *A Wrinkle in Time*, which took me far away from the world of provable fact, frightened so many adults that it was two years before an editor dared risk publishing it; it is fascinating that children will willingly and eagerly accept what terrifies the grown-ups. As I look around me at my own children and grandchildren, at the children I teach, at the children who come to me to talk, it seems that they are a great deal less confused than their elders.

A high school senior told me that he's given up watching most TV programs because of the arbitrary lineup of good guys and bad guys. It wasn't that he objected to having good guys and bad guys; it was that there are no longer any criteria by which he can judge who is a good guy and who is a bad guy. In our permissive society everything is all right. A murderer gets off as having been temporarily insane. A thief has had a deprived childhood. A rapist or a dope pusher was fed cornflakes at the wrong moment by his mother; so it's all her fault. Nobody's really to blame for anything.

If we are freed from any personal responsibility whatsoever for our own actions and errors, what kind of freedom is that? If we are not allowed to feel guilt when we have done wrong—real guilt, not false guilt, which is something else—then we are not free to try not to make the same error again. If I am unjust in my relations with my husband or children and am not free to say, "I was wrong, I'm sorry," and "kiss and make up" and be forgiven, then I am not free at all.

I believe that there is sin and evil and wrong in the world, and that when people do wrong, that wrong has to be paid for. And it is paid for, sometimes, by self-sacrifice, virtue, and nobility—those old-fashioned and embarrassing words.

If I cannot hope to be good of my own virtue—and I cannot—I can hope to be at least a little better because of the virtue of others. Courage, honor, integrity, are as contagious as cowardice, pride, falsehood. But we need to be able to know which is which. And far too often I don't know by myself. Often things which at the time have caused me great pain have led to great good. Things which at the time seemed sweet have turned sour in my mouth.

If I, like that high school senior who wants standards, need help in knowing the difference between good and evil, I find that help in fellow human beings who share in the human condition, and who yet show me structure, service, and sacrifice, and who at the same time are free enough to be open to the glorious freedom of creation.

Finding Something To Live By

The young people who talk to me and teach me have a sense of tragedy about being an American in the world today. Our country has never had this needed sense of tragedy before. We are, as a country, young and brash; we've fallen easily into the trap of a perverse kind of Puritanism and do-it-yourself-ism. Kids are worried about this condition. They have learned that parents who think their children can do no wrong usually produce spoiled, nasty brats. People who think their country can do no wrong usually help to destroy it. Our kids care passionately about their country, about redeeming their flag; this, for them, involves accepting a sense of tragedy which we, as Americans, have thus far refused to face. Too many of us still go along with the unreal idea that there's always going to be a happy ending. America has never lost a war (haven't we?); all we need to do is try a little harder and everything will be all right. We can be perfect all by ourselves. One word for this is Pelagianism: we are perfectible of our own effort. We are basically good and pure. We just need to think more positively.

Alas. It hasn't worked. It never does work.

What does, then? What does?

Not, certainly, the materialism which our television commercials and glossy ads try to titillate us with. I think that we must look to our roots. We have lost the American dream; we have lost our primal humanity. Jung said that the twentieth-century world is in desperate trouble because it has lost a valid myth to live by.

Now, a myth is a verbal icon. That's really the only definition of myth which makes any sense. But both icon and myth are loaded words today. We confuse icon and idol, and this is largely because we tend to turn our icons into idols. We confuse myth with fabrication, with stories which are not true. If I were Satan I would do my best to infiltrate the world of myth and destroy it; it would seem that such has happened. We have tried to kill myth by pretending that it is part of the world of make-believe, of fairy tales, of the world which we ought to discard as soon as we move from childhood into the grown-up world. I will never forget the well-meaning aunt who told me that creatures like Titania and Oberon, Mole and Rat, the Princess and Curdle, aren't real, nor are guardian angels, and I must stop believing in them. I loved and trusted this aunt, and she shook me. Anger came to my rescue. I knew she was wrong. But it took me a long time to get my faith back.

A myth, a verbal icon, like a visual icon, is something which has in it a glimpse of reality far greater than the actual icon itself. Myth is now "in"; we're slowly turning back to the idea that to see iconically is a way of realizing things which can lead us to the living truth which is beyond decaying, time-bound, provable fact. The problem with the current fashionableness of myth is that we now have thousands of conflicting definitions—the devil knows exactly where to infiltrate; and I believe in him, too.

One definition which I find provocative and liberating is an ancient one by that prolific author, Anon:

These things which never were, but always are.
These things which never were, but always *are.*

And even this definition itself is mythic and needs definition. What did Anon mean by "These things which never were"? *Was* Ivan Karamazov, for instance? Did Alice really go down the rabbit hole? Was there really a Hamlet in Elsinore? Or a mole and a rat on the river bank who were friends with an arrogant toad?

A fourth-grade boy asked me if I really and truly believed *A Wrinkle in Time.* I answered with an immediate, "Of course."

To deny the reality of the world of fantasy, fairy tale, and myth makes no sense to me at all. Prospero and Ariel, Frodo and Aslan, Heathcliff and Jane Eyre *are.* They are, perhaps, even more truly than we are. Even if in our limited, finite, rational-proof manner they never were, they give us our only glimpse of what is really real, of the essence of things, of *ousia.*

In a world which is changing radically, and at a rapidly accelerating pace, we desperately need those things which always are. High school and college age students are looking quite consciously for these things which always are. They are looking in all kinds of ways, in astrology, Buddhism, Hinduism, an extraordinarily rigid fundamentalism, and—to my personal delight—they are looking to children's books because they are finding only despair and moralism in adult novels. These young people are insisting on icons, on myth, on ousia, on something to live by. They consider that the values by which their parents live are obsolete, materialistic, and decaying.

Now, to blame the ills of the present on the mistakes of the older generation is a bit simplistic. I'm not going to wallow in the masochistic guilt which comes from blindly accepting this accusation. The world has been in a bad way for a long time. It took many generations to get us to the state we're in now. My own generation has provided us with no small number of superb men and women who have done much to hold the hounds at bay, men and women who have had a vision of freedom and ousia and have managed quite often to keep us from total disaster.

Mythically speaking, trouble started when there was war in heaven, and Michael and his angels battled the dragon. We're still paying for the pride, the hubris, of the first Adam. There is living and liberating truth for me in these verbal icons, these ousic stories.

But we have to be aware of the chilling fact that for every creative icon or myth there is also a destructive one. The powers of darkness do know our vulnerable spots and don't hesitate to rush in. A human being is a searching animal by nature, thirsting for the transcendent, but, as George Tyrrell pointed out a century ago, if we are not fed ousia we will swallow the garbage of any superstition offered to us.

It is dangerous to assume that every spirit abroad today is indeed the Holy Spirit. There are evil spirits in the world and we are foolish if we do not take them seriously. The phenomenal success of *The Exorcist* underlines the awareness of the man on the street of the seduction of evil. Ulrich Simon, in a book called *The Theology of Auschwitz,* says that "Auschwitz is unthinkable apart from enthusiastic ecstasy." Hitler had great charismatic gifts, and total faith in the virtue and nobility of his vision. Communism, likewise, is not a political system, but a powerful religion. The dark myths of the evil angels are flourishing, and are the more frightening because they always masquerade as visions of light.

How do we tell an ousic myth from one which is anousic? The closest I can come to an answer is that it is the nature of love to create; it is the nature of hate to destroy. Wherever killing is involved; wherever treating people as things is involved; wherever having possession of someone or something is involved, the myth is destructive. Wherever life is found, and life more abundantly, the myth is creative and opens us to ousia.

But the youngsters *are* on the right track in looking for something real, something true, something which does not depend on the materialistic culture of television commercials. And I think that they're on the right track in turning to poetry and fantasy, to an ousic language which has not yet been emasculated. I care passionately about language, and I think that language is in need of redemption. I'm helped in my feelings about the English language when I see, more objectively than I can see what is happening to English, what has happened to language in Japan and Russia.

After the Second World War the Japanese lost so many actual written characters that college students today cannot read the great Japanese works of literature, because they no longer know the characters used by the great classical writers. This destruction of language is a curtailment of freedom.

In Russia it is not easy for a Russian to read the works of Alexander Solzhenitsyn (even if these works were readily available), because so much vocabulary was lost in Russia after the Revolution. In one of Solzhenitsyn's books his hero spends long hours reading the great Russian dictionary which came out in the 1890's. Solzhenitsyn himself has one volume of this two-volume work, and in his novels he is forging the Russian language back into vitality, taking the words of the people of the streets and the words of the great dictionary, and pulling these words out of the shadows and into the light. This is what Dante did with *The Divine Comedy*; it is what Chaucer and Shakespeare did; it is what the English language needs to have done in order to survive as a great tongue.

Our vocabulary, too, has been diminished and perverted. We use jargon in order to escape ousia. The two great tools of imagery for the writer are metaphor and simile—metaphor, where "My love *is* a red, red rose," and simile, where "My love is *like* a red, red rose." The two are very different. But current use has distorted *like* so that it is losing its power as a simile word. I've been told on good authority that the man who wrote the famous "Winston tastes good like a cigarette should" did it with deliberate contempt for the public. Diminish and distort vocabulary, and the public will lose freedom to make decisions, and will buy more of the product. Ivan Illich points out the dangers of the present corruption of language, and the unfortunate results of such perversions as using nouns as verbs.

It is a great deal harder for students today to read the great works of the English language than it was for my generation. We have lost so much vocabulary, have blunted so many words, that it is much more difficult for a student to enjoy Shakespeare or Chaucer or Fielding than it was only a generation ago. One of the most contemptible things ever done by publishers and their advisers was the publishing of books for young children using what they called "limited vocabulary." The writer of such books was given a list of words which are—supposedly—within the limits of a six year old, or a twelve year old, and not allowed to use any word that is not on the list. How on earth is a child going to grow if the vocabulary is kept within his or her limitations? No honest writer is going to make concessions to the needs inherent in a story. Beatrix Potter wrote that lettuce had a *soporific* effect on Flopsy, Mopsy, and Cottontail. No publisher would let her get away with that today but it was, it really was, the one word which suited the situation. I think that vocabulary and the writer are in collaboration; the writer may not manipulate vocabulary, but must work with it; we do not possess vocabulary, we participate in it. When we try to possess it then, inevitably, both vocabulary and freedom diminish.

When this happens, what follows? Take Japan once more as an example: there used to be an illusion that the Japanese have become wholly Westernized. Yet a wise chaplain for two New York prisons pointed out to me that Japanese movies are more filled with monsters, with fantastic violence, than anything we've yet produced in this country—and these Japanese movies are avidly watched in the United States. And this, he said, is because we have driven our archetypes below our consciousness, and they are now erupting in subconscious violence—and not only on the screen.

The reaction to such violence takes many forms, including a swing to the extreme right or the extreme left. It takes courage for us to move from the safe area of provable fact into the unknown area of the questions which deal with that part of us which we cannot know, cannot control, cannot manipulate, to those questions which cannot be answered in the language of provable fact. This language is simply inadequate when we try to face the ultimate questions, and only encourages us to limit ourselves.

Mythic, iconic work is often produced in times of darkness and of almost unbearable stress. Think of the condition of the world when the Book of Daniel was written. Remember the brutal place and time in which Dante wrote *The Divine Comedy*. Shakespeare's England was cruel and bloody. It's interesting and tragic to note that the book of the Bible most read in concentration camps during the Second World War was the Revelation of St. John the Divine—the Apocalypse. These beautiful, revelatory works express my own affirmations of light and meaning. I believe in *The Tempest;* in *Tyger, Tyger, Burning Bright;* in Bach's B Minor Mass. I believe in Rouault's Clowns; in the Zeus of Artemission; in Scarlatti's *Cat's Fugue.* What this means is that I acknowledge that we have in that vast, submerged part of us an unquenchable longing for the transcendent, the great world beyond and around our limited world of provable fact where authority belongs to us and we are not free.

Structure: A Proclamation of Freedom

If I seem to equate structure and freedom, I think that probably I do. To write a book involves enormous structure, but it is also a proclamation of freedom, a free affirmation of the reality of creation, and our own active participation in it.

Where and how does one find time to write and run a household? Something has to go. I omitted all kinds of housewifely virtues; my house was tidy, but I did not scrub the kitchen floor daily; commercials of various floor waxes, furniture polishes, and window cleaners go right over my head; they are not within my frame of reference or the structure of my day. It is more important that I have at least an hour a day to read; that I walk at least two miles a day with my dog—this is thinking time; and that I have an hour a day at the piano. This last got squashed with the advent of our third child; I'm only now getting back to it, and I find playing the piano one of the best consciousness expanders there is. When I'm stuck in a story, or in life, if I go to the piano and play Bach for half an hour or so, I usually get unstuck. Also, it is impossible to play Bach's fugues and feel sorry for yourself. You can wallow in self-pity with Chopin or Schumann, but Bach knocks you right back into proportion. So Bach is an important part of my structure.

If I think about structure, structure in life, structure in writing, as something which liberates, as against the structure which imprisons, it is because the kind of structure I am thinking about always implies risk. I am worried that we live in a climate where we are not allowed to fail, and therefore we are encouraged to take fewer and fewer risks.

One reason that children are given fewer fairy tales today than they were when I was little, is that fairy tales are violent, and they involve risk. Why we shudder at the violence in fairy tales and close our eyes to the violence of everyday life in the 1970's is beyond me. As for risk—no risk, no fairy tale. Failure is not only possible in fairy tales, it often strikes. And even when the poor peasant boy or the lovely stepchild succeeds, there is risk first. The young man may not make his way safely through the magic thicket. The power of the evil fairy may be stronger than that of the benevolent godmother. If the princess kisses the beast, he may devour her. Will the frog really be saved from the wicked spell and turn into a prince?

There is risk, risk of failure, of horror, of death, in fairy tales, but there is also an unspoken affirmation of ousia, and of the ultimate "all-rightness" of things.

But before we can affirm this all-rightness we must accept immediate all wrongness. It is in these dark and unknown waters that fairy tales have their home. Although we tend to think of fairy tales as light and crystal clear—glass slippers, enchanted mirrors, vast parties in great ballrooms—they speak to us, ultimately, of dark things. No one is more aware of the disastrous aspects of humankind's overweening pride than the teller of fairy tales. No one is more aware of our ultimate insecurity, loneliness, horror. But the teller of fairy tales, ancient or modern, is also aware of our infinite value; of the extraordinary fact that we often accomplish the impossible.

Therefore the fairy-tale-er must give a far deeper sense of verisimilitude than the writer of slice-of-life stories. We must believe that the stairs of the castle up which George Macdonald's princess climbs to her grandmother are there—that they would be there even if George Macdonald had never written about them; we must believe that it is quite possible that one day we may be asked to plunge our own hands into that terrible burning fire of roses. The fairy-tale-teller writes about a world more real than that of every day. I've experienced this feeling of being jerked out of the really real world back into our daily shadow world when I've been deep in reading a story and somebody has interrupted me; and even more strongly when I've been writing. If I'm fully thrown into the writing, thrown out of myself (ex-stasis) and into the world of the story, when I am interrupted there is a frightening moment of transition when I am jerked out of the *real* world, and must return to the much-smaller-dimensioned world of everyday life.

Fairy tales are at home in the world of magic, but in a true fairy tale this magic is neither coy, nor impossible. If we cannot believe in the magic of a fairy tale, then it isn't a real fairy tale.

But magic, like myth, must be redefined. Words are slippery things, changing in color and shape like oil in water, and if we do not change along with them, our own meanings get distorted.

There is a lot of interest in Black Magic today, and in White Magic, too, along with the illusion that the power of magic, for good or evil, can be separated from the rest of life. Magic is power, and power, in primitive (?) societies, is seen as being both *mana* and *tabu*. The great power lines which stretch across our country and make our lights work, and inform our refrigerators and washing machines are, when used to do this, mana. But if you were to touch one of those power lines with your naked hand that would be the end of you: taboo. Those who tamper with taboo—both in real life and in fairy tales—are arrogant in the ultimate sense of arrogance. They usurp the prerogatives of the gods; they fall into the classical Greek flaw of hubris, putting oneself in the place of God.

Mana is working with God, is part of co-creation. The magic of mana is never a do-it-yourself activity. It is aware of the pain of life, of death, of resurrection. And therefore there is usually at least a hint of eschatology in fairy tales. They break out of chronological time and move into those chronos-liberated waters below the visible tip of the iceberg. Our underwater minds, unlike our conscious minds, are uninhibited by linear time; in our sleeping dreams time is sometimes fantastically condensed; in a few minutes we can dream many hours' worth of adventures. As we go deeper into the world of fantasy, myth, fairy tale, we become even more free from the arbitrary shackles of time.

The teller of tales is always aware (consciously or not, it makes no difference) of taboo. Bluebeard's wife is forbidden to open the door to one room, one room only; Cinderella was not to stay at the party past the stroke of twelve. Peter Rabbit was not to enter Mr. MacGregor's garden. When taboo is violated inadvertently the result is always disaster. Oedipus did not know that the old man he killed was his father, nor that the queen he married was his mother; his innocence of knowledge does not excuse the breaking of taboo; death and madness follow. King Arthur did not know that Morgeuse was his sister. The fact that he did not know the extent of his wrongdoing does not let him off the consequences of his act: Mordred, his son by Morgeuse, looms in a dark and sinister way over the scene as Arthur's armies are defeated, the dream of the Round Table dissolved in betrayal and tragedy; and Camelot is in ruins.

It is only recently that fairy tale, fantasy, myth, have been thought of as being exclusively for children. Originally they were not for children at all. But just as children are learning the letters of the alphabet earlier, so too they must learn the alphabet of myth, because this is the foundation for conceptual thought. It is important that children be taught the Greek and Roman myths which help us to understand our archetypes, and are part of the alphabet with which we may search for ousia.

However, although *Gulliver's Travels* was written for adults, it is found on the children's shelves in most libraries. And the unabridged Malory most certainly was not written for children. No good writer of children's books writes *for* children. A children's writer is writing out of open, intensely aware, questioning, unblunted child's eyes. For children are better believers than grown-ups. They are aware of what most adults have forgotten, that the daily, time-bound world of provable fact is the secondary world, the shadow world; and story, painting, song, give us glimpses of ousia.

Most "children's versions" of the great fairy tales and myths are grossly overcut, and often the wrong sections get deleted, so that the reality of the story evaporates. A librarian pointed out to me recently that there is a new version of George Macdonald's *The Light Princess* which is cut so that the point is lost entirely. "Middle-aged" children love long books: what I wanted during this period of my life was a book so long that it would never end. So I went through volumes of Dickens because most children's books were too short.

Aristotle talks of the willing suspension of disbelief: when I am reading a story into which I enter wholly, with which I participate, I not only suspend disbelief, but I believe in a way in which I am seldom able to believe in everyday life. This world, this vivid world which seizes me and makes me part of it is perhaps a child's world: I am seldom able to become part of the world of many contemporary novels or plays, and most slice-of-life novels for adults or "young adults," because these works, brilliant though some of them be, conform only to the ways of this world and ignore the possibility of a larger universe.

If I am a child, in the sense of having an acute case of Peter-Pantheism, then this is pagan and puerile. But I must, in my journey into adulthood, middle age, and onwards, take all of myself, and this means that I must keep with me the wonder and awareness that was mine.

I remember one time when I was legitimately and bitterly unhappy, out of joint with myself and the world; I slipped out of the house with the dog on a cold winter's evening and there, in an ice-green sky was a tiny crystal sliver of a new moon, and it was as though I had been taken by the scruff of the neck and been shaken back into proportion. It was more than just the beauty; it was a moment of ousia.

Ousia sometimes comes to us when we least deserve it, for surely I did not deserve the radiance of the new moon just then, nor the ability to see it. Pablo Picasso, that giant who painted right up to the end, wrote: ". . . in painting . . . to find is the thing. The one who finds something . . . at least arouses our curiosity, if not our imagination. When I paint, my object is to show what I have found. . . ."—in other words, he seeks to share his vision. It is impossible to judge in the lifetime of the artist whether or not a work of art is great, because great art not only reflects its culture, it transcends it. We will not know for several generations how much of Picasso's work is transcendent. But if we look at another giant, Shakespeare, we see that he reflected the bawdy, cruel, colorful world of the first Elizabeth, and that he also speaks clearly to our world right now, right here, and this is partly because his MTH shared certain basic, archetypical images with ours, because ousia is not limited by time and space.

Out of childhood and youth the mature artist is forged, and to become grown up implies grief and pain and fear and the dark shadow of death—no wonder many artists are considered to be at least slightly mad. But the person who reads, looks at paintings, listens to music, must share in all of this, too. As I learn from the slings and arrows of chronology I must be not just 55 years old, but 1-2-3-4-5-6-7-8-9-10—all of me, not just an isolated chronological fragment. It is only with all of me that I may move into the worlds of fantasy, fairy tale, myth.

How to define these three? Each, to some measure, partakes of the other. The differences are tenuous; they are held together by ousia. But fantasy, more than fairy tale and myth, deals with the embracing of a world which is wider than our daily world, which reaches out to the boundaries of creation. Fantasy is the battlefield of the forces of good and evil. If I did not believe, somewhere in the unknown depths of myself, that the powers of creation will ultimately defeat the powers of destruction, then I would never again write—or read—a fantasy.

A fairy tale is acted out in a small world, and the action deals not only with risk, but usually also with magic: the desire for power in this world.

Myths hold for us glimpses of our archetypes; the characters in myth are usually larger than life, their passions are more violent, their nobility extraordinary.

All three, fantasy, fairy tale, myth, call on us to participate with them and to be co-creators, and so break the boundaries of chronological time. For there is also Real Time, *kairos*, as the Greeks called it, *kairos*, of which we have only occasional glimpses. And then there is Other Time, which is the time of myth, fantasy, fairy tale. Other Time is the most complicated for the human being to understand, since it leaps across our time, and embraces both real-time, and non-time, both good and evil. This is the lure and danger of the world of such tales: we may be given great and lovely gifts, or we may be annihilated.

In Other Time we are given glimpses of ousia, of things as they may be in Real Time.

When I am quiet and unburdened by false guilt at the brook, I can look at a small frog on a cool grey rock and see him as truthfully as the human eye can see. But we don't always see things as they are. When I lie on my back on the stone bridge and look up at the sky to see which way the clouds are moving, so that I can amuse myself by making L'Engle's short-term weather forecast, I see the sky moving past the earth; I see the sun move in this sky; at night I see the sweep of stars and moon. But what I see is not what is. I can see that clouds at different layers are moving at different speeds, but I cannot see that the sun is a revolving atomic furnace about which our earth whirls; I cannot see that the moon is revolving at a different speed from the earth, and is only a mirror of the sun with no light of its own; nor can I see that the stars themselves are suns of wildly disparate size, rotating as they revolve, nor that all stars belong to galaxies which also move at incredible speeds in cosmic dance. I can, to some extent, understand this more, because of my background of fairy tale, fantasy, myth, than the words of science. But I cannot, with my limited human vision, see any of this. What I see is a stable rock, comfortable because it does not betray me by moving under me. Sometimes, lying safely on its strength, I try to feel the movement of the earth, and there are times when I feel that I feel it. But it is something that I can never see.

I look back to the frog, small, cool, unthreatening. I will not hurt it, nor will it hurt me. But given the right (or wrong) stimulation, I could be made to see it as a hideous beast. Mobs have been made to *see* innocent victims as hideous, evil, threatening. Protestant and Roman Catholic Christians have been so terrified of each other that they have been willing to kill. During periods of rampant anti-semitism a gentle old man can suddenly be *seen* with his nose hideously hooked, his eyes blood red, his teeth lengthened into fangs.

But the frog can be seen not only as dragon, it can be seen also as bewitched and beautiful prince.

Rainer Maria Rilke writes: "How should we be able to forget those ancient myths about dragons that at the last minute turn into princesses who are only waiting to see us once beautiful and brave. . . . Perhaps everything terrible is in its deepest being something helpless that wants help from us."

I know that when I am most monstrous, I am most in the need of love. One of our children, when he was two or three years old, when he was naughty used to rush at me and beat against me; what he wanted, by this monstrous behavior, was an affirmation of love, and I would put my arms around him and hold him very tight until the dragon was gone and the loving small boy had returned.

The seventeenth-century poet, Thomas Traherne, wrote: "Certainly Adam in Paradise had not more sweete and curious apprehensions of the world than I when I was a child." Everything was new and delightful for him. The rosy glow of sunrise had in it the flaming glory of creation. The stars at night were a living, heavenly dance. He listened to the grass growing, smelled the west wind, tasted the rain, touched the grains of sand on the sea shore. All his senses, his mind, his heart, were alive and in touch with ousia. "So that," Traherne adds sadly, "without much ado I was corrupted, and made to learn the dirty devices of this world, which now I unlearn, and become as it were a little child again, that I may enter into the kingdom of God."

Unlearning is the task before us now. When I first read those lines of Traherne's I began to realize that what I want to do is to try to share my own unlearning, my own shedding of the dirty devices of this world, my own becoming once more as a little child.

Obviously this doesn't mean that I ought to dress like my daughters, talk in teenage jargon—or any other kind of jargon— or be somebody I'm not. It does mean that I must, as a child does, accept my dependency. I am dependent on my family, my friends, my community. I need help when I abuse my freedom and fall into error. It is through our errors, and accepting them as such, instead of alibi-ing, and rationalizing (as I tend to do) that we learn.

Children accept their dependency, and so are often far more free than their parents. They know they are often naughty, and false pride has not yet kept them from being able to say, "I'm sorry." How many of us can turn to another and say, like my little granddaughter, "I bin very naughty," and then hold up her arms for love and forgiveness? How many of us are free to accept that we are often less than we would like to be, and to move openly and vulnerably into apology? I learn from my grandchildren here, from their acceptance of reality which allows them to look at the world with eyes that have not yet become jaded. When they quarrel they are not ashamed to kiss and make up. They have not yet learned to slam doors on new ideas. And they see beauty all around them.

The All-rightness of Things

One of my students says that his parents never notice the sunset over the Hudson—one of New York's most beautiful sights—and that they mock him for getting excited about such glory. Alas, there are far too many days when I walk home from work and see only grimy buildings, filthy streets, discontented faces, and am unaware of the glory of the sunset, the brilliance of the first star, or the smile on the face of a child who wants to make friends with my dog. I'm stuck in the daily, un-free, time-bound world of provable fact until something—or someone—jolts me out of it.

An old southern woman said that she didn't mind cooking except that *hit's jest so damn daily.* I often feel the same way, not only about cooking, but all the common chores under which I bog down and dwindle and lose sight of ousia.

If we are to recognize the whole of our selves, then we must unlearn some of the dirty devices of the twentieth-century world of provable fact. We don't need to settle for the limited selves we can know and manipulate. This—I'm sure I don't need to point out—does not mean discarding the intellect. Far from it. This is no time to lose our heads. But we are not head alone. We are meant to be whole persons, free to move in that region where Shakespeare and Lewis Carroll and John Donne wandered at will, and where we can all become more fully alive. When we are fully alive we are free enough to move vulnerably into risk, and this freedom involves an intuitive acceptance of the ultimate all-rightness of things, an intuition which underlies all fairy tale, fantasy, and myth.

When a small child is frightened in the night and cries out in terror, the mother's instinct is to pick the child up and cradle it and say, "It's all right, it's all right."

But look at the world around us. What's all right? What was my mother promising me when she held me in her arms and said, "Don't be afraid. Mother's here. It's all right."? What was I promising my children when I did the same thing? I had certainly learned that Mother, no matter how much she may want to, cannot stop accidents, cannot stop wars, cannot stop death. So what am I promising today when I pick up a three year old grandchild and say, "It's all right"?

I think that I am promising that despite the pain and evil with which we are surrounded, there is an underlying all-rightness to things, and I find affirmations of this in all the great works of fantasy, fairy tale, and myth. The astronomer, Leverrier, affirmed this same hope when strange irregularities in the orbit of Uranus were discovered. There appeared to be no explanation for such unstructured behavior on the part of a planet in a reasonable solar system. But Leverrier didn't throw up his hands in horror and say that the heavens were in a mess, as some scientists did; instead, with a basic faith in the all-rightness of the universe, he computed the size, position, and orbit of a planet which, if the strange irregularity of Uranus were to make mathematical and poetic sense, must be in the sky. Because Leverrier had a fundamental faith that the universe is not irrational, he risked predicting that Neptune had to be there. And it was there, just as he had predicted, a hitherto invisible planet, Neptune, causing the seemingly meaningless irregularities in Uranus.

It is all right, Leverrier was assuring himself and the rest of the world. It is all right.

And as far as I am concerned this sheds a good deal of light on the affective.

It is this same faith in ousia, in the all-rightness of the universe, which sends me to the typewriter each day, which enables me to hold and comfort a child, no matter how wrong everything around me may be. In a world which sometimes seems to be without hope, I still affirm hope.

Because I am a human animal, with talks instead of tails or barks or meows, because I can draw on the memory treasure house, the MTH of the past, and risk looking ahead to an unknown future,

I can move from anamnesis to ousia to hope. When I affirm the all-rightness of things this all-rightness for me may be set in the context of pain, of death, of loss; I have often been tested in this affirmation, and I make it austerely and soberly. Nevertheless, in spite of everything, and because of the courage and compassion and vision my family and friends have given me, I can still go to my typewriter to forge a book, hold a child in my arms, and set down on this page the words: Yes, it is all right.

And I call on all who read this to make this affirmation with me. I am able to make this affirmation only because my companions along the way have given me the strength to say my own Yes. We need to remember our MTH, and to build our future on thousands of years of tradition, turmoil, and travail, and say, Yes, it *is* all right. We reverence our past, we are alive in the present, and we look forward to the future with excitement because we know that this is the only hope for humankind. Our search for ousia must show us not only that we can say, Yes, it is all right, but we must believe it, and act on it, too.

5

Perceptions of the Artist About the Affective Domain

Kenneth R. Beittel

Introduction and Argument

*T*he poet, the lunatic, and the lover, says Shakespeare, are possessed of an imagination quite compact. Setting aside the lunatic and the problematic relationship the world may project between the lunatic and the other two, let us concentrate on the bard's simple statement about poet and lover.

The poet, or artist, acts as though the world of experience could be grasped concretely as pure imagination and as that fusion which is fullness of being. The utterances of the poet or artist, be they in words or any medium, are at once symbols of existence and transcendence. They are symbols of existence because one feels and undergoes in order to speak, and they are symbols of transcendence because it is only in speaking and fully living that one can truly feel. The artist's utterances are pure metaphor.

Arting and loving are treated as primary instances of "creative learning" in this paper. Further, it is maintained that this learning is of such a kind that in it everything must be learned at once, even though it is generally alleged that it cannot be taught at all. I certainly do not expect those not in the arts to accept these statements at face value, since they require a leap that apparently comes only with experience with the processes in question.

Creating as Metaphor

In Japanese, the characters for *metaphor* signify "speaking in darkness." Can the artist speak in darkness? Yes, because one cannot live as a fully sentient being in the present by past light, and all light of tradition, technique, theory and training reflects off the moon of past achievements—the culture's or one's own alike. Finding the self in darkness, one chooses to speak. And the speech shines in the dark spaces of the heart and mind.[1]

Given the irreducible absurdity of the Babel of meanings and habit patterns into which one is unceremoniously thrown, the artist ignores or breaks through this plight and speaks as though for the first time. For the primary word of relationship, the I-thou dialogue of which Buber [2] so eloquently speaks, there is nothing one has that is not needed, nor nothing one needs and does not have. One is, in short, origin and agent.

Loving and Actualization of Potential

The lover acts as though nothing exists but the beloved. One sees in the beloved indeed what no one else can see. Far from being deluded (as it might appear from an uncaring externality), the lover releases in the loved one qualities and values that are indeed there, but in that teasing potential that would not be there otherwise, and they stream from the beloved like a radiance. In A. E. Housman's poem, the young man says: "O when I was in love with you/Then I was young and brave,/and miles around the wonder grew/How well did I behave." [3] (We will skip the outcome, when the "fancy" passed by, although it proves out the same point, but in a descending movement.) The former state, however, is the normal one for lover and artist—indeed of humankind generally, at our most vital and creative—that of having one's potential teased out in the very process of living. There is an exfoliation of vivid and vital values—values, moreover, that we are amazed to find through our enlarging repertoire of acts, yet which seem centrally like the self we were destined to become. Love is a movement, says

[1] Martin Heidegger. *Poetry, Language, Thought.* Albert Hofstadter, translator. New York: Harper & Row, 1971.

[2] Martin Buber. *I and Thou.* Walter Kaufman, translator. New York: Charles Scribner's Sons, 1970.

[3] Alfred E. Housman. *The Shropshire Lad.* New York: Avon Books, 1964.

Kenneth R. Beittel, *Professor of Art Education at The Pennsylvania State University has been on the faculty since 1953. His early teacher, then Department Head, was the late Viktor Lowenfeld. His interests in research have concentrated on psychological and phenomenological studies of the world of the artist in the process of making art. He regularly teaches a pottery studio class and has practiced the craft seriously for over 25 years. His studies included an apprenticeship in Japan. He is the author of* Mind and Context in the Art of Drawing *(1972), and* Alternatives for Art Education Research: Inquiry into the Making of Art *(1973). He has advised more than 100 completed doctorates in Art Education. Research studies of his have been supported by the National Science Foundation and the United States Office of Education.*

Scheler,[4] from a lower to a higher center. Far from disdaining the physical, the sentient, and the sexual, it sets off through these and properly restores to these the profoundest of metaphysical reverberations.

The lover's metaphor is to act in fullness of presencing as though never having embraced or caressed the beloved before. As lover touches beloved, an untouched touch pervasively returns the touch. As they embrace, it is again like the purest and most instinctive first time in the early world. The lover, as lover, need not write poetry, but is living it. The warmth of the sun intensifies as it reflects from the moon which reflects from the face of the beloved.

Lover and Artist as True Existentialists

Though it is tautological, the artist "arts" by "arting," and the lover loves by loving. They are always doing their thing—not getting

[4] Max Scheler. *The Nature of Sympathy.* London: Routledge and Kegan Paul, 1970.

ready to do it. There is no lover who is not loving. There is no artist who is not arting.

Both artist and lover are primordially existential—they are the true existentialists whom the philosophers describe. In the midst of absurdity and nothingness, they choose to act in fullness of being. No wonder that both are sometimes tragically broken through their courage to be. They dare to face the existential crises into which they are thrown rather than be defined inauthentically by others— whether that definition proceed from family, church, therapist, job, tradition, the projection of myths upon them, or whatever. For this rebellion toward being, one can be sure, the collective world will try to exact its toll, coming down on what it admires and desires but cannot openly condone because of the fear which is turned back upon itself—the fear of change and the unknown, the fear that one's own existence may be meaningless or inauthentic.

Artist and lover move through commitment. They act as though nothing else existed. They are able to exclude and dampen down equally as well as to embrace and enkindle. They bracket out by bracketing in. Once in action they are single-hearted, forgetful of all but the universe presence-ing in that instant. Their sense of time is all *kairos,* all qualitative, and none of *chronos,* that time that metes out mechanically. A minute fills a lifetime. Life is not measured out in trivia. Artist and lover, in short, shout "yes" to a world that "no's" everything.

Arting and Loving as Learning

Can we speak of "learning" where arting and loving are concerned? Yes and no, or no and yes. Yes, because in both our potential is teased out through being and becoming, encounter and dialogue. We actualize our selves through movement toward and with "otherness." Any mastery accruing, if indeed that word can be used, is seen over against goals clarifying only in process and increments of mystery before the potential toward which we feel ourselves magnetically drawn. Let me set the lover aside, for a while, to better fulfill my topic in the space remaining.

What kind of "learning" is it where everything must be learned at once and where those successful at it say it cannot be taught? And how can everything be learned at once? Or why is there art in schools, or art schools, if it cannot be taught?

Everything must be learned at once because nothing can be learned at all. One cannot learn to speak in darkness by speaking

in the light. The child and the novice are protected by their igno-
rance. The "everything" they must face in their own proper darkness
is commensurate with the scope of their heart and mind. It is even
so with the greatest genius. That is why the work of the child and
of the genius can both address us as art speaking. Origin and meaning shine forth in both through the compact imagination incarnate in
the work's very articulation. Both are finite, but they point to an
infinity opened out whenever language speaks in darkness.

All is ontological, all is I-thou, all is dialogue for the artist. Of
course, no one can sustain only the primary relationship of dialogue
incessantly. The mechanistic world, the social world, will see to
that. The artist, however, will fight against succumbing, but will
maintain emotional honesty. The artist will resist giving in to what
Collingwood [5] called "a corrupt consciousness," a condition characterized by the refusal to clarify feelings through the work of
expression.

How a Beginning Potter Encounters the Total Art of Potting

I am sometimes a potter and a teacher of pottery. Let me focus
on teaching a beginner something about "throwing" (making pots)
on the potter's wheel to bring our questions to a more concrete base.
The beginner, by definition, will usually have little "clay sense."
In our culture, at least until recently with all of the summer arts
festivals, a beginner will have little "pot sense" as well. The latter
lack was clearly brought to my attention when I taught pottery to
a native Japanese student who had never worked on the wheel
before. Even before he could "center" (bring the clay to visual and
tactile stillness on the spinning wheel) he was lifting up his irregular
tea bowls (for which a subtle tradition exists in the Japanese tea
ceremony) and saying, "Ah! I want to drink tea." From his culture
he had absorbed some pot sense but had as yet little clay sense.
If one drinks tea—or Coke—from a styrofoam cup and, in addition,
thoroughly disengages even that experience from the ceremonial and
sacramental aspects of drinking, one cannot be expected to have
much pot sense compared with the young Japanese man.

These cultural differences are intensified and extended by other
variations in readiness and, especially, by the idiosyncratic blend of

[5] R. G. Collingwood. *The Principles of Art.* New York: Oxford University Press, Galaxy Books, 1958.

habits and sensibilities observed and felt intuitively in my *relation-ship* to each new learner. To be sure, as a somewhat skilled potter and experienced teacher, I have a repertoire of expectancies against which to see the unique learner and occasion always before me.

How did potters learn their craft before modern times? By being sons of potters and apprentices of potters. By learning the whole and the parts simultaneously. By moving up a hierarchical scale of mastery in a natural way through their own slow ripening therein. By making thousands of traditionally conditioned minor acts second nature. I know this to be so because the small son of a prior partner in my pottery studio learned, after several summers around the shop, to wedge (knead) more clay than he could lift, and he did this better than most college students I have taught after a ten-week course.

In working with a beginner on the potter's wheel, I try to present an image of the total processes involved: wedging a rela-tively large amount of clay by using a rhythmical rocking method perfected by the Japanese; centering on the wheel by moving the whole mass of clay up and down; opening by thumbs or fingers so that the clay is penetrated, simultaneously broadened out at the base and swept upward into the first thinning toward a cylinder; drawing up by inside and slightly stronger outside knuckle and finger pressure into a cylinder that is straight, centered, true at the top and twice as tall as wide; forming by passage of pressure from inside to outside and back (with little or no pinching of the clay from both sides) into the desired shape; wet-tooling on the wheel, cutting and removing excess clay while wet to reveal the shape of the air around which the clay is wrapped; finish-tooling where desired, in a semi-dry state using clay chucks and metal cutters for footing, balancing, and precision of form; and finally, by the most direct processes, decorating, glazing, and firing.

There are many variations of the total processes briefly sketched in above. They are not a concern here. My point is to indicate that *the total art of potting* is being learned as one engages in the separate parts of what might look like traditional craft techniques. No mere technology (seen as discourse which is informative and prescriptive), not even a "human technology" is here involved. While on one level simple conditioned reflexes, reinforcement, operant condi-tioning, and the like, are involved, on other levels the beginner engages in total plans, images, feelings, dialogues, and encounters between me as teacher and the clay as "other."

The potter uses not just the hands, but the entire body; not just the clay, but all of nature. As one wedges the clay in preparation for throwing, the rocking rhythm flows in one movement off back and shoulders down through the hands into the clay. As one lifts the clay on the wheel, one moves from the balls of the feet, rising with the upward motion as with a breath. When using a bottling tool inside the forming pot to push it out into a pregnant fullness, there are nerve ends at the curved tip of the wooden instrument. In drawing the wall, the hand tenses outside the pot while the one inside relaxes. The potter always "knows" more, as Polanyi [6] puts it, than can be put into words. The fingers talk with the clay and go where needed without instruction.

In Search of the Teacher

It is as though the beginner must walk as a stranger into a new landscape, hopefully as a whole and trusting person. Is the teacher then a guide? Again, yes and no. Yes, because a teacher recognizes many of the geological and botanical features of the terrain. No, because as an other he or she cannot perceive what the beginner perceives—no more than the beginner can perceive what the teacher perceives. Their shared entry into that landscape, to be effective, must be jointly experienced as a unique existential event.

It is obvious to assert that the teacher needs the student in order to be engaged in teaching. The other side of the equation, however, is asymmetrical. The student does not need the teacher to be engaged in learning. One could look upon teaching, then, as Montaigne looked upon doctors—none is better than a bad one, for in the former instance nature can have its way. Besides, ontologically speaking, to be taught, to undergo teaching, is inescapable, thrown as we all are into a human culture. Teaching has already begun for all of us. We cannot undercut it no matter how close we come to the impenetrable fringes of human consciousness. We take in vague meanings with our mother's milk. The "self-taught" are thus also taught by "others." There are so many self-taught artists because it is better by far to come to the arting dialogue at the level of one's own skills as these relate to one's feelings and perceptions than to be inundated by technologies and values which are alien or removed even the slightest distance from one's spontaneity and expressive causality.

[6] Michael Polanyi. *The Tacit Dimension.* New York: Doubleday & Company, Anchor Books, 1967.

Teaching in Relation to Living Tradition and Authentic Self-Expression

It may be obvious to the reader that I use "to teach" largely as an intransitive verb. As will be seen later, however, the teacher's role will seem, on the surface, more non-directively nurturant where there is little tradition and more directively so where there is a living one. It is my feeling, however, that a closer look will show this difference to be one of the surface structure only of the setting provided, dependent on whether or not there is a conscious appeal to tradition. Authority in teaching, then, would seem to refer either to a radical commitment to a vital tradition or a radical commitment to the agency, the art-life connections, of the student. Though over-drawn, these two points of view correspond to what I would term "fine arts education" or "art education."

And even as we cannot avoid "teaching" in being "self-taught," so we cannot avoid teachers. Someone I know has put the case as bluntly as it can be put: "Choose your bastards with care!" Since learning from a teacher, even one consciously sought out by the learner, requires much trust, trust no one! To learn everything at once in something that cannot be taught requires that, even as an apprentice, one must be one's own master. The primacy of the relationship to arting, the arting dialogue, cannot be broken or, if close to being severed, it must be reestablished vitally before all else. Expressing and making have also already begun for us all before we move consciously toward someone with trust in order to learn.

I will now say that living tradition and authentic self-expression have equal cogency in learning in art. To support this two-pronged assertion I will point to my research into drawing, on the one hand, and to my apprenticeship to a master potter, in Japan, on the other. Then I will attempt to return to my prior statement and its apparent paradox: Arting is such that everything must be learned at once, but it cannot be taught.

Learning To Draw in a Traditionless Setting

My inquiries into the making of art have focused largely on drawing.[7] For the last six years I have moved from my earlier more behaviorally oriented studies and the mechanistic world view upon

[7] Kenneth R. Beittel. *Mind and Context in the Art of Drawing.* New York: Holt, Rinehart and Winston, 1972. Also, *Alternatives for Art Education Research.* Dubuque, Iowa: William Brown, 1973.

which they were properly based, toward phenomenological method as applied to the being of the artist engaged in the making of art in a context where the arting is shared and shareable with a "significant other" who is researcher as participant observer. Where, in short, the being of the researcher is also fully involved in an ongoing relationship to creating. The ontological thrust of this study of arting cannot deny the many causal contingencies of my earlier "scientific" studies, but, more importantly, it cannot deny the phenomenological and metaphysical levels of knowledge thus opened up. As my research assistant [8] put it, the study by human beings of the person as artist arting plunges one directly into a "concrete metaphysics."

First of all, there is the problem of the person *qua* artist. In essence, I have had to assume that for arting to be going on, there is, *a priori,* evidence of the artist's artistic causality, idiosyncratic meaning, and intentional symbolization.[9] These fancy word constructions are my attempt to assert that the person as artist must act as origin and agency in a movement toward form where the burden and clash of breaking with one's own past and the culture's modes and meanings are taken on as an inevitable part of the existentiality and self-transcendence of the act of making art.

One of the mysteries of teaching in its relationship to learning as arting is that it occurs most potently when it is least intended. When we set out *not* to instruct but instead to study the person as already arting—to "give the drawing back to the artist," as I like to put it—then everything can be learned at once and the context in itself is educative. Minimal skills (as judged by a nonparticipating external eye) become maximally related to meaning and forming. The beginner almost always assumes a necessity to first master basic skills and then move toward their expressive use. But this view has just enough truth to it to be very dangerous in its clouding over of the necessary tension between mastery and mystery. One must speak in darkness—in metaphor—from the start. As I have suggested and hope to delineate further in speaking later of tradition and apprenticeship, one never learns *only* an isolated skill, a technology—for example, how to center clay on the wheel—but much more above and below and through that. Nor does one ever teach *only* an isolated skill, a technology, for it flows from the authenticity of being of the one who mediates, in a dialogic relationship to the

8 Joan Novosel, conversation with the author, September 1974.
9 Kenneth R. Beittel, *op. cit.*

one who in like or potential wholeness stands within the context of mediation, or else, as Buber [10] put it, teaching becomes a lie.

A lack of conscious tradition or confusion because of weak and conflicting traditions throws the novice first back upon the cultural stereotypes that would have been projected upon a teacher anyway, were one present. The beginner is slowly disabused of these projections, given a nurturant setting, and strengthens slowly artistic causality and accepts the idiosyncratic meanings one cannot help but bring to the arting event. The beginner is, in short, an apprentice who, in the absence of an authentic master, must be apprentice-and-master or apprentice-as-master. One must take the dialogue with each instance of art-making seriously. One is then prepared for the absurdity and paradox which are essentially and inevitably present in his being as person and as artist. How else can this be said? One must already be arting to understand arting. This is a paraphrase of the statement that to understand one must have already understood.[11] Put in terms of thir essay, to learn everything at once, one must already be learning everything at once. The obvious is both profound and overlooked.

How does one step within this circle? By stepping, I am almost drawn to say. This is not nonsensical because expressing and making have also already begun for all of us, no matter how weak and buried that expression and making may appear to be. I have often seen a beginning artist (I call all those "artists" who step intentionally within the context of art-making) set out to copy something. Always one has transcended beginning intentions through the discoveries arising from the process of making. It is a bleak tribute to the awesome tyrannical and inhibiting force of formal education that our potential for expression in various media is often cancelled out for good. Being "self-taught" in any of these would have been vastly superior. Having no teacher is indeed superior to having a bad one in such matters. (Conversely, or positively put, having a good teacher can of course be better than none.)

Vandenberg [12] has said that in the educative setting we are all that our teachers allow us to be. How true this is where we are concerned with the truth of being of the person as artist. Discipline is no problem. It is already implicit in the compact imagination and

[10] Martin Buber. *Between Man and Man*. Boston: Beacon Press, 1955.

[11] Richard E. Palmer. *Hermeneutics*. Evanston, Illinois: Northwestern University Press, 1969.

[12] Donald Vandenberg. "The Pedagogic Atmosphere." Paper presented at Philosophy of Education Conference, Spring 1974.

commitment of poet and lover. It is likewise implicit in the acknowledged finitude through which the infinite potential of metaphor
shines. No artist has enough mastery. No lover is sensitive enough
in loving.

Insofar as the teacher can promote the artist's agency and draw
forth the unlimited meanings unfolding in the art process, to that
extent the learner is allowed to be what can be—to that extent tease
out the potential that would not have been there otherwise. I realize
that my usage of "potential" oversteps some of the definitional
boundaries often set on that word. Suffice it to say that I wish it to
include the meaning that what unfolds could not be predicted but
that it nevertheless seems a natural part of one's being *after* its
appearing.

Expression, arting events, exist as historical and often physical
realities. As such, what one has expressed is part of the context of further expressing. The meaning of a metaphor is problematic. The artist always says more and other than was intended—
or, rather, the meanings are not finished. Expressive acts are thus
texts for interpretation—for, that is, hermeneutics. The artist goes
back to study the expressions. What do they mean? One craves an
other's *authentic* response to one's creations, for, since the other
comes out of a different horizon, new meanings will be thus revealed.
Both a past and a future open up thus in one's present.

The participant observer, like the teacher or the master, is
involved in what I have called [13] "formative hermeneutics." Whether
responding to the artist's expressions nondirectively by always referring back to the artist's feelings and possible meanings or whether
more directly reading and sharing insights with the artist, the observer
participates in the artist's thrust into the newness of the next arting
event. This is especially true where the participant observer (as
researcher)—or where the teacher or master—is interacting with the
artist *in terms of the processes of making*, not just on the finished
expressions. We have done this in my research into drawing [14] by
having a feedback session and inquiry *between* works. Before each
new working session, that is, we have projected on a screen time-
lapse in-process still photographs of the works done the session
before. This stimulated recall keeps the dialogue centered on the
being of the artist in the act of making. The richness of revelation

[13] Kenneth R. Beittel. "Formative Hermeneutics in the Arting Processes
of an Other: The Philetics of Art Education." *Art Education* 27(8): 2-7; December 1974.
[14] Kenneth R. Beittel, *Mind and Context, op. cit.*

and potential which thus accumulates binds artist and participant observer together, for the latter becomes witness, co-discoverer, co-creator in a manner which does not usurp the artist's essential agency, but which brings to bear the fullness of the I-thou dialogue between human being and human being. In brief, we become engaged in philetics: the dynamics of creative love as centered on love of creating.[15]

Here, then, is an instance of how the absurdity and paradox of the being of person as artist is faced in the presence of a significant other in such a way that the spontaneity, agency, and idiosyncratic meanings of the artist are not only preserved but dynamically released under the formative hermeneutics of creative and creating love. What cannot be taught is none the less learned all at once, and a loving community inspires the apprentice to be his or her own master.

Where there is no vital tradition of how to make things, there are no masters, even though there are those who have come to mastery related to their own existence as artists. Without tradition, what one has mastered becomes arbitrary if it is projected upon an other. No one speaks in authority for there is no "right" way to speak. There is no standard which is clearly super-personal. Herein resides the source of what I feel to be the sickness of the American art school. Although there are no masters, because there is no vital tradition, every faculty member is in a position to act as one. How can everything be learned at once in something that cannot be taught at all when the teacher often moves by arrogance, caprice, or seduction? I do not mean that all art teachers intend to move thus toward their students, but that the effect of the context is thus. I do not think that I am unusual when I say that, in thinking back to my days in art school, I can come up with only one teacher who fully allowed me to be as an artist.

The Master-Apprentice Method Within a Vital Tradition

When much later, in my forty-fifth year, I apprenticed to a master porcelain potter [16] in Japan, I felt the power of vital tradition and the meaning of a discipline transcending the individual ego.

[15] *Ibid.*

[16] With Manji Inoue, master porcelain potter of Arita, Saga Prefecture, Kyushu, Japan.

I learned ways of doing things which were traceable back through Korea into ancient China. I felt a creative love which flowed like a broad river from behind me to before me. I was only a traveller on its banks. My master had his master who had his master, and on and on. Though each master differs, no master is that river. It flows through him. The tradition is always and never the same. Everything must indeed be learned at once, though it cannot be taught. It is, in fact, knowing these two things that makes one a master and that makes learning with such a one close to the zen experience.

The master chooses the apprentice perhaps more than the apprentice chooses the master. Once chosen, there is a relationship of perfect trust. If I did not go to the studio, the master came to get me. I did not fret about "self-expression" or "doing my own thing" even though I was a potter—an amateur I then decided—for almost 20 years before this new relationship. I have been largely self-taught—that is, I had learned by my own trial-and-error and through the wisdom capable of being written into books, especially into the English potter Bernard Leach's *A Potter's Book*, already a blend of East and West. I also had watched some of the few remaining American folk potters, like the Owens family around Jugtown, North Carolina, where I saw the effortlessness and fullness of bodily rhythm possible in throwing. Such simple people were all in advance of what my few American "artist-potter-teachers" could show me.

The master works through total concentration and imagery. In all finitude, a master nevertheless embodies perfection as an egoless possibility. As Shoji Hamada [17] has put it, he is not interested in the good potter, but the good pot. To be a good potter will take care of itself, for in working in that disciplined relationship to otherness, one is working on oneself. When my master worked, the reality of the moment of working was supreme. Stillness was imposed on all else. He spun with the wheel. His body was in a ballet with the clay. The images thus aroused are indeed like the dance and like lovers loving, although the intensity of doing depends on no metaphors. When he wedges clay, it moves and rolls upon the board as though it is alive. All energy is toward the clay and the perfectibility of the task. There is an implicit and explicit standard. The porcelain clay needs 300 turns. The potter rests after each hundred, and turns the clay around before rebeginning. If, as

[17] One of the "ineffable living cultural treasures" of Japan, a potter now in his eighties, working at Mashiko, Tochigi Prefecture, north of Tokyo, Japan.

apprentice, I am asked to help wedge the master's clay, he will insist on doing the last hundred himself. At the three-hundredth turn, the clay leaps up and down like a live fish just out of water and comes up in a perfect cone ready for the wheel.

Once on the wheel, the mass of clay is clapped by both hands into place and the wheel set spinning. The clay moves upward effortlessly with the potter's rising hands into a tall cone perfectly on center, as though a steel shaft were at its core. As in yoga, the potter seems at rest, but let a novice try it and the supreme energy and concentration required are seen at once. The potter then leans the clay into the torque of the spinning wheel and just as quietly and calmly the clay transforms into the compact shape from which it started, only to rise again, return, then again, and return. After that, it starts up still a fourth time but stops short of its summit, budding instead into a knob-like shape, the exact amount required for making a traditional form, one of many to come from that mound if the potter is doing production throwing, as of rice bowls. My master could produce in this manner one perfectly shaped porcelain rice bowl after another. A new one was set on the movable board beside the wheel every two minutes. Though identical to the naïve eye—and indeed a check of depth and diameter would show how perfect the control—yet each was alive. No motion was wasted. It was a dance in action, not a machine in mass production. The shape of each at the bottom, where it was lifted from the wheel, both saved the bowl from distortion in movement and also supplied a resting place for a stabilizing finger for centering the bowl, upside down, hanging off a chuck, for later tooling and finishing. Each step hinged on the other, and any departure only compounded difficulties to be encountered later.

The steps for making this simple bowl shape are so clear that they can be enumerated as a basic discipline for the apprentice, thus: (a) wedging the clay 300 turns, (b) raising the clay thrice on the wheel into a tall cone, (c) fixing the knob (required quantity for one bowl) the fourth time up, (d) opening the knob with the thumbs, (e) thinning and raising the wall with a curving, ski-shaped rib, (f) making the first "tweak" (indentation), setting off where the foot will end from the stem where the bowl will be cut off (done with a scissors-like motion of the first and second fingers of the right hand), (g) finishing the rim with a piece of wet leather, (h) pushing out the bowl form with a flat shaping rib to the exact contour desired, (i) giving the stem under the foot limit a final thinning tweak, (j) cutting the bowl free of the mound at the stem line (while the wheel is in motion) with a braided string knotted at one end, (k) lifting the bowl from the mound at the stem cut (the wheel still spinning), and (l) setting it on the movable board. These basic steps toward the rice bowl shape constituted the discipline set for the new apprentice. Typically, an apprentice worked through a year without saving a single bowl.

The steps in tooling are equally clear and require a like mastery. The tools permit no basic departure from the model of perfection which the tradition has winnowed out. For throwing, they must be from the right wood, suitably aged (the curved shaping rib, for example, is carved from green Chinese lilac wood and aged and dried, soaking in water for several months, or it will crack). The grain must run just so, the metal tools used for finishing must be bent and filed just so.

When, several years after my study in Japan, I was able to bring my master to the University where I work to teach for one ten-week period, I received further proof that the tradition-full and the tradition-less kinds of learning in the arts are related. Contrary to my fears, those students in a graduate course who were most into their own creative development and self-expression were those who could commit themselves most fully and selflessly to the discipline required—and this, though porcelain was new to them and the wheel direction was new also: clockwise (because shaping is from the inside and shaping tools are held in the right hand within the evolving bowl).

Space will not permit the full description of the impersonal beauty of the discipline toward perfection existing at each stage of the work. The river of tradition lives on and the apprentice willingly assumes a radical commitment toward its validity and vitality. All is not well, understand, in Japan and its traditional arts, but while there can be as Koestler [18] put it, "a stench of zen," there can also be, and was for me, a strength of zen.

To say that the master taught through imitation is too simplistic a reduction. He taught through embodiment, wholeness, and imagery. Imagery was especially important to me, for from that came feel and flow prior to the analytical acts of my mind which were always self-defeating until I learned to overcome them.[19] Small cues became part of the total concentration. "No breathing,"

[18] Arthur Koestler. *The Lotus and the Robot.* New York: Harper & Row, 1966.

[19] Eugen Herrigel. *Zen in the Art of Archery.* New York: Pantheon Books, 1953.

he might say at some point, and that would communicate to me my lack of total bodily immersion, in which the breath would be held almost instinctively. Or, without a word he would move my hand with his behind it. I doubt whether one can attend with a more searching eye than that of an apprentice who, having tried and failed in imitation of the master, sees the master perform anew. What does one see? All the minor acts are interlocked in one massive hierarchy held together by what seems effortless grace. The clay literally throws itself. It is again, a dance, all-process beauty in movement. The resultant object is good only if the making is good. One cannot, as Yeats put it, tell the dancer from the dance.

I could go on and on about both the traditionless learning I have uncovered in my inquiry into drawing and also about the radical commitment to vital tradition of a master-apprentice relationship. The result of both is the same: one learns to be a person as artist to the extent that one is allowed to be as a person and artist; one learns to speak in darkness; and one learns everything at once in something which cannot be taught but nevertheless can be enveloped in a trust and creative love which is the ground of all good teaching and learning.

The artist, then, with compact imagination, with courage to be and to change, and with insistence that the laws of the heart be given equal footing with the mind, has much to tell us about the affective domain. The journey through life is both personal and mythical. Experiencing and expressing have their own meaning and validity and are, at bottom, one thing, for the one enlarges the other as the other enlarges it, and the act of expression itself is primordial and pure experiencing. In the center of meaninglessness, the artist says "Yes" to life and action. The artist lives feeling and making ontologically, as movements of a compact imagination penetrating the darkness and speaking within it. Do not look at the artist and the lover with a cold and external eye. *Learn to become being with them. Learn to become becoming with them.* Do not presume to teach the artist anything, at whatever stage of his journey you meet—in an other or in yourself. Being as arting, I have argued, is a movement in which one takes responsibility for speaking in darkness and for learning everything at once, accepting the profound truth that it cannot be taught at all. Yet, in the way of being, the artist is the model for us all. As with the child's nonsense poem about the purple cow, I have never seen a total artist or a total lover. But I can tell you anyhow, I would rather be than see one.

6

The Reluctant Student: Perspectives on Feeling States and Motivation

Charles M. Fair

I have been asked to write a chapter in which "attention will be given to new theories, practices, concepts or research in one or more of the natural sciences that shed new light on our understanding of the affective domain." This assignment entails three principal difficulties.

The first is that over the past decade or so, no strikingly new or important discoveries appear to have been made in the sciences relevant to this discussion. And even in the light of what we already knew ten years ago, the relation of feeling-states to "motivation," or of both to performance, remains unclear.

The second difficulty is that the existing evidence from those same sciences has for the most part a limited application to the kinds of human understanding we are concerned with here.

The third difficulty arises from my own point of view. The problems that particularly occupy teachers today can best be understood, I believe, when seen as part of a much larger complex of changes affecting our society as a whole, that is, the historical approach may have as much to tell us as the scientific; and what it tells us may be less reassuring, if only because science confines itself to supposedly manageable facts, whereas those of history are often beyond anyone's control. The chapter which follows takes these points up in order.

Motivation, Emotion, and the Mechanics of Underperformance

Certain basic relations between emotion and "motivation" have been demonstrated in operant conditioning experiments with animals, and seem to have clear parallels in human experience. If an animal is required to solve a problem in order to earn a reward or avoid a punishment, it will be "motivated" to do so roughly in proportion to the apparent intensity of the pleasure it gains or the pain it precludes. And if the problem is a simple one, the animal may show few signs of emotion while solving it.

As the problem is made progressively more difficult, the animal's actions may at first become more brisk and efficient, suggesting that it is responding with an increased outlay of energy and a corresponding sharpening of its perceptions. An EEG taken at the same time would very likely reveal an intensified "arousal" pattern (normally accompanied by mild to intense stress-like bodily reactions—changes in heart-rate, in circulatory levels of norepinephrine, for example).[1]

Epinephrine and norepinephrine (adrenaline and noradrenaline), also known as catecholamines, are associated with stressful states such as anger or fear. The EEG or electroencephalogram records the electrical activity of the brain by means of electrodes variously positioned on the scalp. In human adults, the waking resting-state EEG frequency is generally the alpha (8-10 cycles/sec). During "arousal" that frequency increases over most or all of the cortical surface, and the various areas recorded from will cease to be in phase or synchronous. During "slow wave" sleep, by contrast, many cortical areas show a high degree of synchrony.

If now, the experimental problem is made next to insoluble, two things may happen. The animal's behavior may lapse from a trial-and-error pattern into one which is either randomly start-and-go or blindly perseverative and "superstitious." That is, it may begin compulsively repeating actions which were effective before but are so no longer. And simultaneously, it may begin to show signs of quite violent emotion, most notably fear.

What this sequence tells us is something fundamental about the relationship between motivation and emotion. It is probable that all of our actions are emotional in the sense that we perform

[1] See, for instance: W. G. Steiner. "Electrical Activity of Rat Brain as a Correlate of Primary Drive." *EEG and Clinical Neurophysiology* 14(2): 233-43; 1962.

Charles M. Fair is the author of four published works. One of those, and several technical papers, deal with the structure and functions of the central nervous system. He is a former Guggenheim Fellow (an award granted for study at UCLA's Brain Research Institute, 1963-64), a former member of the Neurosciences Research Program of the Massachusetts Institute of Technology, and researcher at Massachusetts General Hospital. Two of his books, The Dying Self (Wesleyan, 1969) and The New Nonsense (Simon & Schuster, 1974) present a new, scientifically based view of what is sometimes called the Human Condition.

them in a definite climate of feeling—eagerness, enthusiasm, resentment, indifference, impatience, and so on. The man who says he is "anxious" to get a particular job done may be literally that, as appropriate physiological measures (of skin-resistance, EEG, circulatory catecholamine levels, for example) might show. The word *meticulous* comes from the Latin meticulosus, meaning fearful.

What we *call* emotion is not intentional states as such; for so long as our intentions seem practicable, what occupies us is not how we feel but what we are doing. Emotion, in those circumstances, is a background element, a part, simply, of the gross energy supporting our actions. It is when our intentions are not practicable—when, for instance, we are hopelessly thwarted in love or in our life's ambition, or when someone close to us has died—that that same energy, having no useful outlet, manifests itself as sheer feeling. We then become conscious of our emotions partly because, being blocked from expression, they are more intense than usual, partly because we are denied the distraction of doing something. In short, when we are "frustrated"—when we have strong motives we see no way of putting into practice—our behavior tends to disintegrate. Its intentional component, and the corresponding organized actions, drop out, and what remains is undischarged raw energy. We feel emotion in this form to be threatening because, lacking a definite object, it may, as it accumulates, push us into relatively blind, directionless behavior which may take the form of finding butts on which to vent our feelings.

In popular language, we are reaching the point at which we shall have to "blow off steam"—often not as harmlessly as that phrase suggests. A physiological psychologist would see the same phenomenon as representing a back-up of central nervous excitation to the point that "arousal" itself contributes to the disorganization of thought, producing a corresponding impulsiveness or irrationality in our actions. Denenberg[2] and others have proposed this as a general principle which would define the coherence or efficiency of behavior as an inverted U-function of the degree of arousal. Everyday experience appears to confirm that hypothesis. Most of us do tend to function best when moderately keyed up, but above a certain level of excitement find ourselves impeded or blocked— it being at this stage that we are apt to become aware of our feeling-state as such, whether it be rage (at the difficulty of the task facing us) or anxiety (to cope with it) or fear (that we will fail).

Certainly all of us have seen this principle in action in the classroom. A student called upon to answer a question he knows is beyond him may flush or go pale, and as he does so, may "jam up," becoming mute and then perhaps rebounding into some form of rage—defiance, a chip-on-the-shoulder flippancy. The essential point is that under these circumstances, he is apt to perform *below* normal, seeming more stupid than he really is. On the same principle, repeated failure of this kind may generate an expectancy of further failure amounting to certainty. That is, the student's emotionality may, through a process of inadvertent conditioning, increase to the point that motivation to do well in school is effectively destroyed; and instead of small incidental failures he now inclines to large climactic ones. In spirit, if not in fact, he is reaching the dropout stage.

The practical question is why students, often of nearly the same intelligence, differ so enormously in their threshold to this sort of emotional disorganization. A most important factor here is what one could call the intentional component in their behavior. Other things (native intelligence, stability of temperament) being equal, the student who comes from a family of literate, hardworking, reasonably cultivated people is likely to have acquired some respect for intellectual achievement, and by emulation, some start toward it.

[2] V. H. Denenberg. In: D. C. Glass, editor. *Neurophysiology and Emotion.* New York: Rockefeller University Press, 1967. p. 172ff.

For respect, as such, is a true motive, in that it involves not only a logical component but an emotional one—in this case an affectionate approval transferred from parents one loves to the kinds of character and achievement they seem really to value and to represent. The word "really" here is not meant as a casual qualifier; for children do appear to have the ability to distinguish what older people wholeheartedly believe in from what they merely endorse—and that as much in the case of teachers as of Mom and Pop.

It follows then that if parents don't really believe in or act according to the principles they endorse, the children they send to school will be undermotivated in the sense just defined. Such children will be deficient in respect—the predisposing emotional component—if not in in-formation (sic) or mental readiness—the predisposing intellectual one.

The same deficiency can arise in children whom parents, from choice or necessity, simply neglect. Such children may come, for instance, from households in which both parents must work; in which there are few or no books; in which no one shows any interest in art or the theater or music; in which such things are regarded as "frills": and life is shown, by parental example, to be a matter of hardship and drudgery, intermittently relieved by cheap entertainment. No matter how naturally able, children with this sort of background are apt to be difficult to educate.

In school they will find themselves in competition with children who at home have had books read to them, have heard ideas discussed, and have perhaps become readers themselves at a relatively early age. Even though they may have as great, or greater, intellectual potential, these children find themselves so far behind in preparation, in readiness to learn, that they simply cannot keep up. And exactly in proportion as they are natively intelligent, they will be aware of their predicament and sense that they are being forced to play against a stacked deck.

A natural reaction is to become angry, to see the tasks of the classroom as having no merit in themselves. They experience them as a kind of punishment, a pointless daily humiliation which other students no better or smarter, really, than they, are spared. With this, undermotivation turns to antimotivation; failures accumulate and their emotional threshold goes down. Instead of trying harder they start to rebel.

To the extent that their parents and peers may have accustomed them to physical violence and taught them to regard the more fortunate classes as natural enemies, they may now treat Teacher as one. Teacher is not there to help; Teacher is The Enemy, pushing them around the way the powers in the grown-up world push around Mom and Dad.

So, in effect, they become proto-revolutionaries, gang members dedicated to disrupting all order in the classroom, or to terrorizing fellow students on the playground, well-to-do "sissy" types in particular. (When I was living in Manhattan in the early 1950's, shakedown rackets in the schools there were already beginning to attract attention. Two sons of a friend of mine were in fact paying "protection" to a group of armed students who made regular collections on a schoolwide basis. Reports made to Senator Birch Bayh's committee in the spring of 1975, by students and educators both, make it plain that the spread of violence in our schools, including murder, rape, and assults on teachers, is now a national phenomenon, and increasing at an alarming rate.)

Insofar as the educational system itself has the effects I have described on the "underprivileged" undermotivated student, one can say that it aggravates the hostility between classes and contributes to its own impotence in the face of them.

The later Victorians supposed that class-structure was the result of Natural Selection—meaning that the difference in educability between upper and lower class students was primarily genetic. In the light of recent developments in this country, that explanation sounds rather too simple. For if one were to single out *the* most striking development in American education in the past decade, it is the spread of undermotivation from ghetto students to students from the middle and upper classes.

The no-grading system was in part, perhaps, a concession to this phenomenon—a way in which all of us, students, teachers, and parents, could minimize the extent of it by avoiding anything that could be regarded as a quantitative measure of scholastic competence. One such measure—the recent ten-year decline in Scholastic Aptitude Test scores for language ability and mathematics [3]—suggests that the phenomenon itself may be real enough. If so, how are we to interpret it? Several points here are important to note. The numbers and class origins of the students tested were approximately constant for the period sampled, and the decline in scores

[3] *The New York Sunday Times*, December 16, 1973, p. 1, Section I. " 'The question of what is causing the drop is something none of us can answer' said Dr. William Angoff, Executive Director of College Board programs for the Educational Testing Service of Princeton, New Jersey."

was consistent and greater during the second five years than during the first. My own belief is that a strict scientific approach to the problem is likely to yield little beyond what we already know. The next section explains, in brief, why I think so.

What Hard Science Can and Cannot Tell Us About Ourselves

The lines of scientific inquiry which bear most directly on humankind's understanding of itself are ethology, or the comparative study of behavior, experimental and physiological psychology, and clinical psychiatry. Of these the last seems, in recent years, to have become the most static. The type of psychiatry descended from Bleuler and Kraepelin has never had much following in this country whereas that descended from Freud, while still dominant here, has had, on the whole, only moderate therapeutic success [4] and as a theoretical system has evolved hardly at all. One might, for example, infer that the undermotivation of some students is due to their narcissism, the further inference being that there may have been a statistical shift toward arrest in the early "oral" stage of development. An analysis, à la Kinsey, of current adolescent sexual practices might even support such a conclusion, the question then being—so what? What can one do with this sort of information?

Among early Freudians, a key article of belief was that "repression," especially of the sex drive, gave rise to much of the strain in modern societies.[5] Some saw the thwarting of Eros as a great motive force behind the sadistic excesses of fascism or the violence so prevalent in American movies and American life. But over the past ten years, we seem to have made considerable progress in disinhibiting ourselves sexually, a change accompanied by an increase, not a decrease, in various forms of violence.

In ethology, a more modest and careful science, we find a grab-bag of possibly useful facts drawn mainly from the observation of

[4] See: Allen Wheelis. *The Quest for Identity.* New York: W. W. Norton and Co., 1958. p. 124ff. Also, Percival Bailey. "A Rigged Radio Interview, with Illustrations of Various Ego-Ideals." In: *Perspectives in Biology and Medicine* 4(2): 239; 1961. A follow-up study aimed at assessing the effectiveness of psychoanalysis as therapy is reported in: P. H. Hoch and J. Zubin, editors. *Current Approaches to Psychoanalysis.* New York: Grune & Stratton, 1900.

[5] Sigmund Freud. *Civilization and Its Discontents.* New York: Doubleday, Anchor Books, 1958. In his final paragraph Freud expresses the hope that Eros, freed presumably of old-fashioned constraints, may now "put forth his strength" and save us.

animals and therefore to be applied with caution to ourselves. It is probable that we, like other species, have a sizable repertoire of innate behavioral patterns, some of which can be greatly modified by experience, and some not. Whether we pass through an early "imprinting" stage, as Money has proposed,[6] and whether this in turn (the "imprinting" of Mother or Father) determines our later sexual preferences, remains to be shown.

Tinbergen [7] has pointed out many elements apparently common to human and animal behavior—among them a responsiveness to "innate releasers" such as the bulging foreheads of human and animal young which trigger parental behavior and which, like Disney's Bambi, we find "cute" or automatically appealing. As animal societies do, ours arrange themselves into pecking or butting orders. Both in pattern and function, our national flags bear a striking resemblance to the colored wing-stripes found in various species of ducks. The almost mystical importance we traditionally attach to owning land may trace to a territorial instinct we share with creatures such as the stickleback or the Greenland Eskimo dog.

As popular writers such as Robert Ardrey [8] have pointed out, our friendships may be less a matter of spontaneous warmth than of an instinct to form useful alliances. Even erotic attachments, once their basic adaptive purpose has been served in the first days or months of frantic mating, tend to pass. Likewise, parents' love for their children, and of their children for them, often lessens as the children grow up, and may turn to active dislike when parents and children view each other solely in the light of adult standards— that is, without the softening influence of dependence and those innate releasers which make children seem to us cute or appealing.

I mention these points as indicators not of what we necessarily are but of a condition to which we may be regressing. The effort of Western civilization in past centuries has been to transcend these purely animal elements in our nature—to make sexual ties more enduring than lust alone would make them, to raise friendship from a relation of mutual utility to one of disinterested respect and affection, to set a value on learning not for what it can do for us in a

[6] J. Money. "Components of Eroticism in Man." In: J. Wortis, editor. *Recent Advances in Biological Psychiatry.* New York: Grune & Stratton, 1960. p. 215ff.

[7] N. Tinbergen. *The Study of Instinct.* New York: Oxford University Press, 1961. *Passim.*

[8] R. Ardrey. *The Territorial Imperative.* New York: Atheneum Publishers, 1966.

practical way but as a good in itself. Today we seem determined to reverse this trend—to live closer to our instincts, to be more "realistic" in all our relations. The results in family life and in education are what one would expect: instability, rising divorce rates and a tendency to treat learning not as a "higher" human undertaking but as a set of adaptive gimmicks, a means to advancement in the tribe.

The neurophysiological study of perceptual mechanisms, in particular in the auditory and visual systems,[9] has produced a body of evidence to date somewhat ambiguous, in that we cannot yet say to what extent our primary mode of apprehending the world is "wired in" from early infancy. Other studies, for instance of rats raised in "enriched" versus barely adequate environments,[10] indicate that proper maturation of the neocortex, hence presumably of intelligence, may greatly depend upon early stimulation or psychological nurture. What these experiments suggest is that, nutritional factors aside, cultural deprivation may in some children critically retard the early growth of the brain, with the result that at maturity the cortex is thinner than it might have been, essentially because of the underdevelopment of its fine-structure (dendritic networks, glial cells, possibly vascular supply).

Since nutrition is also known to be a factor important to the proper development of the central nervous system, it follows perhaps that some of the supposed racial differences in brain mass or structure[11] may actually have been due to differences in class— in the case of some Blacks or American Indians, the result of mental and nutritional deprivation combined. In any case, the data from animal studies, showing a close connection between early behavioral stimulation and later maturation of the cortex appear to confirm an intuition which educators have had at least since the time of J. S. Mill, namely that the sooner one can set a child to thinking, the

[9] For an excellent summary of recent work in these fields and related ones (for example, hemispheric dominance), see: F. O. Schmitt et al., editors. *The Neuroscience Third Study Program*. Cambridge, Massachusetts: The MIT Press, 1974. 1107 pp. See also: John Szentagothai and Michael A. Arbib, editors. *Neuroscience Research Program Bulletin* 12(3): 307-510; October 1974.

[10] M. C. Diamond et al. "Increases in Cortical Depth and Glia Numbers in Rats Subjected to Rich Environment." *Journal of Comparative Neurology* 128(1): 117-25; 1966.

[11] One of the most careful and critical reviews of data relating to differences in brain weight or cortical structure between ethnic groups was made by Percival Bailey and Gerhardt von Bonin in *The Isocortex of Man*, Urbana: University of Illinois Press, 1951.

better he or she is apt to be at it. Conversely, the later one is started, the more of one's potential may irreversibly have been lost.[12]

In the field of experimental psychology, Skinner's generalizations, drawn mainly from work done with animals, do not seem to me to have the revolutionary implications which Skinner and others suppose. The idea that what we decide to do or refrain from doing depends upon our estimate of the "contingencies of reinforcement"—that is, the rewards or punishments likely to result—is hardly news. "As the twig is bent . . ." "Spare the rod . . ." and "Money makes the mare go" are Skinnerian statements. What we gain by rephrasing them in the bleak jargon of behaviorism is not immediately apparent, at least to me.

In one handbook of Skinnerian child management,[13] the emphasis seems to be on positive reinforcements. "Catch the children being good rather than bad" we are told. "Ignore disruptive behaviors. Do not attend to the behaviors you wish to weaken or make less frequent. Get involved with other children showing behaviors you wish to strengthen." To judge from recent reports [14] on the spread of violence, and not in our large urban schools only, I suspect that this method of controlling "disruptive behaviors" may not quite suffice.

In other branches of experimental psychology, it has been shown that conditioning in young animals is favored if learning (of the conditioned stimulus) is accompanied by some form of

[12] The question of whether human beings go through "critical learning periods" is still unsettled. It is certain, however, that fine motor skills such as dancing or playing a musical instrument are most apt to be mastered by those who start learning them very early (ages 5-10). Other evidence from neurophysiology shows that the eyes of newborn kittens deprived of patterned input, may later learn to see patterns but apparently with some deficits. The same principles may apply to learning motions of the mind; if some of these are not started soon enough, they may never be easily or wholly learned.

[13] Wesley C. Becker. *Parents Are Teachers.* Champaign, Illinois: Research Press Co., 1971. Reprinted by permission.

[14] See, for instance, a Knight News Service item, dated May 10, 1975, reporting on the survey made by the Judiciary Subcommittee To Investigate Juvenile Delinquency—a survey which, according to Senator Birch Bayh, Chairman of the Committee, "reads like a casualty list from a war zone."

According to the news story, "two years ago, inside the schools of about 500 of the nation's larger districts, 100 children were murdered, several hundred thousand more were assaulted, almost 70,000 teachers were attacked, and $500 million worth of property was destroyed. . . . In Kenosha, Wisconsin, in-school robberies went from six in 1970-71 to 53, two years later. In Clark County (Las Vegas) instances of major school vandalism jumped from 19 to 671 in the same two-year period. In San Francisco during January 1973, four students were expelled for carrying guns in school. Three of them were girls."

doing.[15] This finding suggests that feedback from the motor systems acts in some way to "consolidate" the recall of sensory data being taken in at the same time. In turn this fact, if it is one, provides physiological support for our long-held belief that performance rather than passive understanding is the *sine qua non* of intellectual mastery, performance here being understood to mean interim performance or practice.

The point is important because in our competitive society, many of us, adults and students alike, are afraid to commit ourselves to interim performance for fear of public failure and ridicule. It should consequently be the object of any good educator to discourage this sort of shyness in every way possible, since it may retard the learning process to an extent not heretofore recognized. (Indeed, in my own school days, it was not unusual for the teacher to ridicule a student who had made a poor recitation, apparently on the theory that the student might be nettled into doing better the next time. In my own case, at least, the method was a total failure.)

The recent work in "biofeedback," which shows some promise as a method patients can use to manage such conditions as high blood pressure, heart arrhythmias, or tic douloureux, has little application that I can see to education. The fact that one can learn to control the frequency of one's own "brain waves" has been shown both by the traditional techniques of Yoga and by modern laboratory methods in which the subject watches his or her own "brain wave" output on an oscilloscope. For a primer in this field, I refer you to Robert Ornstein's *Psychology of Consciousness* (Freeman, 1972), which considers Sperry's "split-brain" data in relation to biofeedback and to the meditation techniques. Ornstein believes we can achieve what he calls a synthesis between the active go-getting mode of existence and the passive contemplative one, between the verbal-logical left hemisphere and the "lunar" or intuitive right. Eventually meditation may become standard practice in the classroom; however, in many schools at the moment it might be difficult to institute. Practitioners of Transcendental Meditation or related techniques of EEG control maintain that in the alpha wave state, learning is greatly facilitated. I know of no experiment that convincingly shows that to be the case; and there is other electrophysiological evidence which suggests that learning is in fact a more

[15] R. Held and A. Hein. "Movement-Produced Stimulation in the Development of Visually-Guided Behavior." *Journal of Comparative and Physiological Psychology* 56(5): 872-76; 1963.

active process, involving "fast" beta rhythms in the EEG and a moderate level of general arousal.

In concluding this section, I should mention the various studies which have been made in an attempt to correlate violent behavior, distractibility, "absences," or extreme anxiety, with abnormalities in brain structure or function.[16] To date this work has yielded results of only marginal interest. It is probably true that a small percentage of unmanageable pupils suffer from recurrent subclinical anterior temporal lobe seizures and should be classed as psychomotor epileptics. The fact is that, taken together, all such detectable abnormalities probably account for a negligibly small fraction of the students we now classify as unruly, weak in concentration, or in other ways "exceptional." In short, gross brain disorders may tell us as little about our present problems in the classroom as the XYY chromosome abnormality tells us about our rapidly rising crime rates.

In the later 1960's and early 70's, there were a number of well-publicized attempts to apply brain science to the problem of violence in our society. Most neurophysiologists would, I think,

[16] I recall, for instance, a clinical study involving a patrolman who felt himself becoming more and more inclined to impulsive violence. His difficulty was traced to a focal brain tumor. At about the same time, it was reported in the press that Charles Whitman, who had gone on a shooting spree and killed several people in Austin, Texas, might have been suffering from a tumor of the hypothalamus. The latter is a small subcortical structure in the brain which is vital for the regulation not only of vegetative states such as hunger and thirst, but of emotional and "drive" states as well. Very small lesions of the hypothalamus, depending upon their location, can cause hyperactivity or somnolence, compulsive feeding or fasting, changes in pituitary secretion, and so on.

Another clinical case I remember was that of a young woman who became violently nymphomaniacal while remaining in most other ways perfectly normal. Tests showed that she had an apparent thinning in parietal cortex, opposite a medial cortical area which figures in regulation of the sex drive. (Tumors in the latter area had been known to produce bizarre effects, such as a vaginal hemi-anesthesia.) The inference was that the woman had incurred brain damage at some earlier time, and that cells in the damaged area, by their tendency to seizural firing, were overdriving cells in the nearby sexual area. The woman was put on Dilantin, an anti-seizural drug used with epileptics, and her nymphomania abruptly ceased. A Mr. Dreyfus, founder of the mutual fund of the same name, was apparently cured of his seizural anxiety attacks when his psychiatrist put him on Dilantin, and as a result did much to promote use of this drug for miscellaneous psychic disorders.

Mr. Dreyfus was, in that effort, perfectly sincere and dedicated, as have been a number of scientists in trying to encourage a physiological approach to psychological problems. The fact remains that *most* criminals, juvenile delinquents, or habitual drug users, can probably not be cured by removal of focal brain tumors or going on daily maintenance doses of anti-seizural drugs.

agree with me in saying that these investigations accomplished very little, and were in some cases disingenuously undertaken. At a time when grant money for purely scientific work was becoming harder and harder to get, it was understandable that some researchers would try to improve their chances by making their field of study seem more relevant to pressing social problems than it actually was.

Such "Mickey Mouse" projects, particularly when carried out by mature, highly qualified, seemingly honest investigators, represent a serious breach of the code which, since Francis Bacon's time, has made understanding, rather than fundability, the prime object of scientific inquiry. With the emergence of government-supported Big Science in the past two decades, there has undeniably been some erosion of that traditional standard—a fact which should be kept in mind by anyone studying the supposedly "hard" evidence of the laboratory and the clinic for clues to such things as ineducability or intractable violence in the young.

Perspectives on the Ineducability Problem

My assumption to this point has been that the issue is not so much how to improve our teaching methods as how to adjust them to compensate for the increasing resistance of the taught. The indifference of students of all classes, both to the substance of learning and to the idea or ideal of it as something besides a means to social promotion; the prevalence of cheating and of demands for "relevance" in curricula; the rise in vandalism specifically directed against schools; [17] the increase in "disruptive behaviors" to the point that in some classrooms teaching reduces essentially to an exercise in riot control, all argue that in some crucial way we are failing.

The question is why, at this stage in our educational history we should be fighting not to gain ground but to keep from losing it. The anti-motivation of students from the Black ghetto or of first-generation Puerto Ricans, who have language problems added to those of low economic status, is self-explanatory. The reasons for the poor motivation of middle and upper middle class white students

---

[17] See note 14 earlier. I have on file many similar news stories, for instance one from the *New York Sunday Times*, April 19, 1970, which reported that for the Greater New York area, school vandalism (destruction of labs and classrooms; arson) rose 20% in 1969 from the year before and resulted in losses estimated at $3.2 million.

are less clear. In a recent paper,[18] Bronfenbrenner devoted much attention to this problem, concluding, among other things, that many of our young people are "alienated" because they are in effect rejected by their parents. "The vacuum created by the withdrawal of the parents and other adults" he says "has been filled by the informal peer group. A recent study has found that at every age and grade level children today show greater dependence on their peers than they did a decade ago."

In Bronfenbrenner's view, the "generation gap" was not the spontaneous drawing away we chose to think it but a choice we forced upon our own children. He cites studies which show how little time per day many fathers spend with their kids, adding that "the growing number of divorces is now accompanied by a new phenomenon: the unwillingness of either parent to take custody of the child." Children driven to peer-dependence . . .

have a rather negative view of their friends and of themselves. . . . They are pessimistic about the future, they rate lower in responsibility and leadership. . . . The more serious manifestations are reflected in the rising rates of youthful runaways, school dropouts, drug abuse, suicide, delinquency, vandalism and violence documented for the White House Conference on Children in 1970 and in more recent government publications. . . . What is the ultimate source of these problems? Where do the roots of alienation lie? [19]

The popular explanation is that we live in an Age of Anxiety the causes of which are chiefly external and technological. Students are demoralized because they have grown up in the shadow of the Bomb, and of the slower, seemingly more inexorable catastrophes promised by overpopulation and the accumulation of industrial wastes.

In science, where the trend has been away from the radical environmentalism of a few years ago, a small but growing minority is beginning to think that nature may after all matter more than nurture. This group might be inclined to regard our educational problems in general, and the recent decline in Scholastic Aptitude Test scores in particular, as signs of a genetic change affecting all levels of society.

The latter view has, of course, a long history. Since Darwin's time, its proponents have argued that modern medicine and the protectiveness of civilized life generally have reversed the course

[18] Urie Bronfenbrenner. "The Origins of Alienation." *Scientific American* 231: 53-57, 60-61; August 1974.
[19] *Ibid.*

of natural selection. Wild Norway rats are said to lose much of their wildness, stamina, and intelligence when cage-raised for several generations. Domestic dogs or cats are apt to show less sensory acuity and poorer cerebral development than their feral relatives. Might not the same principles apply to humankind?

It has been argued that the human gene pool is so large and the course of natural selection among us so uncertain and slow that significant changes, for instance in our inherited intelligence, are unlikely to occur on a time-scale of decades. At least one scientifically oriented writer [20] has disputed that conclusion, maintaining that over the past 75 years we have undergone a statistically significant decline in IQ. He cites an experiment in artificially managed selection by which a population of rats, originally of the same strain, were divided within six to seven generations into two distinct groups, one "maze bright," the other "maze dull." More recently it has been shown that mouse populations go through quite short (two to three years) cycles of growth and diminishment, and that these cycles are accompanied by clearly definable genetic changes.[21] It is just possible, but far too soon to conclude, that we like other species (mice, arctic lemmings, the Rocky Mountain hare) show cyclical variations in population growth, possibly accompanied by changes in dominant psychological types and in general intelligence.

I mention this view because, like those of Shockley and Jensen, we are certain to hear more of it, notwithstanding that scientists themselves are continually warning us of the dangers of generalizing from other species to humans. One cannot, however, discount the possibility that genetic changes, in us as in other forms, may occur far more rapidly than we have been accustomed to think. Nor can the argument that civilization is itself, in some ways, counterselective be dismissed out of hand.

[20] Charles L. Fontenay. *Epistle to the Babylonians*. Knoxville: University of Tennessee Press, 1969. pp. 132ff and 174ff. Fontenay's argument is intricate and somewhat difficult to follow, but he seems to be comparing median IQ for (American) populations born between 1891 and 1895 (which he calls "the 1940 population"), and between 1911 and 1915 (which he calls "the 1960 population"). He is led to the conclusion that "the median IQ level in the third generation of the 1960 population would drop to 90 points (only one point above the comparable fourth-generation projection of the 1940 population)."

It is interesting, in this connection, to note that in the ten-year decline in SAT scores mentioned in note 3 earlier, the overall decline in language ability was 6.9 percent.

[21] J. H. Myers and C. J. Krebs. "Population Cycles in Rodents." *Scientific American* 230: 38; June 1974.

The more pertinent question is whether it is specifically counter-selective for intelligence, and here, it seems to me, the evidence points the other way. Certain kinds of intelligence, at least, are at a far higher premium in societies such as our own than in tribal ones. And it is reasonably safe to assume that the students who provided the data for the ten-year study of Scholastic Aptitude Test scores mentioned above were drawn from classes representative of exactly that sort of selection-pressure. Their parents, as relatively prosperous business or professional people could be regarded as demonstrably superior in certain mental skills. The Darwinian argument would explain the parents' preferred status, and the argument from genetics would predict that the traits responsible for their success should appear in greater-than-average measure, in their children. How then do we account for the decline in effective intelligence implied by the SAT figures?

Presumably, as Bronfenbrenner suggests, environmental and psychological factors are chiefly responsible. But here again, I do not think the usual methods of analysis will tell us very much. One of the "factors" supposedly angering our young people and turning them off to schoolwork, was the Vietnam War. Why didn't the same thing happen during the Korean War, whose official rationale was no better and whose draft calls were even larger? And if the liberal argument, which directly connects crime, delinquency, truancy and the like with poverty, is correct, why shouldn't these have been more of a problem during the Great Depression of the 1930's, than they came to be in the relatively prosperous 60's?

The answer, I think, lies in the fact that we may be dealing with a phenomenon which cannot be satisfactorily explained either in biological or sociological terms. It can only, I believe, be understood if we view it from the longer perspective of history. One might define the *Geist* as that body of beliefs, ideas, and feelings which generate the major movements of an age often without becoming fully conscious in the minds of those who act on them.

One of the most significant features of the *Geist* today is what it is not—what is being dropped from our stock of root-ideas. We live in a predominantly skeptical era, and a fact we seem little disposed to face is that skepticism is almost by definition a self-eroding philosophy. However reduced the stock of traditional beliefs, the skeptic always finds grounds for reducing them further, to the point finally that mental and moral amorphousness may become the prevailing state in society. One ground for the skeptic's reducing the stock of traditional beliefs is self-indulgence—a determination to have done with moral constraints which stand in the way of the Good Life and which can be dismissed as survivals from the ages of superstition.

It is that amorphousness—the lack of warmth of conviction or of an essentially idealistic concern with The Other—which appears to be destroying our family life and undermining our children in the ways Bronfenbrenner has described. We seem as a people to be approaching the state prophesied in Yeats's poem *The Second Coming*—to be undergoing a loss of psychic structure so extreme that it is turning up as a measurable loss of self-restraint and of intellectual power or motivation in the generations now rising. In other publications [22] I have given, in some detail, the rationale for supposing that such a regressive change is in fact occurring in our civilization.

The past, and indeed the present, are strewn with the wrecks of societies which lost what Walter Bagehot [23] called "the secret of progression." The problem, as he saw it, was one of balance; a "progressive" society neither broke with its own past nor lived in blind subservience to it, but maintained itself in a state of rational emergence, in which it respected and profited from what it had been. The Lord Mayor of London once described this as peculiarly the English genius—never to be parochial-modern. But skepticism carried far enough results in a parochial modernity such as we see in America today; it amounts to a break in that fundamental continuity on which the "progression" or even the survival of great civilizations depends. It is essentially that break that we may be seeing in our classrooms. By a kind of profound consensus, we seem to be declining the task of our own further growth—turning away from the past, demanding only what is "relevant," the "nowness" of cheap entertainment or immediately useful knowledge. In a most basic sense we lack respect—for each other, for our heritage, for the value once attached to culture or learning as such—*humanitas*.

I doubt that in education proper or in any other special field, we are going to develop the ideas and techniques needed to change this basic drift. But in education, more than in most fields, we can certainly see where it may be taking us.

[22] Charles M. Fair. *The Dying Self*. Middletown, Connecticut: Wesleyan University Press, 1969; also, Charles M. Fair. *The New Nonsense*. New York: Simon & Schuster, 1974.

[23] Walter Bagehot. *Physics and Politics*. Cedar Knolls, New Jersey: Colonial Press, 1900. p. 26.

7

Insights About Persons: Psychological Foundations of Humanistic and Affective Education

Cecil H. Patterson

Formal education always and everywhere has been based on a theory (in the broad sense), or (more accurately) certain preconceptions about the nature of the person, or (more specifically) the nature of the child as a learner. These preconceptions have more often been implicit rather than explicit. They have more often been based upon armchair theorizing than upon empirical observation or research. And they have usually been projections of adult characteristics onto children.

Until relatively recently, little in the way of either theory or empirical or research data has existed in the field of human development upon which to base a theory of instruction. Montessori was perhaps the first to attempt to develop a system of education based upon extensive observation of children (48). Research in child development, especially that of Piaget (48), has now reached the point where it provides a basis for the beginnings of a theory of instruction. Theoretical work in humanistic psychology, as well as theory and research in counseling or psychotherapy have reached the point where they can contribute to the theory as well as practice of a humanistic education, which includes concern with affective as well as cognitive development (45).

It is the purpose of this chapter to review selected materials in psychology, related to the nature of man and his development, which are relevant to a humanistic system of education. Humanistic is used to indicate a concern with the learner as a human being (rather than simply an organism), and as a whole person, rather than simply a disembodied intellect or repository of cognitive processes.

The Nature of Man

Gordon Allport (2) described three images of man, which determine, or influence our activities and relationships, professional as well as nonprofessional, with people.

Man as a Reactive Being

This view of man, called behaviorism, sees the person as an organism which responds to and is shaped by its environment. In this respect, a human being is no different from any other biological organism, although his greater complexity requires some additional concepts beyond those sufficient to account for the behavior of the rat and the pigeon. But it is behavior—essentially overt, motor behavior—which is the focus of study. As it is unnecessary—and of course impossible—to know what goes on in the brain of the rat or the pigeon, so it is unnecessary to know what goes on in the brain—or mind—of the human being. Behavior is a direct response to environmental stimuli. If one can control the environment, one can predict and control behavior.

Behaviorism is associated with John B. Watson and B. F. Skinner. Watson's behaviorism was essentially limited to the classical conditioning paradigm of Pavlov's research with animals. Classical conditioning (or respondent conditioning) consists of attaching reflex behavior, which is the organism's natural, unlearned response to a specific (unconditioned) stimulus to a new, (or conditioned) stimulus by means of associating the conditioned stimulus to the unconditioned stimulus by repeated pairings of the two.

A second kind of conditioning is instrumental conditioning, or, to use B. F. Skinner's term, operant conditioning. In this kind of conditioning, so-called spontaneously emitted or operant behavior is strengthened by positive reinforcement (reward) or by negative reinforcement (the removal of a stimulus which prevents or inhibits the behavior), and is discouraged or weakened by the lack of or the withholding of positive reinforcement (extinction) or the application

C. H. Patterson *is Professor of Educational Psychology at the University of Illinois, Champaign-Urbana. He is a graduate of the University of Chicago (major, Sociology) with an M.A. (Child Psychology) and Ph.D. (Educational and Counseling Psychology) from the University of Minnesota. He is a Fellow of the American Psychological Association (Divisions of Counseling Psychology, Rehabilitation Psychology and Psychotherapy) and a past president of its Division of Counseling Psychology.*

He has published several books in the field of counseling and psychotherapy, including the standard text, Theories of Counseling and Psychotherapy, *and* Relationship Counseling and Psychotherapy. *He is also the author of* Humanistic Education *and of the forthcoming (tentative title)* Foundations for a Theory of Instruction and Educational Psychology.

During 1972-1973 Professor Patterson was a senior Fulbright-Hays lecturer at Aston University, Birmingham, England. He identifies himself with the humanistic psychology of Carl Rogers and Abraham Maslow.

of aversive stimuli (punishment). (Michael and Meyerson provide an excellent brief discussion of conditioning [40].)

Behaviorism is not as simple as it appears at first glance, or as it is made to appear in popular presentations or in paperbacks for classroom teachers. Its oversimplification is misleading, though it is no doubt one of the reasons for its wide appeal. Another reason for its appeal is its association with science, with the scientific method and the research tradition, and with the tremendous amount of research which has been done with animals and in laboratory studies with first-year college students. The behaviorists repeatedly emphasize that their approach is experimentally based on laboratory studies. Another basis for its current appeal is its extension beyond what might be called classical behaviorism; behaviorists have broadened their view, and have encompassed or incorporated much of the total field of psychology, particularly cognition, and are now appropriating the term humanistic to apply to themselves. Thus we have progressed through periods of neobehaviorism and neo-neobehaviorism; behaviorists are now talking about fourth and fifth generation behaviorism.

The nature of what the newer behaviorists include under behaviorism is indicated by the work of Albert Bandura (5). Bandura rejects many if not most of the concepts traditionally accepted as the core of behaviorism. He states that "the fabled reflexive conditioning in humans is largely a myth." Automatic conditioning does not occur automatically but is mediated by cognition. It is not the repetitive pairing of experiences which results in learning, but the recognition that the paired events are related. "Behavior is influenced by its consequences much of the time. . . . But external consequences, influential as they often are, are not the sole determinants of human behavior, nor do they operate automatically." Consequences influence behavior because they impart information, and because they represent anticipated benefits, which thus give them incentive or motivational value. It is anticipated consequences rather than actual consequences which influence behavior.

Bandura refers to the nature of intermittent reinforcement which is a paradox for traditional behaviorism, since only a minority of responses may be reinforced, so that "behavior is maintained despite its dissuading consequences." Expectations and beliefs are involved, in opposition to actual consequences. Bandura also finds a place for internal influencers of behavior, through the operation of self-produced or self-reinforcing consequences. Thus, behavior is not entirely under environmental control, and there is room for the concept of personal freedom. This is a far cry from Skinner's statement that behavior is controlled solely by environmental contingencies (except for genetic or constitutional factors) (61). It is beginning to appear that Skinner is almost alone, as a radical behaviorist, in taking this extreme position.

That behaviorism is broadening, expanding, and moving toward humanism is heartening, though many of those who are espousing humanism are apparently not clear about its nature—for example, Skinner, who calls himself a humanist, and is a signer of the Humanistic Manifesto II (23). To be sure, there is perhaps no clear agreement as to the essential nature of humanism, or even whether those who call themselves humanists have anything fundamental in common. (We shall consider the nature of humanism, or humanistic psychology, later.)

Yet a question must be raised about the use of the designation behaviorism. It is confusing, and misleading, to apply the term to the position of Bandura. The question can be asked: What is meant by behaviorism when the word is used in such different ways? It becomes impossible to criticize or evaluate behaviorism when in effect the definition changes so radically. Bandura represents a small, but growing, development among behaviorists. But the majority (and this applies particularly to those who are applying behaviorism in various situations, such as education and school classrooms) appear to share a basic attitude or assumption. That is, that behavior, and thus the behaver, or the person, is an object to be changed, or manipulated, by external methods. This raises questions about the ethics of such influence and control, and the nature of the changes which are attempted, or the goal of programs to change behavior (47).

If any theoretical or systematic approach dominates education at the present time, it is behaviorism, represented by the emphasis on the use of teaching machines and methods of classroom management. The behavioristic system employed is derived from traditional behaviorism, rather than the approach being developed by Bandura. While hope exists that this situation will change in time, we are now under the influence of this earlier behaviorism, which will continue for some time until those in education who are technicians begin to be influenced by leaders in psychology such as Bandura. In the meantime, we are seeing the results of a narrow behaviorism in our classrooms. The nature of these results is indicated in the title of an article which surveyed target behaviors used in studies involving normal classrooms: "Current Behavior Modification in the Classroom: Be Still, Be Quiet, Be Docile" (72). One study (63) classified classroom behaviors as inappropriate or appropriate. The former included the following: getting out of seat, standing up, walking around, running, hopping, skipping, jumping, moving chairs, racking chairs, tapping feet, rattling papers, carrying on a conversation with other children, crying, singing, whistling, laughing, turning head or body toward another child, showing objects to another child, and looking at another child. What is there left to do? Not much: the appropriate behaviors included attending to the teacher, raising hand and waiting for the teacher to respond, working in seat on a workbook, and following in a reading text. No doubt some of the inappropriate behaviors would interfere with learning. But it is clear what the conception of education and learning is in such a classroom—education is teacher-controlled, and learning is passive. The good classroom is the quiet classroom with pupils fixed in their chairs staring at the teacher. One wonders if behaviorists are so enamored of conformity and so ignorant of the nature of human beings and of human learning in natural environments as to accept such behaviors as desirable, or are they indeed, as they often claim to be, technicians at the service of educators who have these behaviors as goals.

This is no place for a critique of behaviorism. The reader who is interested in such a critique will find it in Bandura's paper referred to above, as well as in other sources, including a chapter in the 72nd Yearbook of the National Society for the Study of Education (39, 58, 64).

The basic difficulty with behaviorism is not that it is wrong, but that it is incomplete and inadequate as applied to the total human being. There is no question that man is a reactive being. At birth he is little more. But as the human being develops, he becomes more. His first move away from simple reflex behavior is toward a hedonistic approach to the environment—the avoidance of pain and the satisfaction of needs, or pleasure. This is the simple operant conditioning model. But the course of normal development is away from depending on reflexes for survival, and away from simply *reacting to* one's environment, to *acting on* one's environment. The sign of maturity is autonomy, or relative independence of one's environment. Behaviorism is a "nothing but" model, equating humans with animals. But the individual is "something more" than a reactive being, and this something more is significant, even crucial, in understanding the person and facilitating his development as a human being.

The great danger in behaviorism, then, is not that it is wrong, but that, being right, it could lead to a view of man as nothing but a reactive being. And if man is treated as such, he could in time actually become simply a reactive being, or at least become less human and more like an animal. Paradoxically, he would be under the control of others who claim that they are not free, but who yet take on the responsibility of controlling others.

Man as a Reactive Being in Depth

The second image of the person described by Allport is that of so-called depth psychology, or of psychoanalysis. In this model, man is determined by his innate, instinctive needs and drives. In its emphasis upon the avoidance of pain and the seeking of satisfaction or pleasure, it is similar to the operant or reinforcement model of the behaviorists.

It is not necessary to elaborate upon this view, first, because it is well known, and second, because it has had little influence upon education. Among the few attempts to apply psychoanalysis to education are those of Isaacs (25), Jones (26), and Neill at Summerhill (43). Its influence is declining in psychology and psychotherapy. Its major contributions have been the recognition of the importance of early childhood influences and experiences upon later personality and behavior, and of the importance of the nonrational or affective and emotional nature of man.

This model is similar to the behavioristic model in that man is determined, in this case by the past rather than by the environment. In both cases he is a victim of forces beyond his control, in one case from within and in the other from without.

Man as a Being in the Process of Becoming

Allport's third image of the person is the existential model. Man is seen as personal, conscious, future-oriented, feeling as well as thinking. He is free and in control of his behavior (within limits, of course). He is an active being, or as Allport terms it, proactive; he searches for stimuli and seeks experience. He organizes stimuli and the environment, and creates, to some extent, his own world. Rather than being manipulated by the environment, he manipulates the environment for his own purposes. He is not a creature of instinct or of environmental stimuli alone—of the past and present alone. The human being is the only animal with a future, and is influenced by the future. He is forward-looking and is influenced by anticipations, expectations, hopes and fears. In addition, the person's past is not fixed or constant—an individual can reconstruct or reconstrue the past, and thus deal with regrets and guilt deriving from past behaviors. The fact that the human being has some degree of freedom means that he can and must make choices. And since he is free to choose, he is responsible, to some extent, for his choices and his behavior. A completely deterministic view of humankind relieves him of responsibility for his behavior, a state of affairs which would have important, if not catastrophic, consequences for society.

It is this view or image of the person which seems to be the core of humanistic psychology. Although it would appear that this view would be in direct conflict with the image of the person as a reactive being, requiring that one make a choice between them, this is not necessarily the case. There is overwhelming support in psychology for the case that the person is a reactive being. But as indicated above, this view is limited and restricted. As Allport notes (2), "the trouble with our current theories of learning is not so much that they are wrong, but that they are partial." Thus, the reactive model must be supplemented by a model which recognizes other characteristics of the person. That the behavioristic model is inadequate is indicated by the movement of behaviorists, such as Bandura, to expand the model, even to the extent of incorporating aspects of humanistic psychology. It appears, then, that we are on the way to developing a model of the person which will include his most human aspects. This model will, inevitably, minimize the purely reactive aspects of human behavior.

Let us proceed to a consideration of some of the major aspects of this view of the nature of humankind. Whether we call it humanistic behaviorism, behavioristic humanism, or some other name is irrelevant. However, at the risk of offending those behaviorists who may not want to give up the term behavioristic, we shall call it humanistic psychology.

Humanistic Psychology

Humanistic psychology crystallized in the early 1960's representing, in Abraham Maslow's term, a "third force" in psychology, in contrast to psychoanalysis and behaviorism. Those who were involved in its development were concerned with the increasing deindividualism, depersonalization, and dehumanization becoming apparent in society, a trend supported and fostered by the applications of behaviorism. The focus of this approach, as noted above, is upon the person and his total experiencing—of emotions, feelings, affects, and valuings as well as cognitions. The experiencing person is not a passive recipient of stimuli—experiencing involves selecting and giving an organization and meaning to the stimuli which surround him, and using them to develop his potential and create a life. The following is a description of the nature of man from a humanistic viewpoint. Although based upon a number of humanistic psychology sources, it is an attempt by the writer to provide an integration of these sources.

Man Is Inherently Good

One of the issues which divides us in our views of the person is whether he is innately good or bad (or indifferent). Many, if not most, religions view humankind as innately depraved. Freud was pessimistic regarding human nature. He believed that the individual's instincts were antisocial, and must be controlled by culture or society. He wrote: "It does not appear certain that without coercion the majority of human individuals would be ready to submit to the labour necessary for acquiring new means of supporting life. One has, I think, to reckon with the fact that there are present in all men destructive, and therefore anti-social and anti-cultural, tendencies, and that with a great number of people these are strong enough to determine their behavior in society" (18). Man is not only antisocial, but actually hostile to others, according to Freud: "Civilized society is perpetually menaced with disintegration through this primary hostility of men toward one another. . . . Culture has to call up every possible reinforcement in order to erect barriers against the aggressive instinct of man" (17).

Aggression has long been considered a basic instinct. Adler originally proposed that aggression was the single basic motive or instinct of the human being (4). The strength and practical universality of aggression argue for it as innate. However, many have questioned its innateness or instinctiveness. Anthropologists have found societies with little trace or evidence of aggression (1). Ashley Montagu, an anthropologist, writes: "My own interpretation of the evidence, strictly within the domain of science, leads me to the conclusion that man is born good and is organized in such a manner from birth as to need to grow and develop his potentialities for goodness. . . . [The view that aggressiveness is inherited] is not scientifically corroborated. In fact, *all* the available evidence gathered by competent investigators indicates that man is born without a trace of aggressiveness" (42). He refers to Lauretta Bender's finding that hostility in the child is a symptom complex resulting from deprivation in development. Charlotte Buhler in her studies of infants also found that "they give evidence of a primary orientation toward 'reality' into which the baby moves with a positive anticipation of good things to be found. Only when this reality appears to be hurtful or overwhelming does the reaction become one of withdrawal or defense" (8, p. 71). Maslow also declares that impulses of hate, jealousy, hostility, etc., are acquired. "More and more," he writes, "aggression is coming to be regarded as a technique or mode of compelling attention to the satisfaction of one's need" (36). There is thus no instinct of aggression that seeks expression or discharge without provocation or without regard to circumstances.

In other words, aggression is not primary, but a reaction to deprivation, threat, or frustration. This was the thesis of the frustration-aggression hypothesis put forward by the anthropologist Dollard of Yale and his psychologist associates in 1939 (14). A more general term for the stimuli which provoke aggression is threat. Aggression is universal because threat, in some form or other, is universal. The psychoanalyst Bibring, in criticizing Freud's theories, questions "whether there are any phenomena of aggression at all outside the field of the ego-preservative functions," noting "the empirical fact that aggressiveness appears only or almost only when the life instincts or the ego instincts are exposed to harm" (6, pp. 474-98). A widely read novel purporting to demonstrate the innateness of aggressiveness in humans inadvertently supports the view that aggression is the result of threat, since its development in the group of boys in the novel occurred under conditions of fear and feelings of being threatened (22).

There is evidence that man is inherently good in the continual striving toward an ideal society, with the repeated and independent development of essentially similar religious and ethical systems whose ideals have withstood the test of time. In spite of conditions of deprivation, threat, and frustration these ideals have been held and practiced by many individuals. Humankind has developed systems of government and of law which, though imperfectly, especially in their applications, represent these ideals.

It might actually be argued that goodness or cooperation has a survival value (41), and that innate aggression would be selectively eliminated by evolution. If there were not an inherent drive toward good in humankind, or if aggression were innate, it is difficult to understand how the human race could have continued to survive. The potential for good has survived in the face of continued threat and frustration. When we can reduce deprivation and threat the manifestations of good will increase and aggression will decrease. It is important to add as an addendum that aggression does not include assertive behavior, initiative behavior nor even much of competitive behavior. The confusion of these kinds of behavior with aggression has perhaps contributed to the belief that aggression is innate.

Man Is an Active as Well as (or More Than)
a Reactive Being

This point has been made above. It is obvious that the human being is physically active, even in the absence of environmental stimulation. To be sure, internal stimulation is present, and in the infant these stimuli are mainly the physiological drives or needs seeking satisfaction. One of these needs, however, is the need for activity, a need whose satisfaction is necessary for physical growth and development. Later, these internal stimuli include psychological drives whose satisfaction is necessary for psychological growth and development.

Behaviorists recognize the activity of the organism, calling it operant behavior, though extreme or radical behaviorists would insist that this behavior is environmentally determined (if not genetically or constitutionally determined), and that the behaviorist simply shapes it or brings it under the control of different environmental conditions. The greater the extent of one's control of environment, the greater is the extent of the control of the organism. Behaviorists insist that if one had complete control of the environment, then behavior could be completely controlled. Perhaps the greatest extent to which the environment can be controlled is in prisons or concentration camps. Yet even here, there are differences in the way in which individuals behave, as Frankl (16) clearly shows.

Whether one sees the individual as selecting stimuli (or rewards or reinforcements) and thus creating an effective environment, or whether one sees the individual as being controlled by the environment (through rewards or reinforcements) depends upon one's point of view. The behavioristic terms "instrumental response" and "operant response" suggest that the individual responds purposefully to obtain some goal—the response is instrumental to its attainment—or operates upon the environment to achieve something. The cartoon depicting a rat in a Skinner box pressing a bar and receiving a pellet, with the caption reading (if I remember correctly) "Look how I've got him conditioned. Every time I press this bar he gives me a pellet," illustrates this. Skinner might reply that although the rat might think it was controlling the receipt of the pellet, it was not in fact doing so. Yet one might well ask who is controlling whom in situations where children receive rewards (candy, tokens, etc.) for certain kinds of behavior. It's all in one's point of view.

Behavior Is Determined by the Individual's Perception

The behaviorists insist that behavior is determined by external stimuli, while depth psychology insists that it is determined by internal stimuli. Neither is entirely correct. Stimuli, internal and external, do influence behavior, but do not determine it. The individual reacts to stimuli in terms of his perceptions of them, what they appear to be, what they "mean" to him. The same objective stimuli are perceived differently by different individuals. In this sense we do not react to any "reality," but to what we perceive. We can only know the world through our perceptions, and reality is thus what we perceive. Our perceptions are our only reality; we cannot react to what we do not perceive. "We see things," says Gibson, a perceptual psychologist, "not as *they* are but as *we* are" (19, p. 98). In other words, it is not "seeing is believing," but "believing is seeing." Beliefs, attitudes, expectations, wishes, and desires influence our perceptions, and thus our behavior. "What is perceived is not what exists, but what one believes exists . . . what we have learned to perceive as a result of our past opportunities and experiences" (10, pp. 84, 85).

The evidence for this point of view is overwhelming, beginning with the discovery by experimental psychologists that the same physical stimulus is not reacted to in the same way by different subjects. A thirsty person perceives water or an oasis in the desert; a hungry person, when presented with the word "cat" for an interval too short to be able to read it sees it as "eat."

This is a simple, common sense theory of human behavior, but nonetheless a very useful one, in that it enables us to understand the apparently unreasonable behavior of others. For a simple example, take the case of an automobile driver who stops at a stop sign, then immediately proceeds again right into the path of a car coming into the intersection from the left, or right. "That person must be blind," is the most charitable reaction of an onlooker. The driver of the other car will no doubt have a much more derogatory reaction. The first driver's behavior seems ununderstandable. But, if one recognizes that the driver perceived the intersection as a four-way stop, such behavior is at once clear and understandable.

The importance of perception in behavior is not adequately recognized, except by those who call themselves phenomenological psychologists (10, 29, 44). Yet all psychologists, including the behaviorists, must, in a basic sense, be phenomenological psychologists.

Man Has a Single Basic Motivation

The single basic motivation of all human beings is the actualization of one's potentials. A number of psychologists have reached this conclusion, apparently independently, including Goldstein, Angyal, Rogers, and Combs and Snygg. Angyal defined life as "a process of self-expansion" and added: "We can say that the tendency of the organism is toward increased autonomy," or a tendency toward self-determination. He also refers to self-realization as being the intrinsic purpose of life (3, pp. 29, 47, 354). Lecky, impressed by the integration and organization of the self, felt that a need for self-consistency and its preservation is the single basic need of the organism (30). Self-actualization is a part of Rogers' general organismic actualizing tendency: "The organism has one basic tendency and striving—to actualize, maintain, and enhance the experiencing organism" (53, p. 487). Rogers also uses terms such as independence, self-determination, integration, and self-actualization.

Combs and Snygg have perhaps developed the unitary theory of motivation most extensively. They state: "From birth to death the maintenance of the phenomenal self is the most pressing, the most crucial, if not the only task of existence. . . . Man seeks not only the maintenance of *a* self. . . . Man seeks both to maintain and enhance his perceived self" (10, p. 45).

The use of the terms maintenance and preservation along with enhancement and actualization poses the question of whether there aren't actually two motives. Maslow perhaps was influenced by some such consideration in his concept of deficiency motivation and growth motivation (37).

But preservation or maintenance, and enhancement or actualization, may be seen as two aspects of the same motive, operating under different conditions. Adler recognized the different expression of the same motive in neurotics and normals. The neurotic, threatened and compensating for deep feelings of inferiority, reacts to preserve or restore his self-esteem, or to overcome the feelings of inferiority with superiority through a striving for power. The normal individual, on the other hand, free of threat and without feelings of inferiority, can strive for completeness or perfection (4, p. 114). In the unhealthy, disturbed, or abnormal individual who is under stress and is threatened, enhancement or positive striving is impossible. He must defend himself against attack or threat, and strive to safeguard, defend, or secure what he is or has. His energies are absorbed in preservation. Goldstein has made the same point. He considers the drive for self-preservation a pathological phenomenon. The drive for self-actualization, he suggests, undergoes a change in the sick (or threatened) individual in whom the scope of life is reduced, so that he is driven to maintain (or defend) a limited state of existence. Preservation or maintenance of the self is thus the pathological form of self-actualization, the only form of self-actualization left to the disturbed (in Goldstein's case, brain-damaged) or threatened individual (21).

A more serious question can be raised against the concept of a single basic motive by those who contend that the individual has many motives, and who propose various hierarchical orderings of them. The most widely known proposal of this kind is that of Maslow. Maslow's hierarchy starts with the basic physical needs, which are prepotent, taking precedence, when they are unmet, over all other needs. When these basic needs are met, the safety needs emerge. Then come the belongingness need, the love need, the esteem need, and then the need for self-actualization (38, pp. 35-47). The problem arises that the order is not invariant, as Maslow himself recognizes. It is not always true that the lower, more basic physiological needs take precedence over the higher less prepotent needs. A person may sacrifice life for honor. We need, therefore, some organizing principle to explain this apparent inconsistency.

The concept of self-actualization as the single basic need provides this principle. It clarifies, or eliminates, the confusion we face when we attempt to understand and order, or integrate, the multiplicity of specific drives or motives, often contradictory or opposed to each other, which are attributed to human beings. There is no need to attempt to order drives or needs in a hierarchy. There *is* no hierarchy in the sense that certain needs always take precedence over other needs. All the specific needs are subservient to the basic tendency for the preservation and enhancement of the self. The individual's specific needs are organized and assume temporary priority in terms of their relationship to the basic need for self-actualization. That specific need which is most relevant assumes priority or prepotence, or, to use Gestalt terminology, becomes the figure against the ground of other needs (49). When it is satisfied, the next most relevant need in terms of self-actualization assumes prepotence, or figure, while the others recede into the background. All specific needs are organized by the basic need for self-actualization, and their significance or relevance is determined by this basic need.

The Perception of the Self, or the Self-Concept
Is the Most Important Determiner of Behavior

Perceptions are influenced by our needs, beliefs, and attitudes. Our perceptions of the world are influenced by our perceptions of our selves. The self is the most important part of the individual's phenomenal field, the center around which all other perceptions are organized. Other perceptions derive their meaning or significance from their relevance to the self-concept, in terms of their contribution to the maintenance and enhancement of the self, or to self-actualization. The person who views himself as a failure expresses this in his perceptions of the behavior of others and in his own behavior in response to the behavior of others; in other words, he becomes a failure. The child who perceives himself as a nonreader does not read. Many children do not learn to read because they are convinced they cannot read. With this conviction they do not attempt to read, and thus do not learn. This vicious circle operates in the case of children who believe they are failures in other areas, or indeed that they are failures in all areas. The individual with strong feelings of inadequacy is threatened by requests and demands made upon him. He perceives the world as a dangerous place, presenting situations with which he is unable to cope.

The relationship between the self-concept and school achievement is now clear. Purkey (50, p. 27), in summarizing the evidence, notes that "there is a persistent and significant relationship between the self-concept and academic achievement at each grade level, and that change in one seems to be associated with change in the other. ... Although the data do not provide clear-cut evidence about which comes first—a positive self-concept or scholastic success, a negative self-concept or scholastic failure—they do stress a strong reciprocal relationship and give us reason to assume that enhancing the self-concept is a vital influence in improving academic performance." Scholastic achievement is not determined by scholastic ability alone. The self-concept, among other factors, appears to be involved.

If behavior is determined by the behaver's perceptions, or phenomenal field, particularly the perception of self or self-concept, then it should be clear that to be able to understand and to predict another's behavior one must know that person's phenomenal field. That is, it is not what we know *about* the individual and his environment—the so-called objective facts—that is important, but whether we are able to put ourselves in another's place and to perceive him and the world as he perceives them. In other words, we must be able to take an *internal* rather than the usual *external* frame of reference if we are going to understand people.

Man Is a Social Being

The concept of man as a self-actualizing being eliminates the individual versus society dilemma. The notion that a self-actualizing person is antisocial, or at least asocial is a misconception which has been put forward by so many well-known writers that it requires correction.

Maddi (34), criticizing self-actualization as the good life, writes "Actualization will tend to take place without the aid of socialization. Indeed, society is usually regarded, in this view, as an obstruction, because it forces individuals into molds, roles, conventions that have little to do with their own unique potentialities. The best thing society can do is impinge upon the individual as little as possible." In another place (33), he writes: "According to Rogers . . . what blocks individuals is society, in the form of persons and institutions reacting with conditional positive regard and therefore being too judgmental to be facilitative of self-actualization. . . . The definition of the good life involved emphasizes spontaneity rather than planfulness, openness rather than critical judgment, continual change rather than stability, and an unreflective sense of well-being. Enacting this, one would more likely live in the woods than enter public life."

The idea that the self-actualizing person is—or can be—antisocial has been expressed by E. G. Williamson. Pointing out that human nature is potentially both good and evil, and that "man seems to be capable both of becoming his 'best' bestial and debasing self, as well as those forms of 'the best' that are of high excellence," he contends that it cannot be accepted that "the nature or form of one's full potential and self-actualization will thus be the 'best possible' or the 'good' form of human nature" (71, p. 195). While one could contend that counseling would provide conditions for the actualizing of one's "best" potential, Williamson questions the "implicit assumption that the 'best' potentiality will be actualized under optimum counseling relationships" (70). He appears to believe that counseling, by accepting self-actualization as its goal, is in danger of encouraging "growth through demolishing all barriers restricting free development in any and all directions, irresponsibly and without regard for the development of others" (68). He questions the assumptions that "any and all forms of growth contain within themselves their own, and sufficient, justification," and asks "Do we believe that the fullest growth of the individual inevitably enhances the fullest growth of all other individuals?" (69).

Smith (62) appears to accept this view of self-actualization as including undesirable, or antisocial, behaviors: "and the problem of evil remains: People may realize their potentialities in ways that are humanly destructive, of others if not of themselves."

Even White (66) sees self-actualization as self-centered or selfish. Recognizing that Maslow included "focusing on problems outside oneself and being concerned with the common welfare" in the concept of self-actualization he questions its inclusion: "To call working for the common welfare 'self-actualization' instantly falsifies it into something done for one's own satisfaction." Thus it is apparent that he views self-actualization as self, or selfish, satisfaction. "I ask readers to observe carefully," he writes, "whether or not self-actualization, in its current use by psychological counselors and others, is being made to imply anything more than adolescent preoccupation with oneself and one's impulses." This, in my opinion, is an unfair and unwarranted characterization of counselors who accept the concept of self-actualization.

The implicit assumption in this conception of self-actualization is that there is an inevitable conflict between the individual and society, and that the full development (or self-actualization) of individuals is inimical to the self-actualization of other individuals.

The formulations by Rogers of the self-actualizing person deal with this issue. The individual lives, and must live, in a society composed of other individuals. He can actualize himself only in interaction with others. Selfish and self-centered behavior would not lead to experiences which would be self-actualizing (or satisfying) in nature. The self-actualizing person "will live with others in maximum possible harmony, because of the rewarding character of reciprocal positive regard" (54, pp. 234-36). "We do not need to ask who will socialize him, for one of his own deepest needs is for affiliation and communication with others. As he becomes more fully himself, he will become more realistically socialized" (55, p. 194). He is more mature, more socialized in terms of the goal of social evolution, though he may not be conventional or socially adjusted in a conforming sense. "We do not need to ask who will control his aggressive impulses, for when he is open to all his impulses, his need to be liked by others and his tendency to give affection are as strong as his impulses to strike out or to seize for himself. He will be aggressive in situations in which aggression is realistically appropriate, but there will be no runaway need for aggression" (55, p. 194). The self-actualizing person needs to live in harmony with others, to love and to be loved, to meet his own needs, to be a self-actualizing person. Thus, the self-actualizing person provides the conditions for the self-actualization of others, rather than being a negative social influence.

To Change Behavior We Must Change Perceptions

If perceptions, particularly perceptions of the self, determine behavior, then it becomes clear that we must change perceptions in order to change behavior. Perceptions change in those situations which have relevance to the self and thus involve the basic need for the preservation and enhancement of the self. Other situations or stimuli are simply ignored or not even perceived. This is why so much of what children are exposed to in school has little if any effect. It is not seen as relevant; it is simply not perceived.

The first condition for perceptual change is thus an experience which is relevant to the self and the self-concept, that is, it has personal meaning. If the experience is consistent with the self-concept, there will be no, or little, change. It will be accepted and reinforce the self-concept. An experience which is consistent with a self-concept of failure does not change this perception of oneself. The experience must be inconsistent with the existing self-perception, thus raising a question or posing a problem. But, since one naturally attempts to preserve the existing self-concept, there is resistance to change, and experiences which are inconsistent may be ignored, resisted, distorted, rejected, or denied.

These reactions of preservation of the self-concept are the characteristic reactions to threat. An individual who feels threatened does not easily change his perceptions but becomes resistant to change. To be sure, his behavior may change under coercion, but the change does not persist when the coercion is removed. The experience which leads to change must raise a question or pose a problem in a challenging rather than a threatening way. The distinction between threat and challenge is important in learning or behavior change, since what is a challenge to one child is a threat to another. The teacher of a large class of children is in a situation where attempts to challenge some children are threatening to others. This would seem to support grouping for instructional purposes, though there are other factors involved. It also supports the desirability of individualized instruction.

This concept of the need for challenge and the avoidance of threat is an extension of Piaget's concept of optimal discrepancy between the child's cognitive structure and a new situation, which leads to interest, motivation, and learning (52), and of Hunt's "problem of the match" (24, pp. 267ff).

Disturbances in learning (of a psychological nature) are the result of threat to the self or self-concept. The person under threat restricts his perception, becomes defensive, withdraws, and narrows and restricts his range of activity or exploration. He doesn't "see" all aspects of the problem or situation, such as alternative solutions to the problem, he ceases exploration, and engages in repetitive or stereotyped ineffective behavior. In extreme cases he "freezes" and is unable to function at all. Every teacher has seen such behavior in students who are called upon in class, or in examinations. Learning does not occur when the individual feels threatened.

Humanistic Education

Humanistic education is based upon the principles and concepts of humanistic psychology. There are two major aspects of humanistic education. They are (a) the general psychological conditions for learning; (b) affective education. Space does not permit extended discussions of either. More has been written about the latter. A more extended discussion of both will be found in an earlier publication of the writer (45).

The Goal of Humanistic Education

Education has traditionally focused mainly upon the cognitive or intellectual development of the student. Recently there has been emphasis on preparing students for work or employment (career education). Although there has been much talk and some effort to educate students for citizenship and in mental health, little if anything has been accomplished. The Educational Policies Commission in 1938 (15) listed four objectives for education: education for self-realization, education for good human relationships, education for civic responsibility, and education for economic efficiency. Twenty years earlier the Report of the Commission on the Reorganization of Secondary Education (12) proposed similar objectives. Conant in 1948 (13) listed three objectives for education: education for citizenship, education for the good life, and education for a career or vocation. But little was or has been done since to implement these objectives. Humanistic education is now calling attention to such objectives.

It is becoming increasingly obvious that the problems which we face require more than intelligence and technical know-how for their solution. They are basically problems of living together, of human relationships, of cooperating in making the planet earth a place where people can live in peace. We need people who can understand others, who can accept and respect others as well as themselves, who are honest and responsible. If the schools are society's means of preparing people to live in society and the world, they must be concerned with these objectives. Silberman, in his critique of American education, wrote: "Our most pressing educational problem . . . is not how to increase the efficiency of the schools; it is how to create and maintain a humane society" (59, pp. 196, 203).

Education must become concerned with the development of individuals not as disembodied intellects, nor even as citizens of a single nation, but as persons, as members of a world community, as members of the human race. "Where the actions of one can drastically affect the lives of others far distant, it will be crucially important that each person master the skill of feeling what others feel. This skill, more than new laws or new politics, will soon become crucial to the survival of the race" (32, p. 127).

These are the goals which those interested in humanistic education are proposing for the schools. They are aspects of what Rogers calls the fully functioning person (55), a person who is open to and aware of his feelings, who is able to relate to others, and who is developing and utilizing his potentials. Other terms referring to the same concept are self-realization, self-enhancement, and self-actualization. The last, self-actualization, is becoming generally accepted. Combs (11, pp. 23-24) states that it is the primary goal of humanistic education. Since few if any persons can be said to be fully self-actualized or expected to reach this state, the goal is actually a process, the development of self-actualizing persons.

In adopting this goal, education is not at odds with other institutions in our society. The production of self-actualizing persons is—or should be—the goal of all our social institutions: the family, the church, the economic system, and the social and political systems. Such a goal is not inconsistent with, but includes, those things with which the school has been traditionally concerned. The self-actualizing person must be able to read and write, and must be well informed if he is to utilize his potentials, but cognitive development is only one aspect of the total development of the individual. To be sure, cognition and affect interact and neither can be neglected.

The point is that education has neglected affective development; it must be attended to without neglecting cognitive development.

This goal is not something that is external to the individual, that is imposed upon him. It is not inconsistent with the individual's nature and needs. Indeed, this goal is inherent in the human organism. It is the objective of the single basic drive of the organism, the preservation and enhancement of the self.

Psychological Conditions for Learning and Self-Actualization

Recent research in counseling or psychotherapy has confirmed the existence of several conditions, or aspects of a personal relationship, which have been included, implicitly if not explicitly, in every major theory or approach to counseling or psychotherapy. The presence of these conditions appears to be necessary for voluntary behavior changes of a positive or learning nature. The nature and kind of changes which occur are broad, including quite specific outcomes similar to the cognitive and academic objectives of education as well as the personal characteristics of self-actualizing persons, which include the conditions themselves.

Three basic conditions are empathic understanding, respect, and genuineness. Brief definitions of these conditions follow.

Empathic Understanding. There are two kinds of understanding. The first is knowing about something. It is objective understanding from an external frame of reference. The object of such knowledge or understanding is just that—an object. This is the common, as well as the scientific meaning of understanding.

There is another kind of understanding. It is the knowing of another being which is achieved from putting oneself in the place of another, so that one sees the world, and him, as closely as possible as he does. It is understanding from the internal frame of reference. In the example above of the automobile driver at the four-way intersection, it is the understanding of the driver's behavior made possible by putting oneself in his place. This is a highly personal understanding. Atticus Finch, the lawyer in the novel *To Kill a Mockingbird,* in trying to help his children understand the behavior of others toward him, says, "You never really understand a person until you consider things from his point of view—until you climb into his skin and walk around in it" (31, p. 24).

Respect. The second condition is a deep respect for another, an acceptance of him as a person of worth, without judgment or condemnation. It is unconditional, not dependent on his behaving as we would like him to or agreeing with us. It is a caring and valuing of him as a person, a human being, with a deep concern for him.

Facilitative Genuineness. Being genuine is being real, honest, open, sincere, as contrasted with being deceptive, maintaining a facade or playing a role. There is no incongruence between what one is thinking and feeling and what one says. Authenticity and transparency refer to the same thing.

Genuineness is not to be confused with so-called "brutal honesty or frankness." It does not require that one express all of one's negative feelings, momentary irritations and hostilities, as some encounter leaders advocate. These feelings are often more related to one's own hang-ups or condition than to the behavior of the other person, and are not facilitative in relationships with others. Facilitative genuineness does not require that the person express all his feelings; it only requires that whatever he does express is real and genuine and not incongruent with what he is thinking and feeling.

A major characteristic of these conditions is that they are non-threatening. They provide the atmosphere in which real learning can take place, with a minimum of anxiety, and without the restrictions and inhibitions which accompany threat. The basic indictment of our schools by those critics who are concerned about more than academic achievement is that these conditions do not exist in many of our schools. Children are not respected, they are not liked by teachers and administrators, they are not really understood, they are not treated as human beings. In an atmosphere characterized by the lack of these conditions children not only do not grow and develop as persons, they do not achieve academically.

The essence of teaching is the relationship between the teacher and the student. Rogers writes:

I see the *facilitation of learning* as the *aim* of education. . . . We know . . . that the facilitation of such learning rests not upon the teaching skills of the leader, not upon his curricular planning, not upon his use of audiovisual aids, not upon the programmed learning he utilizes, not upon his lectures and presentations, not upon an abundance of books, though each of these might at one time or another be utilized as an important resource. No, the facilitation of significant learning rests upon certain attitudinal qualities which exist in the personal relationship between the facilitator and the learner (56, pp. 105-106).

These conditions for learning are not techniques—they are attitudes. One would hope that those people who select teaching as a profession would have a high respect for children, a concern and a caring for them and for their development. One would hope that they were open and honest in their classroom behavior, rather than playing the role of a teacher. One would hope that they really understood children—how they think and feel and how they perceive things.

This is not always the case, however. That it is not the case raises questions about the selection and education of teachers. It suggests that selection should pay attention to the personal characteristics of those who would become teachers. And the education of teachers should pay attention to the attitudes of teacher education students and provide the conditions and opportunities for the development of those attitudes which facilitate learning. These conditions are the very conditions which we want teachers to manifest. We should teach teachers as we want them to teach. Teacher education should include an affective aspect also, including helping teachers learn to implement the conditions and attitudes in the classroom (see 45, Chapter 8).

Learning takes place in the student. It is an active process, not simply a passive absorption of information and knowledge, as many educators, including Montessori, Dewey, and Piaget, have recognized. There are thus some characteristics of, or conditions in, students which are necessary to facilitate learning.

Motivation

One of the ubiquitous problems in education is that of motivation—how to motivate children to learn, or to want to learn. Teachers are expected to motivate children in some way, though it is not clear how they are to do so. The behaviorists offer an answer in their use of extrinsic reinforcers—candy, tokens, transistor radios, etc. But they recognize that these are not sufficient in the long run, and that intrinsic reinforcers—such as satisfaction in learning—should replace extrinsic reinforcers.

The behaviorists remind us of a basic fact—learning is, or should be, pleasant, satisfying, rewarding. It is so in the infant and young child. Infants and young children are constantly active, engaged in developing physical capacities through exercise, exploring the environment. They learn to sit up, crawl, walk, and talk, even without direct instruction or training. There is no problem of motivation. As Skinner says, "No one asks how to motivate a baby.

A baby naturally explores everything it can get at, unless restraining forces have been at work, and this tendency doesn't die out. . . ." (60, p. 101). *The child is a natural learner,* he is motivated to learn. The process of striving for self-actualization, to use and develop one's potentials, is the process of learning. Learning is the normal state of the healthy organism. We should not have to motivate children to learn.

Young children learn most of what they do learn by themselves, without instruction. What we call play is the principal means of learning before school age. Moreover, the most significant learning of many older children occurs in play outside of the school. We thus do not need to teach in the sense of imposing something on the child or putting something into him. In an appropriate environment children learn by themselves.

Why is it, then, that there is such a problem regarding learning in school, and so much concern with motivation to learn? In the first few years of school the curiosity, interest, enthusiasm, and persistence in learning of many children are destroyed. They become passive, silent, bored, resistant. Leonard (32, pp. 110-11) reports his observation of children in kindergarten and those in fourth-grade classes (nine year olds), comparing the spontaneity, naturalness, and responsiveness of the kindergarten children with the controlled, quiet, inhibited behavior of the fourth graders. Something happens to kill the natural learning of children. This something must be related to what goes on in the classroom. The school environment, rather than facilitating learning, often retards or destroys it. Children are exposed to conditions which are threatening, even fearful; these conditions inhibit and eventually destroy the desire to learn.

Learning Requires Activity on the Part of the Learner

Real learning is an active process, a process in which the learner engages in exploration, on a concrete or abstract level, of the subject matter or material to be learned, until it becomes personally meaningful to the learner. This is something which occurs in natural learning, when the child is free to learn, and where appropriate materials are available to manipulate and explore. The concept of active learning has been recognized by almost all the major figures in education from Socrates through Dewey to Piaget. Piaget emphasizes the need for education to "give broad scope to the spontaneous research of the child or adolescent and require that every new truth to be learned be rediscovered or at least reconstructed by the student and not simply imparted to him." Information or knowledge acquired passively is not retained. "A student who achieves a certain knowledge through free investigation and spontaneous effort will later be able to retain it" (51, pp. 15-16, 20, 93).

The psychological conditions for learning in both the teacher and the learner recognize the importance of the nature of the learner as a human being. Learning is not a purely cognitive process—cognitive learning involves noncognitive elements, since it is the total person who is engaged in the learning process. Learning is a highly personal process, and as such is influenced by the personal characteristics of the teacher and the learner. Teaching involves a relationship between the teacher and the learner, and the characteristics of the relationship which facilitate learning constitute the core of humanistic education.

Affective Education

If education is concerned with the total development of the individual, then it must go beyond the facilitation of cognitive development. Education must become involved in the child's personal development—his feelings, emotions, values, and interpersonal relationships. This aspect of humanistic education is becoming known as affective education, or psychological education.

There are three major aspects to affective education: (1) modeling; (2) didactic instruction, (a) indirect and (b) direct; and (3) experiential.

Modeling

The humanistic teacher is a model or a personal example to students. Students learn from this example. The humanistic teacher, by being empathic, respecting, and genuine thus not only facilitates cognitive learning, but the learning of empathic understanding, respect, and genuineness.

Modeling is a most effective method for teaching complex behaviors, particularly social behaviors. It is a widespread and powerful method of teaching. Children learn what the teacher does rather than what the teacher says if there is a conflict, even though they may be told: "Do as I say, not as I do." If the teacher is not the kind of person he is trying to teach students to be, no matter what he does he cannot teach this. But he will teach whatever he is, whether he is aware of it or not.

This is the problem of many of the attempts to teach attitudes and values. The principles of democracy are taught in a classroom and a school which are anything but democratic.

Instruction in Affective Education and Human Relations

Indirect. The standard curriculum can be used to teach humanization (as Wilhelms calls it [67]) and human relations. It requires that materials be selected and used toward this end, as well as for the specific subject matter content. An attempt to introduce affect into education through the curriculum is described by Jones (26).

The use of existing subject matter in affective education is much easier in some areas, such as the social sciences, than in others such as mathematics. In the standard curriculum the education of the emotions and the learning of interpersonal relations are likely to be viewed as by-products, in which case they may be neglected or "tacked on." But if these outcomes are not viewed as simply by-products, this can be a most effective approach (as illustrated by Jones [26]), since the history of the development of humankind and the customs and practices in different cultures provide inherently relevant content for understanding the problems humans have faced in living together.

Direct. Although there have been attempts to teach mental health or mental hygiene in the schools for many years, they have not been successful. The materials have been academic and abstract, with little personal relevance, unrelated to the actual experiences, or feelings and attitudes of students. Teaching methods have been structured, and instructors have not been adequately prepared in what they are teaching.

Recent attempts at direct affective education have departed from the standard content and materials of mental hygiene, and from the standard methods of instruction. The number and variety of materials and methods are too great to attempt to summarize. Four of the most extensive proposals are those of Castillo (9), Brown (7), Mann (35), and Weinstein and Fantini (65).

There are a number of difficulties with most of these direct approaches to humanistic education. One is that they are often forced into a standard curriculum format. They may become subject-matter oriented rather than person oriented, and they may lead to the teacher following the material rigidly as a lesson plan. Another difficulty, which often results from the structuring of the experiences in a curriculum, is that they become techniques. Although they may be used successfully by some teachers, many other teachers cannot use them effectively because they do not fit the teacher's personality or methods. Techniques must actually cease to be mere techniques, and become a part of the genuine teacher, before they can be effective in the everyday, continuing classroom. Techniques can be built into a role, making the teacher a showperson, performer, or director, unable to function without them. Techniques become a crutch. Another difficulty with structuring the approach into games, exercises, simulations, etc., is that the teaching situation is not natural, spontaneous, or real, but tends to become contrived. This preoccupation with structured, planned, contrived experiences leads to the development of materials, props, and equipment, including pictures, posters, films, filmstrips, cassettes, all in expensive kits, with teachers' manuals and students' guides.

It appears that many teachers, and/or their supervisors and those concerned with curriculum, feel that teachers are afraid to face a class of children without an armamentarium of techniques and materials and are uncomfortable in an unstructured situation, or it may be that such an unstructured approach is considered undesirable and is not education. As educators (teachers) take refuge in lesson plans, they can also take refuge in techniques.

The overemphasis upon techniques and structured, teacher-controlled procedures, complete with predetermined specific objectives, is inconsistent with the goals of affective education, which include spontaneity, student-initiated activity, open and free discussion in a natural setting, and self-directed exploration and learning.

This overemphasis upon techniques and materials leads to the necessity of warning teachers (and student teachers) that the adoption of any or all of the techniques, games, and exercises in the various sources will not necessarily make a humanistic teacher or facilitate affective learning.

A basic issue in the area of affective education or education in interpersonal relationships is the extent to which emphasis is placed upon skills rather than upon attitudes. It appears that in programs of affective education the focus is upon the former. It can be argued that if behavior is changed, then attitudes will change, and there is some truth in this. But this is not always the case, and human relations skills can be practiced as techniques without the basic attitudes of respect, acceptance, and a desire to understand the other person. And it is also true that changes in attitudes lead to changes in behavior; such changes are more genuine and real, and thus the behavior is more effective in terms of developing good relationships with others, and probably more persistent.

Perhaps the greatest difficulty or deficiency in current approaches to affective education is that they are not based upon an adequate understanding of the nature of affective development, or on any systematic theory of human behavior and interpersonal relations. It is only recently that such a foundation has been available for cognitive education, with Piaget's studies and theories being the most comprehensive. It would appear that before we can develop a curriculum of affect, of human development, or of psychological education, we must have more knowledge, understanding, and agreement upon the nature of emotional development. Piaget has manifested an interest in affective development and believes that the process of affective development follows stages such as those he has found for cognitive development. His work in the area of values has been built upon by Kohlberg (27, 28).

The Experiential Approach

The value of learning by experience has long been recognized. It would appear that experiential learning would be particularly relevant in the affective and human relations area. We learn to live with others by living with others. Interpersonal relationships are not structured in advance—they are usually spontaneous encounters.

The need for structure, control, planned specific outcomes and content materials is probably a need of teachers more than a need of students, particularly younger students. Children appear to be able to relate to each other in a natural and spontaneous, honest, trusting, understanding way unless they have been hurt and mistreated by others. *Teachers don't need techniques to relate to children* nor do children need techniques to relate to each other. In fact, techniques can interfere with establishing a real relationship with children.

Affective education should include group experiences of a natural, spontaneous nature, such as the basic encounter groups of Carl Rogers (57, 45, 46). The mushrooming of the group movement has led to the entrance into the field of many who are inadequately trained in psychology, and to the proliferation of methods and techniques some of which are at least potentially harmful. As a result, there has been a reaction against encounter groups in schools. This is unfortunate, because groups are natural ways for individuals to relate and to learn to relate to others. The schools should utilize this natural resource in affective education.

While the facilitation of encounter groups requires some training of a psychological nature, such training need not be extensive. The conduct of encounter groups consists of providing the same conditions as those described above for humanistic teaching— empathic understanding, respect, and genuineness or honesty. Teacher education students should, and could easily, be provided the necessary preparation in teacher education programs (45, Chapter 12).

William Glasser proposes the use of groups in schools to reduce failures in school (20). He recommends "classroom meetings," led by the teacher, beginning with the first grade. But these classroom group meetings, in addition to being planned and structured to deal with specific topics or problems, are too large for experiential human relations groups.

Actual experience in groups seems so clearly superior to any other method of learning in human relations that it is amazing that it has not been widely used in human relations education. There is no substitute for learning to relate to others through interacting with other people. This is, of course, the way everyone actually learns, but in a haphazard, inadequate way. Sitting in a classroom while actually being psychologically alone, not really knowing the other students or relating to them in any close, meaningful way, and listening to a teacher talk about "mental hygiene" or "human relations" is not an adequate way to learn, nor is being in a classroom and going through a series of exercises and games; while involving some interpersonal reactions, they are not "for real" or natural.

In the small (encounter) group of six to ten students, without assigned subject matter or an agenda other than to talk about themselves or whatever is of concern to them, students can learn through experience:

    To listen to others
    To accept and respect others
    To understand others
    To identify and become aware of one's feelings
    To express one's feelings
    To become aware of the feelings of others
    To experience being accepted and understood by others
    To recognize basic commonalities in human experience
    To explore oneself

To develop greater awareness of oneself

To be oneself

To change oneself in the direction of being more the self one wants to be

To help others accept themselves

To help others understand themselves and each other.

In such groups learning occurs without the input of external content, in contrast to other approaches to affective education. Groups provide the materials or content for learning through their interactions with each other, without content or techniques which put distance between the learner and what is learned. It is not necessary, nor desirable, for the facilitator, or teacher, to focus cognitively upon, or analyze, what is going on in the group. To do so leads to self-consciousness and artificiality, reducing or eliminating the naturalness and spontaneity of the interaction. The teacher or facilitator promotes learning essentially by modeling the qualities of empathic understanding, respect, and genuineness.

Conclusion

Our educational system is obsolete. It is obsolete not only in curriculum, but in methods. Methods of instruction ignore much of what we know about the conditions of learning. Our curriculum focuses upon cognitive development and ignores affective development. In the world in which we live, and will be living, we need persons who are not only mature intellectually but affectively. Even though our science allows us to reach the moon, it will help us little if we can't live together on earth.

Humanistic education addresses these problems of education. It provides an understanding of the psychological conditions of learning, the characteristics in a teacher which facilitate learning. It also provides a systematic foundation upon which affective education can be built. Although much is being written about affective education, most of it is by those who have little understanding of psychology or the nature of man. While it is true that we know less about the nature of affective development than about cognitive development, we know enough to begin a program of affective education which goes beyond the methods and techniques now being suggested.

Opposition to affective education appears to come from those who see it as displacing or detracting from cognitive education. But affective education is an addition to our present system. Moreover, it is a part of the larger concept of humanistic education. And humanistic methods of education do not ignore or de-emphasize cognitive learning; they provide the conditions for better, more effective cognitive education.

We now have a basic understanding of the nature of man. To be sure, many details remain to be filled in, but it is not necessary to wait for these details to begin to implement what we know. The principles of good human relationships are now known; in fact, they have been known for centuries, and are epitomized in religious and philosophical statements such as the Golden Rule. The psychological conditions for personal development—both cognitive and affective—are the conditions for the survival of society and the human race. Society could not exist if these conditions did not exist to a minimal degree. These are the conditions, or values, which are necessary if human beings are to live together and survive. If the outlook appears rather gloomy at present, it becomes exceedingly important that these conditions be taught and practiced by an increasing number of individuals. Perhaps, hopefully, the evolutionary development of the human race has led to the survival of those who have the potential for developing these conditions. But we cannot expect that they will develop without nurturance. It is the function of education to provide this nurturance.

References

1. A. Alland, Jr. *The Human Imperative.* New York: Columbia University Press, 1972.

2. G. W. Allport. "Psychological Models for Guidance." *Harvard Educational Review* 32:373-81; Fall 1962.

3. A. Angyal. *Foundations for a Science of Personality.* New York: Commonwealth Fund, 1941.

4. H. L. Ansbacher and Rowena R. Ansbacher, editors. *The Individual Psychology of Alfred Adler.* New York: Basic Books, 1956.

5. A. Bandura. "Behavior Theory and the Models of Man." *American Psychologist* 29:859-69; December 1974.

6. E. Bibring. "The Development and Problems of the Theory of Instincts." In: C. L. Stacy and M. F. Martino, editors. *Understanding Human Motivation.* Cleveland: Howard Allen, 1958.

7. G. I. Brown. *Human Teaching for Human Learning: An Introduction to Confluent Education.* New York: Viking Press, 1971.

8. Charlotte Buhler. *Values in Psychotherapy.* New York: The Free Press, 1961.

9. Gloria A. Castillo. *Left-handed Teaching: Lessons in Affective Education.* New York: Praeger Publishers, 1974.

10. A. W. Combs and D. Snygg. *Individual Behavior: A Perceptual Approach to Behavior.* Revised edition. New York: Harper & Row, 1959.

11. A. W. Combs. *Educational Accountability: Beyond Behavioral Objectives.* Washington, D.C.: Association for Supervision and Curriculum Development, 1972.

12. Commission on the Reorganization of Secondary Education. *Cardinal Principles of Secondary Education.* U.S. Bureau of Education Bulletin 35. Washington, D.C.: U.S. Government Printing Office, 1918.

13. J. B. Conant. *Education in a Divided World.* Cambridge: Harvard University Press, 1948.

14. J. Dollard, L. W. Doob, N. E. Miller, O. H. Mowrer, and R. R. Sears. *Frustration and Aggression.* New Haven: Yale University Press, 1939.

15. Educational Policies Commission. *The Purpose of Education in American Democracy.* Washington, D.C.: National Education Association, 1938.

16. V. Frankl. *Man's Search for Meaning.* Revised edition. New York: Washington Square Press, 1963.

17. S. Freud. *Civilization and Its Discontents.* New York: Harrison Smith, n.d. Quoted in: D. E. Walker. "Carl Rogers and the Nature of Man." *Journal of Counseling Psychology* 3:89-92; Summer 1956.

18. S. Freud. *The Future of an Illusion.* London: Hogarth Press, 1949. pp. 10-11. Quoted in: D. E. Walker. "Carl Rogers and the Nature of Man." *Journal of Counseling Psychology* 3:89-92; Summer 1956.

19. J. J. Gibson. "Theories of Perception." In: W. Dennis, editor. *Current Trends in Psychological Theory.* Pittsburgh: University of Pittsburgh Press, 1951.

20. W. Glasser. *Schools Without Failure.* New York: Harper & Row, 1969.

21. K. Goldstein. *The Organism.* New York: World Book, 1939.

22. W. Golding. *Lord of the Flies.* New York: Coward McCann, 1955.

23. *Humanistic Manifestos I and II.* Buffalo: Prometheus Books, 1973.

24. J. McV. Hunt. *Intelligence and Experience.* New York: The Ronald Press Company, 1961.

25. S. Isaacs. *Social Development in Young Children.* London: Routledge, 1933.

26. R. M. Jones. *Fantasy and Feeling in Education.* New York: New York University Press, 1968. (Also Harper & Row Torchbooks.)

27. L. Kohlberg. "Moral and Religious Education in the Public Schools: A Developmental View." In: T. Sizer, editor. *Religion and Public Education.* Boston: Houghton Mifflin Company, 1967.

28. L. Kohlberg. *Development of Moral Thought and Action.* New York: Holt, Rinehart & Winston, 1974.

29. A. E. Kuenzli, editor. *The Phenomenological Problem.* New York: Harper & Row, 1954.

30. P. Lecky. *Self-Consistency: A Theory of Personality.* New York: Island Press, 1945.

31. Harper Lee. *To Kill a Mockingbird.* Philadelphia: J. B. Lippincott Company, 1960. Copyright © 1960 by Harper Lee. Reprinted by permission.

32. G. B. Leonard. *Education and Ecstasy.* New York: Delacorte Press, 1968. Copyright © 1968 by Delacorte Press.

33. S. Maddi. "Ethics and Psychotherapy: Remarks Stimulated by White's Paper." *Counseling Psychologist* 4(2): 26-29; 1973(a).

34. S. Maddi. "Creativity Is Strenuous." *The University of Chicago Magazine,* September-October 1973(b), pp. 18-23. Copyright © 1973 by The University of Chicago. Reprinted by permission of *The University of Chicago Magazine.*

35. J. Mann. *Learning To Be: The Education of Human Potential.* Riverside, New Jersey: The Free Press, 1972.

36. A. Maslow. "Our Maligned Human Nature." *Journal of Psychology* 28:273-78; October 1949.

37. A. H. Maslow. "Deficiency Motivation and Growth Motivation." In: M. R. Jones, editor. *Nebraska Symposium on Motivation, 1955.* Lincoln: University of Nebraska Press, 1955. pp. 1-30.

38. A. H. Maslow. *Motivation and Personality.* Second edition. New York: Harper & Row, 1970.

39. F. W. Matson. *Without/Within: Behaviorism and Humanism.* Monterey, California: Brooks/Cole, 1973.

40. J. Michael and L. Meyerson. "A Behavioral Approach to Counseling and Guidance." *Harvard Educational Review* 32:382-402; Fall 1962.

41. A. Montagu. *On Being Human.* New York: Henry Schuman, 1950.

42. A. Montagu. *The Humanization of Man.* Cleveland, Ohio: World Publishing Co., 1962. Reprinted by permission of the author and publisher.

43. A. S. Neill. *Summerhill.* New York: Hart Publishing Co., 1960.

44. C. H. Patterson. "Phenomenological Psychology." *Personnel and Guidance Journal* 43:997-1005; June 1965.

45. C. H. Patterson. *Humanistic Education.* Englewood Cliffs, New Jersey: Prentice-Hall Publishers, Inc., 1973.

46. C. H. Patterson. "The Group Relationship in the Elementary School." In: M. M. Ohlsen, editor. *Counseling Children in Groups.* New York: Holt, Rinehart and Winston, 1973.

47. C. H. Patterson. "Humanistic Concerns and Behavior Modification: Toward a Basis for an Ethics of Behavior Control." Paper presented at Conference on Moral and Ethical Implications of Behavior Modification, School of Education, University of Wisconsin–Madison, March 20-21, 1975.

48. C. H. Patterson. *Foundations for a Theory of Instruction and Educational Psychology.* New York: Harper & Row, Publishers. In press.

49. F. S. Perls. *Ego, Hunger, and Aggression.* New York: Random House, Inc., 1969.

50. W. W. Purkey. *Self-Concept and School Achievement.* Englewood Cliffs, New Jersey: Prentice-Hall Publishers, Inc., 1970. Copyright © 1970. Reprinted by permission.

51. J. Piaget. *To Understand Is To Invent.* New York: The Viking Press, Inc., 1973.

52. J. Piaget and Barbel Inhelder. *The Psychology of the Child.* New York: Basic Books, 1969.

53. C. R. Rogers. *Client-centered Therapy.* Boston: Houghton Mifflin Company, 1951.

54. C. R. Rogers. "A Theory of Therapy, Personality, and Interpersonal Relationships, as Developed in the Client-centered Framework." In: S. Koch, editor. *Psychology: A Study of a Science.* Volume 3. *Formulations of the Person and the Social Context.* New York: McGraw-Hill Book Co., 1959. pp. 184-256.

55. C. R. Rogers. *On Becoming a Person.* Boston: Houghton Mifflin Company, 1961.

56. C. R. Rogers. *Freedom To Learn.* Columbus, Ohio: Charles E. Merrill Publishing Co., 1969.

57. C. R. Rogers. *Carl Rogers on Encounter Groups.* New York: Harper & Row, 1970.

58. M. Scriven. "The Philosophy of Behavioral Modification." In: C. E. Thoresen, editor. *Behavior Modification in Education.* Chicago: National Society for the Study of Education, 1973. pp. 422-44.

59. C. E. Silberman. *Crisis in the Classroom.* New York: Random House, Inc., 1970.

60. B. F. Skinner. *Walden Two.* New York: Macmillan Publishing Co., 1948.

61. B. F. Skinner. *Beyond Freedom and Dignity.* New York: Alfred A. Knopf, Inc., 1971.

62. M. B. Smith. "Comment on White's Paper." *Counseling Psychologist* 4(2): 48-50; 1973.

63. D. R. Thomas, W. C. Becker, and V. M. Armstrong. "Production and Elimination of Disruptive Classroom Behavior by Systematically Varying the Teacher's Behavior." *Journal of Applied Behavioral Analysis* 1:35-45; 1968.

64. T. W. Wann, editor. *Behaviorism and Phenomenology: Contrasting Bases for Modern Psychology.* Chicago: University of Chicago Press, 1964.

65. G. Weinstein and M. D. Fantini, editors. *Toward Humanistic Education: A Curriculum of Affect.* New York: Praeger Publishers, 1970.

66. R. W. White. "The Concept of Healthy Personality: What Do We Really Mean?" *Counseling Psychologist* 4(2): 3-12, 67-69; 1973.

67. F. T. Wilhelms. "Humanization via the Curriculum." In: R. R. Leeper, editor. *Humanizing Education: The Person in the Process.* Washington, D.C.: Association for Supervision and Curriculum Development, 1967.

68. E. G. Williamson. "A Concept of Counseling." *Occupations* 29:182-89; November 1950.

69. E. G. Williamson. "Value Orientation in Counseling." *Personnel and Guidance Journal* 37: 520-28; April 1958.

70. E. G. Williamson. "The Societal Responsibilities of Counselors." *Illinois Personnel and Guidance Association Newsletter,* Winter 1963, pp. 5-13.

71. E. G. Williamson. *Vocational Counseling.* New York: McGraw-Hill Book Company, 1965. Copyright © 1965 by McGraw-Hill Book Company. Reprinted by permission.

72. R. A. Winett and R. C. Winkler. "Current Behavior Modification in the Classroom: Be Still, Be Quiet, Be Docile." *Journal of Applied Behavioral Analysis.* 5(4): 499-504; 1972.

8

The Person in Community: The Need To Belong

Elizabeth Léonie Simpson

Unity is indeed the vital need of Man. He is surrounded by magnetic pulls and stresses, but to embrace life in its diversity is impossible. The Don Juans die without a wife; the eternal travellers without a bed; the Jacks of all trades without talent; the little girls who wanted to be everything . . . soiled, unbalanced, empty-handed. It is through one single person or one group of people that one has to embrace all people; through one single craft all the possibilities of action; through our one soul all the heroes, all the murderers, all the saints, all the cowards that we are capable of being.

—Jean Anouilh [1] (Emphasis added)

༄

*O*n December 12, 1967, Louis Fieser, the developer of napalm, was quoted by the New York *Times*. Asked his views about how the material might be used, Fieser answered, "It's not my business to deal with political or moral issues." Thus neatly separating his personal actions from responsibility for their consequences, he

[1] J. Anouilh. "Letter to a Young Girl." *The Daily Telegraph Magazine* 363: 9-14; October 8, 1971.

denied the significance of his involvement. Try as he did, to many readers of the newspaper Fieser could not justify his stand by avoiding the question. He had been raised as a member of a group in which individuals are responsible for the political and moral choices which they make, even when the effects of their actions are much less widely effective than his were. Fieser's attempt to avoid responsibility was designed to keep him free from the consequences of his deeds. If it was not his business, then he could not be blamed.

Others may agree with Louis Fieser. The settlement of political and moral issues is often not simple. Responsibility can be difficult, even painful, and avoided. Franz Stangl, Kommandant of the Treblinka concentration camp during World War II, like many members of armed services, believed that by obeying orders he removed himself from personal responsibility. He wrote, "What I did without or against my free will, for that I need not answer." Like Lieutenant Calley at My Lai, he rejected his independence and saw himself as subject to, and dependent upon, others. He did as he was told to do and refused blame for not acting as he knew was right.

Calley, shooting unarmed, helpless, hungry women and crying children, believed his antihuman actions were protected in the same way. Others agreed with him. When a national survey was taken, 51 percent of the respondents said they would have acted as Calley did; 67 percent thought that most people would do so, too. But, who were the people who agreed with Calley's behavior? Largely, Calley's supporters came from among those with relatively low levels of education, income, and social status—people who saw Calley, like themselves, as having to do what other people told him to do without free choice and, therefore, without responsibility or guilt.[2]

During World War II, there was a widely heard joke about the impossibility of finding just one Nazi in a full room. The implication was clear that collective morality may be destructive of individual morality. Personal integrity may be lost when individuals are exculpated through foisting the blame onto others within the group who are "in charge" and therefore responsible. If I do what everyone else does (or what many others do), am I to blame? Don't I do what I am told to do? Am I not (especially in the Army) supposed to obey orders? Calley, like the other Americans who agreed with his

---

[2] H. C. Kelman and L. H. Lawrence. "Assignment of Responsibility in the Case of Lt. Calley: Preliminary Report of a National Survey." *Journal of Social Issues* 28 (1): 177-212; 1972.

Following a middle-aged Ph.D. at the University of California, Berkeley, in 1970, **Elizabeth Léonie Simpson** became Associate Director of the Center for International Education at the University of Southern California. Since that time, she has taught at USC and (as Visiting Associate Professor) at the University of California at Irvine in Social Ecology. Before the development of her interest in psychology and education, she had published fiction and poetry. More recent interests center on political and moral development. Some of the more recent useful work is to be found in Democracy's Stepchildren: A Study of Need and Belief (San Francisco: Jossey-Bass, 1971), a criticism of Kohlberg's work in "Moral Development Research: A Study of Scientific Cultural Bias" (Human Development 17(2): 81-106; 1974), and "A Holistic View of Moral Development"—a chapter in Lickona's Moral Development and Behavior (New York: Holt, Rinehart and Winston, 1976). She has co-authored Harcourt Brace Jovanovich's innovative series The Social Sciences: Concepts and Values. National consultancies include the Ford Foundation, National Institute of Education, and the United States Office of Education. Pi Lambda Theta awarded her its 1970 National Distinguished Research Award.

Lifelong interests include three children and figure ice-skating.

actions, had learned how to think and to behave as a member of groups within his culture. Like Fieser, he had learned to separate his personal actions from the responsibility for consequences. He was a "good soldier"—a killer who obeyed orders. He was responding on the basis of his earlier learning experiences, as well as to the external stimuli of the particular situation.[3] In Calley's culture,

[3] D. Goslin, editor. "Introduction." Handbook of Socialization Theory and Research. Chicago: Rand McNally & Company, 1969. p. 20.

responsibility for evil is greatly mitigated if it is performed as an act of obedience.[4]

The Search for Meaning Beyond Self

I alone, I with others, I with all—out of this enlargement of self-knowledge comes the search for meaning beyond the self and beyond the present. I identify with others (and differentiate myself from them). I interact with others according to group-sanctioned rules, making choices and defining my encounters as the members of my groups would do so. My identity, its differentiation, and the meaning of my images grow out of these groups, not only from my shared humanity. Much of what I have learned as a group member—my socialization—has been neither formal nor intentional. Like you, like each of us, I have learned to do and to be what I have observed being and done. Because I am a twentieth-century American, rather than a nineteenth-century Eskimo, I have perceptions and concepts based upon the habits and rewards of my present culture which I have learned. I may, for example, use eight different shades of red as my lipsticks, but not distinguish among eight different kinds of snow, a habit which was learned because rewarded within the Eskimo's culture.

I am not the inevitable and predictable product of organismic—biological and psychological—evolution alone. Like all humans, in the midst of differing physical worlds, I have been developed by other humans, as well as myself. Like other humans, I am a part of an everchanging but patterned matrix of social relationships through which all children become adults, persons unique but not alone, shaped and developed by shared people, shared places, and shared times.

Where more than one person share time and the opportunity for action, socialization is inevitable. Sometimes known as enculturation, it is "the process by which individuals acquire the knowledge, skills, and dispositions that enable them to participate as more or less effective members of groups and the society."[5] This learning of the knowledge, skills, and values of the culture, or smaller groups,

[4] Hannah Arendt points this out clearly in her discussion of the Nazi Eichmann's post-war trial in *Eichmann in Jerusalem*. New York: The Viking Press, 1963.

[5] O. G. Brim, Jr. "Socialization Through the Life Cycle." In: O. G. Brim and S. Wheeler. *Socialization after Childhood*. New York: John Wiley & Sons, Inc., 1966.

assures the continuance of social patterns. It communicates a body of expectations and ways to fulfill them which are shared by the members of a group. Learned by individuals and often unconsciously, these exist beyond the life span as a part of the common social milieu.

All human development is social-situational—that is, it is the result of continued interaction between personal maturation and socialization into group life. "The study of enculturation becomes the study of interaction between cultural beliefs transmitted to the child through teaching and social experience, on the one hand, and universal stages of cognitive development, on the other."[6] The characteristics of its members determine the nature of a group, just as the nature of the group—its past history and present practices— determines the manifestations of members and the definition of acceptable, or even possible, behavior for those members. From group to group, these social aims may differ widely. Some of the most vivid accounts of modern environmental sources of the development of common political values have come from descriptions of the collectivization of child rearing in Israel and the Soviet Union.[7]

For most Americans, it is families and schools under whose direct influence a large proportion of preadult life is spent.[8] Within these communities are subgroups based on age, sex, socioeconomic class, and the various kinds of adult and child work and play. But, as Maslow has convincingly reported, the need for group membership is not simply that of children. It is lifelong, for we are characterized by the human need to belong.[9] More, we are all shaped by the values held in common within these enduring groups. To a large extent, these become acceptable and desirable guides and control our behavior and our goals. We learn them as *norms* when we learn how to perform specific roles within our groups. Because we learn the same expectations of each other and acquire mutual values and

[6] R. LeVine. "Culture, Personality, and Socialization: An Evolutionary View." In: D. Goslin, editor. *Handbook of Socialization Theory and Research.* Chicago: Rand McNally & Company, 1969.

[7] See, for example, J. Azreal. "Soviet Union." In: J. Coleman, editor. *Education and Political Development.* Princeton: Princeton University Press, 1965. pp. 257-58; B. Bettelheim. *Children of the Dream.* London: Macmillan, 1969; and U. Bronfenbrenner. *Two Worlds of Childhood.* New York: Russell Sage, 1970.

[8] A. J. Schwartz. *The Schools and Socialization.* New York: Harper & Row, 1975.

[9] A. Maslow. *Motivation and Personality.* New York: Harper & Row, 1954.

behavior, membership within our group satisfies the need for recognition and belongingness.

This need to belong is the need to fulfill the human capacity for intimacy and interaction which have meaning and positive emotion embedded in them. It is based on the sense of unity, membership, and identification which derives from the expression of self against a nexus of common meanings. To belong to a human group is to be able to make mutual predictions with the added dimension of mutual, reciprocal satisfactions. The idiosyncratic person finds human completion as a part of some larger whole. As Angyal wrote,

Human behavior cannot be understood solely as a manifestation of the trend toward autonomy. Seen from another angle, human life reveals a basic pattern very different from self-assertiveness, from striving for freedom and mastery. A person behaves as if he were seeking a place for himself in a larger unit of which he strives to become a part. In the first orientation he is struggling for centrality in his world, trying to mold and organize objects and events, to bring them under his own control. In the second orientation he seems rather to strive to surrender himself and to become an organic part of something that he conceives as greater than himself. . . . The wish to be in harmony with the unit one regards as extending beyond his individual self is a powerful motivating source of behavior.[10]

In its most humane and useful sense, membership within a democratic group develops the participant as both creator and creature of the culture. Individual development and societal goals are integrated into likenesses and commonalities shared by the members of the group. But if the group is democratic, and wishes to continue to be so, its social ecology must satisfy the psychological needs of the individual participants. Recent research has shown that the kinds of values which humans hold—including the desire to be democratic—are closely related to their needs. Stanley Renshon, for instance, has demonstrated that factors such as a democratic family structure are important effects in the development of the child's sense of personal control. By far more important, however, is the degree to which each parent feels he or she has personal efficacy. When parents do not believe in their capacity to control their lives, the Hobbesian social environment in the home tends to produce Hobbesian, conforming children who are obedient to authorities and intolerant of nonconformity.[11]

[10] A. Angyal. *Neurosis and Treatment: A Holistic Theory.* E. Hanfmann and R. M. Jones, editors. New York: John Wiley & Sons, Inc., 1965.

[11] S. A. Renshon. *Psychological Needs and Political Behavior.* New York: The Free Press, 1974.

These findings support those of a recent study of three groups of adolescents which showed a clear relationship between the loss of belief in personal efficacy and control and the lack of feelings of security, belongingness, or social esteem and acceptance by others. Such psychological deprivation was found to be significantly related to the failure of democratic socialization—in this case, that is, to lack of belief in positive human nature, personal efficacy, open-mindedness, tolerance or acceptance of others, and the rights of others. In the case of every belief examined, the percentage of subjects who held it declined as the number of total needs which motivated the individual increased. For almost every subtype of need (including physiological, security, belongingness, self- and other-esteem), mean scores for each democratic value differed significantly between those whose needs had been gratified and those who were psychologically deprived. Clearly, the individual must be *capable* of holding democratic values; learning that they exist is not enough.

If continuing, formal, institutional socialization, however reinforced, will not alone induce democratic values, we must find another answer, an answer which may lie in an environment which is deliberately planned, as an integral part of a curriculum commitment, to gratify the basic needs of the child. If the antecedents of democratic values are indeed the satisfaction of these needs and a major objective of the school is democratic political socialization, the school must be prepared to contribute far more than it has in the past to the gratification of these needs (p. 134).[12]

A member who is unsure of his feelings about self and his right to membership will compare his own beliefs and attitudes with others in order to establish the validity of his feelings and his views.[13] It is the insecure who are most given to conformity; they need to see themselves as compatible with others in their social world and, more than compatible, as truly belonging to—that is, being a part of—a group. That is why Maslow described the need to belong as a lower, more basic human need than the needs for self- or social-esteem from others.

Nor may the sense of membership always be based on affection or on the belief that other members of the group are good or loving. In fact, while "community is a shelter, a base, and a psychic home . . . it may be one in which this quality is its sole positive attribute." [14]

[12] E. L. Simpson. *Democracy's Stepchildren: A Study of Need and Belief.* San Francisco: Jossey-Bass, 1971.

[13] L. Festinger. "A Theory of Social Comparison." *Human Relations* 14: 48-64; 1954.

[14] Simpson, *op. cit.*, p. 125.

As Erich Fromm pointed out in his essay on selfishness and self-love, hatred against oneself is inseparable from hatred against others.[15] The individual who distrusts himself is likely to distrust others. High self-regard is associated with belief in positive law—belief that the authority for judgments rests in the laws and norms which humans have developed collectively. Accepted memberships and highly gratifying interactions root the individual's sense of authority to the groups which satisfy his needs. ". . . because acceptance gratifies one's needs for self-esteem, it generates attraction [to the group]. However, this general statement [is] complicated by the desire to have others provide accurate evaluation. . . . Social identity is only partly determined by self-conception. Other influential factors include the characteristics and the behavior of others toward us, the environment at the moment, and our motivation." [16]

While sharing our humanity, we differ from members of other groups around the world and through time because the groups within which we interact, while fulfilling much the same human needs, differ in values and in action.[17] The universal process of learning to empathize with others takes place as the child matures from an *egocentric* view of the world to a *sociocentric* one. With a sociocentric view, the child can perceive accurately what those around him or her are feeling and doing and the child's knowledge and perceptions are shaped by his/her observations.[18]

The child matures and changes, but the need to belong, to share meaningful interaction, and to be accepted is not outgrown. It is a lifelong process and probably as old as humanity itself. Thousands of years ago, Homer wrote of "the tribeless, lawless, heartless one" who had no ties and belonged nowhere, wandering the world beyond fellowship, trapped in desperate regions beyond acceptance, community, and kin. Many have written of the alienated and outcast, lost, rejected, and estranged from people who were rightfully friends

[15] E. Fromm. "Selfishness and Self-Love." *Psychiatry* 2: 507-23; 1939. Reprinted in C. Gordon and K. J. Gergen, editors. *The Self in Social Interaction.* Volume 1. New York: John Wiley & Sons, Inc., 1968.

[16] K. J. Gergen. *The Concept of Self.* New York: Holt, Rinehart and Winston, 1971. p. 90.

[17] U. Bronfenbrenner. "Socialization and Social Class Through Time and Space." In: E. E. Maccoby, T. M. Newcomb, and E. L. Hartley. *Readings in Social Psychology.* New York: Holt, Rinehart and Winston, 1958. pp. 400-25.

[18] J. Piaget. *The Moral Judgment of the Child.* New York: The Free Press, 1948. (First published in English in 1932.)

and kin and places which were rightfully theirs.[19] Long before sociology was invented, Aristotle defined humanity as the sharing of life within a society. The function of patterned and orderly existence within human groups has been further described by the philosopher, John Locke, and the French sociologist, Emile Durkheim. More recently, the reciprocal influencing of socialized persons within a group has been referred to and studied as *symbolic interaction.* It is social interaction through the means of communication and often implies that the behavior of the two or more people who are interacting is changed. In the United States, Cooley, Dewey, and Mead have written about symbolic interaction from a social psychological point of view.[20]

It was Paul Tillich, using a historical-anthropological approach to analyzing the functions of education for interaction within a culture, who described them as three.[21] First, is *induction,* that is, socialization or enculturation which teaches the participant the acquisition of shared symbols, traditions, and appropriate responses to objects, events, and persons, as well as the group's view of social responsibility. Second, there are general and professional skills of a *technical* nature to be learned for the sake of subsistence. Lastly, there is the *humanistic* function which is the development of all positive human potentialities, "releasing creativity and discovery." In Tillich's view, induction and technical skills confer group identity on the person, while the humanistic function, involving discipline and criticism but not subjection, creates the self. The child is seen as a participant-observer while the adult (who may be a parent) is a major source of feedback. Because the humanistic function of the school may not be valued similarly in differing cultures, induction and technical learning are the processes common to all human groups.

[19] "Where is my *home?*" cried Nietzsche. "For it do I ask and seek, and have sought, but have not found it. O eternal everywhere, O eternal nowhere, O eternal in vain." Quoted in: W. Lippmann. *A Preface to Morals.* New York: Macmillan Publishing Co., 1929. p. 7. Colin Wilson's *The Outsider* and Albert Camus' *The Stranger* are also moving fictional accounts of the homeless, alienated, and outcast.

[20] See, for example: C. H. Cooley. *Human Nature and the Social Order.* Revised edition. New York: Charles Scribner, 1922; J. Dewey. *Human Nature and Conduct.* New York: Holt, Rinehart and Winston, 1905; G. H. Mead. *On Social Psychology.* A. Strauss, editor. Chicago: University of Chicago, 1964. (First published in 1956 as *The Social Psychology of George Herbert Mead.*)

[21] P. Tillich. *Theology and Culture.* New York: Oxford University Press, 1959.

The Effects of Not Belonging

Both symbolic interaction and induction are learned means of protecting the individual group member through communalization. But, seen as a source of mutual prediction and reciprocal satisfaction, belonging and its opportunity for social identification may enhance self-discovery, extending and varying relationships and the opportunity for communication and interaction. The self is located, extended, and—at least partially—defined by membership. Even when it is seen as protective self-abandonment by the insecure, membership may be desired as an external psychic anchor where the individual may have usefulness, function, and roles defined for him/her. For the insecure, limited self-destruction may be seen merely as the greatly desired anonymity obtained by identifying with the group. Robert Lane has described homelessness or lack of membership as the root of political alienation:

. . . (the) homeless man seeks a penetrating intimacy in human relations, which he may not be able to find. . . . (He) constantly finds himself as the outsider, the stranger trying to enter or find a "we group" to join. . . .[22]

Social or political homelessness may degenerate quickly into a threat to existence itself, for belonging is the *sine qua non* of human effectiveness. A person without the protection of the group has only the stripped-down defenses of the loner. He has lost, as Arendt [23] has documented, the rights of man, for these rights adhere to the individual only insofar as the individual is a member and the group, in defining its boundaries, grants him the privileges and protection which it affords all its constituency. Natural rights, rights apart from human covenants, do not exist. They are, as Jeremy Bentham graphically wrote, "nonsense on stilts."

In practical demonstration, no historical inalienable rights exist at all. The minority treaties guaranteed by the League of Nations, for example, clarified what had previously been implicit—that only nationals could be citizens and enjoy the full protection of legal institutions. Group interest held priority over the law, and, where shares were not held in that interest, laws were inapplicable to the individual situation. The new totalitarian Europe emerging during

[22] R. Lane. *Political Ideology.* New York: The Free Press, 1962.

[23] Hannah Arendt. *The Origins of Totalitarianism.* Second enlarged edition. New York: Harcourt Brace Jovanovich, Inc., 1958. This thought-provoking work, like her *On Revolution* (New York: Viking, 1963), is scholarly, original, and deeply compassionate. Reprinted by permission.

the late thirties and forties of this century drove prosperous and educated citizens, as well as the poor, to cross national boundaries without passport, money, or nationality to become unidentifiable beggars. Such forced migrations and loss of homes have hardly been unprecedented in history; what has been unprecedented in the twentieth century is the impossibility for enormous groups of people of finding a new home. The fulfillment of the need for belonging has been elevated to a permanent, existential problem.

There have been over ten million displaced persons who were victims of World War II. Repatriation, when the refugee did not want to return to the country of his or her origin, and naturalization, which affected the precarious social position of earlier naturalized citizens of the same origin, have both failed. The logical solution has been found in the internment camp which substitutes for a non-existent homeland. Thus, loss of acceptance by a national group results in the annihilation of humanity, role, and rights, and ultimately deteriorates into loss of the right to life itself. "The prolongations of their lives is due to charity and not to right; their freedom of movement, if they have it at all, gives them no right to residence which even the jailed criminal enjoys as a matter of course; and their freedom of opinion is a fool's freedom, for nothing they think matters anyhow." [24]

Many of the Vietnamese who fled their country at the close of the war there now wish to return from the United States or other countries to which they attempted to make a transition. For these people, loss of home has become identical with expulsion from humanity, for, John Henry notwithstanding, a man who is nothing but a man has lost the attributes which make it possible for others to regard him as a fellow human being. The paradox lies in the fact that, at the same time that a person is becoming more individual, he or she is also becoming more generalized or abstracted into the mold of the universal species and losing humanity as it is usually defined. Deprived of its expression within a specific shared world, uniqueness loses its significance. The United States (or any other alien nation) may simply not provide a possible or acceptable mode of belonging for these refugees. Certainly it would not provide one which was comparable to the society into which the refugees were socialized.

Manifest affection is often part of the positive gratification pattern of the need to belong, although (as was pointed out earlier)

[24] *Ibid.*, p. 293.

it is not necessarily so. Unlike the lower need for contact, the love which gratifies the need to belong may not be merely received; it may also have an active, reciprocal nature, and assume a measure of control and some efficacy in shaping its course. It may involve giving as well as getting, although not always in obvious displays, and result in mutual gratification through the nurturing process.[25]

Early deprivation of this love may result in permanent inability either to give or to receive it. In his chilling account of the *hibakusha* of atomic-bombed Hiroshima, Robert Lifton describes the effect of parental loss on these tainted survivors.[26] Loss of one's mother resulted in a basic deprivation of essential nurturance and created a profound mistrust of subsequent relationships, which might also be terminated. When both parents were killed, the children became permanently vulnerable, faced with "a lifelong struggle against total incapacitation." As an adult, the prototype of the atomic bomb orphan was a profoundly disaffected individual, "working irregularly at low status jobs, moving about frequently and having no permanent address, diffusely anxious and in poor health . . . on the fringe of society . . . sometimes in difficulty with the law." [27] Deprivation left the survivors with a sense of abandonment and vulnerability toward further victimization by bad luck or being looked down on by those without the death-in-life stigma of being affected by the blast. Their interpersonal relationships were permanently impaired.

How vital acceptance and concern are for socialization and the development of mature ethical values may be seen in Sheldon and Eleanor Glueck's work.[28] After many years of carefully controlled comparisons between delinquent and nondelinquent male youth, they concluded that juvenile delinquency is 90 percent predictable where five "highly decisive factors," all related to belongingness needs, are unfavorable in family life. Where, first, the father's discipline is harsh, erratic, and unsympathetic; second, the mother's supervision is indifferent or unconcerned; third, the mother's affection is cold, indifferent, or hostile; fourth, the father's affection is lacking; and fifth, family cohesiveness is lacking so that the group is unintegrated and empty of companionship, children become delin-

[25] H. S. Sullivan. *The Interpersonal Theory of Psychiatry.* New York: W. W. Norton and Co., 1953.

[26] R. J. Lifton. *Death in Life: Survivors of Hiroshima.* New York: Random House, Inc., 1967. Copyright © 1967 by Robert Jay Lifton.

[27] *Ibid.,* p. 259.

[28] S. Glueck and E. Glueck. *Predicting Juvenile Delinquency and Crime.* Cambridge: Harvard University Press, 1959.

quent. Where these five factors were favorable, the Gluecks found virtually no serious delinquency.

From his comparative study of dropouts and high school graduates, Lucius Cervantes developed a dropout prediction table based on school, family, and peer relationships.[29] Failure, lack of participation, a sense of not belonging at school added to problems at home, few close friends and even these not approved by parents and not school-oriented, produce a weak self-image, little ability to defer gratification, and much resentment toward authority. Dropouts, as Miller reminds us, are the "displaced persons of the affluent society."[30] Under social pressure, they may return to school, but as exiles only, in many cases to again become expellees and refugees from an unchanged situation. Most important to the destruction of this pattern are adolescent face-to-face memberships. "If the teenager has a primary relationship favorable to his remaining in school, all disadvantages are fairly readily overcome."[31]

Like other fearful, lower class persons who have abandoned their autonomy where it is most loudly claimed, the aggressive boys whom Albert Bandura and R. G. Walters studied were forced to inhibit their dependency relations.[32] Parent-child relationships were characterized by lack of warmth and affection and, in every case, the fathers showed little acceptance or esteem for their sons and were more punitive than the fathers of nonagressive boys. Although value standards were upheld within the household, they were not internalized since, for those deprived boys, family life provided no rewards for identification with their fathers.

The child's ability to live happily in a given society depends upon the specific contents of his/her conscience. This vital social and emotional learning occurs through motivation, performance, and reinforcement—through trial and error, direct tuition, and role practice which he or she is most likely to undertake if the dependency motivation is strong and he or she identifies with the main caretakers as a means of satisfying his/her needs. "An important motive leading to role practice is the child's desire to reproduce pleasant experiences" or "worry about whether or not he has his parent's affection

[29] L. G. Cervantes. *The Dropout: Causes and Cures*. Ann Arbor: University of Michigan Press, 1965. Copyright © 1965 by the University of Michigan.

[30] In: D. Schreiber, editor. *Profile of the School Dropout*. New York: Random House, Inc., 1967.

[31] Cervantes, *op. cit.*, p. 199.

[32] A. Bandura and R. Walters. *Adolescent Aggression*. New York: The Ronald Press, 1959.

and approval." [33] The home is central to the child's community. There the child will learn to do whatever he or she must to obtain the love needed, and withdrawal of love given is powerful motivation to develop a conscience, that is, to learn the values of the withholder. But what happens to the child who is not receiving love? What is not given cannot be withdrawn, and if acceptance and recognition are not rendered the child, unsatisfied needs will continue. The child's role playing may be an endless search for identification or an authority which is external to him- or herself to replace the missing internal one.

Damaged community and family relationships are also associated with loss of political values. Where problems existed between fathers and sons, Lane, for example, found limited political information, authoritarianism, a need to stifle anti-authority feelings expressed as inability to criticize legitimate political figures, and a pessimistic view of social improvements.[34]

In the United States, much public dismay was shown over the 21 soldiers who defected to China after they had been taken prisoner in Korea.[35] Assumed to be traitors to the values they had learned as Americans, 18 of these young men turned out to be non-Americans: They had not learned to be part of their cultural group life. They had not found their place within society in the way in which every child must—from the inside out, from membership and acceptance in home and school. None had close family ties nor had they taken part in school activities or sports during school. Just how hard is it to abandon a group to which you have never truly belonged?

Maslow believed that the human needs he described are species-wide and anthropological studies seem to bear out this supposition. Gregory Bateson and Margaret Mead, for example, have made a study of Balinese character which concluded that, by Western standards, these people are far from loving as adults.[36] As children they are rejected and slapped for demanding attention and they do not like it—they cry and, in many other ways, show that they want the love which is denied them. In Israel, the ego-strong, well-adjusted

[33] R. R. Sears, E. E. Maccoby, and H. Levin. *Patterns of Child Rearing.* Evanston, Illinois: Row, Peterson, 1957.

[34] R. E. Lane. "Fathers and Sons: Foundations of Political Belief." *American Sociology Review* 24: 502-11; 1959.

[35] V. Pasley. *21 Stayed.* New York: Farrar, Straus, 1955.

[36] G. Bateson and M. Mead. *Balinese Character: A Photographic Analysis.* New York: New York Academy of Sciences, 1942.

children of the *kibbutzim*—the collective communities—find their belongingness needs abundantly supplied within societies which are structurally, but not functionally, family-less. To them, the whole *kibbutz* is the family and their peers are the shared occupants of an intimacy which begins at birth and may end only at the grave. So deep and intense is the feeling invested in these communal relationships and meanings that, during the Six Days' War with Egypt, fighters from the *kibbutzim* were unable to abandon their comrades under any conditions and, consequently, were very poor soldiers, in the sense that they often were injured or killed unnecessarily.[37] To the dead Israelis, the extent of their communality hardly proved to have survival value. Under almost any conditions, a group which truly incorporates the self may guarantee the survival of the group, but it equally assures the destruction of the individual.

"Inference," wrote Bruner, "depends upon the establishment of rules and models." [38] Where social contracts and the texture of interaction within families and communities are maintained, even without affection, personal knowledge and cognitive growth occur. When affection or acceptance occur at school, they may be compensatory for some children. Taylor found in "overachievement" a compensatory, pseudo-love fulfillment which substituted identification with the school for love missing at home. "Underachievers," in another deficiency response, reduce their anxiety about their status through their peer group affiliations.[39]

The gratification of belongingness needs seems also to be related to the achievement of certain types of moral judgment. Kohlberg, studying the movement of children from one type of moral judgment to another at a higher level of development, found that children with peer group participation ("integrates") advanced more rapidly than isolates of matched socioeconomic status and IQ.[40]

In this aching world, distintegration and re-formation lie about us everywhere. The shape of human interaction is being altered, apparently for all time. Yet out of the emerging structure of mass industrial life has come no functional substitute for human communication on a personal, intimate, and primary level. Shall we become

[37] B. Bettelheim, *op. cit.*, p. 264.

[38] J. Bruner. "The Cognitive Consequences of Early Sensory Deprivation." *Psychosomatic Medicine* 21: 89-95; 1959.

[39] R. G. Taylor. "Personality Traits and Discrepant Achievement: A Review." *Journal of Counseling Psychology* 11: 76-82; 1964.

[40] L. Kohlberg. "Moral Education in the Schools: A Developmental View." *School Review* 74: 1-30; 1966.

what Emile Durkheim has called "a society made up of a boundless dustheap of unrelated individuals"? Or, from the dissipating ashes of the small town and the extended family, will new structures of intimacy arise, close and tightly woven, with a dynamic warp and woof from neither kin nor the fictional boundaries of the polity?

As George Homans has pointed out, small groups—interest groups, kin and clan, economic and ethnic groups—have survived the massive destructive forces which have destroyed empires, religions, cultures, and civilizations. The only historical continuity of humans in society has been through the small groups they have established to serve their most fundamental human needs. "All grander sociologies must be true to the sociology of the group," for only at this level have societies invariably been able to cohere.[41] Inclusion in such groups means the taking for granted which permits extended activities instead of a constant and fearful reassessment of the environment. If human life as we know it in its highest form is to stand, some of the intimate features which characterize the small group must be preserved in some form as communities accessible to each of us. Their boundaries would serve not only to present the nature of their membership to outsiders, but also to provide that crucial labeling, the identification of themselves to those who belong.

The Future

To those who belong, what the nature of their membership in certain groups or communities means to outsiders is important, but more so is their identification of themselves as group members. Such groups, as Christian Bay has written, provide the "most important front line . . . in the struggle for self-determination in our daily lives; that is, for an effective voice in deciding about the rules under which we live and work." [42] The enduring task is the never-ending choice of joint environments as optimal for the developing personalities within the group. Rebellion against what exists, as Camus' rebel demonstrated so clearly, may be the birth of consciousness, dissatisfactions, and action which leads to further serious struggles.[43] Those

---

[41] G. Homans. *The Human Group.* New York: Harcourt, Brace, and World, 1950. p. 21. This beautifully written book is broadly useful and wise.

[42] C. Bay. "Access to Political Knowledge as a Human Right." In: I. Galnoor, editor. *Government Secrecy in Democracies: A Comparative Perspective.* New York: Harper & Row, in press.

[43] A. Camus. *The Rebel.* New York: Vintage Books, 1956.

who would rebel, who know themselves oppressed, must be able to transcend their "culture of silence"—to label their own world, rather than to have their oppressors do that for them. As Paulo Freire has written, the need for these community members, who recognize their marginality within the group, is to identify themselves as those who legitimately belong.[44] Importantly, beyond that is the need for "problem-solving education" consisting of discussion and comprehension which lead to the devising of strategies for change. This process becomes a re-definition of membership for the persons who belong and comes—can come—only from those members within a community who are determined to join others in making it their own, directing its shape, its purpose, and its usage.

What will result? That remains to be seen as experimental responses to environmental changes take place. What actions would once have been attacked or thwarted as inappropriate may gradually be accepted without undue consequences. For those who would create change, a powerful question is which features of the environment facilitate or inhibit the learner's assessment of his or her behavior and provide accurate information on what is expected of him/her, as well as what he/she can expect of him-/herself. External sanctions provide formal or informal instruction about performance and are responded to by the learner's feelings and, over time, by the internalization of others' responses to them. Whose responses are internalized, and how, are the crucial questions. Young individuals have enormous malleability. Socialization is extremely effective in producing adaptive skills in growing persons, but to see accurately where we do belong and to claim that right is a lifelong problem.

Some questions about the nature of socialization into groups remain to be answered. For instance,

1. What is the relative influence of early as opposed to later life experiences?

2. What are the relative emphases to be placed on the influence of individual drives, motives, and needs in the process?

3. What is the comparative value of studying process as opposed to content as a basis for predicting and understanding social behavior?

4. To what extent are the properties of socialization unique, rather than experienced in common?

[44] P. Freire. *Pedagogy of the Oppressed.* New York: Seabury Press, 1971.

5. What are the causes of anti-social deviation from norms of a group? What are the causes of conformity to normative (group) expectations? [45]

These questions are not new. Many have been raised continuously and partially answered, even utilized, in the many ways in which such information could be politically useful.

Within a society building toward the ideal, the personal pattern of living must adjust itself to human needs and human needs must not be forced to adjust themselves to invalid, preexisting routines if individual or group life is to be productive and humane. Democratic social structure depends upon the democratic beliefs, attitudes, and values of its members which underlie and support it. Indeed, it depends upon the satisfaction of the basic needs of human beings which act as their superordinate values. These values shape the choices that the individual, as a group member, will make for action. Within communities, basic agreement on these values will shape the creation of future settings and societies. As Sarason suggests, this creation involves in an organized way the most productive attributes of the human mind.[46] What is entailed is not simply spontaneous and mechanistic development, but consciousness as to the desired end, an outcome of reflection and calculation. Participants with their heightened awareness become part of an organized and dynamic effort to create a new reality, a desired whole, which may require the subordination of other parts of themselves.

Within such groups, communities, or societies, problems are never solved once and for all. Whether a new effort or one continuing for centuries, tensions of varying dimensions will always exist between the desires for maintenance and those for social change. The capacity which must be sought is that of using new knowledge for the betterment of the group, the implementation of its human values. To quote Sarason once more, "Action based on behavioral principles unrelated to social principles is a guarantee of failure." [47] We are our memberships, as well as our selves.

[45] Goslin, *op. cit.*, pp. 1-2.

[46] S. Sarason. *The Creation of Settings and the Future Societies*. San Francisco: Jossey-Bass, 1972.

[47] *Ibid.*, p. 270.

Part Three

Humankind and Schooling: The Affective in Practice

Persons are feeling, valuing, and growing beings. Through enriching, nourishing, sometimes painful, and sometimes ecstatic experiences, persons learn to make sense out of their own living. Some persons gain meaning out of happenstance. Other individuals are fortunate enough to gain the kind of strength that is needed to manage life's vicissitudes through agencies, such as the school, designed to serve the public.

It is our contention that schools can help persons become feeling, valuing, and growing individuals. Schools can provide settings designed to evoke feelings—settings in which persons can experience pleasure, passion, delight, and spontaneity. Schools can provide settings in which provision is made for valuing—settings in which interests, judgment, intention, decision, and reflection are necessary components of a person's repertoire of behaviors if the potentials of the person within the setting are to be realized. Schools can provide settings designed for the art of growing—settings in which extending ideas, commitment, striving, revising, transforming, and developing wholeness are evident. In other words, schools can provide for development of the affective as it has been discussed in this book.

The authors who have written this section have examined the schools from three different vantage points. Roderick takes an unusual slant in her chapter, likening the concept of involvement to aspects of the affective domain. She discusses a path educators can follow if they wish to gather on-the-spot information relative to how students react to the joys of life's treats and the sorrows of life's disappointments. Inherent in her chapter are assumptions and procedures relative to evaluation in the affective domain.

Hedges and Martinello move from the descriptive techniques of the Roderick chapter to prescribing how schools can give students opportunities for experiences designed to enhance development in the affective domain. Attention is given to such skills as deciding, problem solving, communicating, and perceiving as means of promoting affective growth. It is interesting to note that the Hedges-Martinello chapter (10), like Webb's, tends to grow out of the uneasy student movements of a few years back. Chapter 10 contains many valuable insights relative to what interested teachers can do so that students receive guidance in growing as whole persons.

Harking back to Yamamoto's earlier analogy between play and aspects of the affective domain, Berman considers the curriculum worker as a player. The spectrum of human qualities characteristic of the affective domain can be found in certain basic qualities of play such as enjoying, transcending, questing, mastering, renewing, and expressing.

Theories and procedures for planning and implementing affective education can come about in a variety of ways. One way is through the exploration of a cross-disciplinary concept such as play. An analysis of this area was conducted by .Yamamoto and Berman. Affective education can come about through the development and implementation of a typology or schema such as the one worked out by Phenix. Or affective education may be the result of an encounter with an often unfriendly environment such as the ideas proposed by Webb and Hedges-Martinello.

As the challenges of the chapters that follow and those of the preceding chapters are considered and implemented in classrooms, we may see more persons grow into healthy, mature individuals.

9

Describing Persons in Settings: Making the Affective Explicit

Jessie A. Roderick

Many a liberal educational reform has foundered on lack of specific tools for accomplishing its purposes—even if a tool may be something as simple as knowing precisely when to leave the learner entirely alone.

—George Leonard [1]

◦⌒◦

A Path to Knowing What the Schools Are Doing

We become more enlightened about the nature of the person with his unpredictable and predictable qualities when we view him from many perspectives. We can gain this understanding of the person in different contexts by vicariously experiencing the work of an artist as we read a description of how she prepares for, accomplishes, and critiques a creation. Or, we can accompany the psychologist, philosopher, or biologist on a walk through developments in a field of inquiry. On each of these journeys, we observe a sifting, sorting, synthesizing, and analyzing of perceptions from one or more

[1] George Leonard. *Education and Ecstasy.* New York: Delacorte Press, 1968. p. 18.

disciplines which can be the genesis of a theory or model—a theory or model unique to the experts making the journeys.

The paths to learning about the person are many and varied. They can include reading about another's explorations, talking with persons, experimenting with materials, and carefully watching events and interactions. Individuals select a path or paths on the basis of their interests, background, and the questions that haunt them and will not let them abandon the search for increased understanding. For example, a teacher who seeks to learn how students in his class view their learning experiences observes and listens to learners engaged in planning sessions, informal discussions, and individual conferences. The search, no matter which path it takes, results in the ability to make more informed decisions. The success of this search and the quality of the subsequent decisions are enhanced by the utilization of tools or procedures which match the question being probed.

In this chapter, a path to learning about individuals interacting with settings is proposed. Settings may be places where individuals work, live, care, become committed, or engage in any type of living. The path consists of observational and reflective techniques that may be fruitfully used by educators or any persons interested in enhancing the understanding of an individual as a whole being. The substantive focus of the path is involvement—the degree of self an individual invests in or brings to an interaction. In addition to the techniques and substantive focus of the path, personal qualities that facilitate one's traveling it are discussed.

The path sketched in this chapter is but *one* way in which schools can contribute to our knowledge of the person. Individuals of all ages and backgrounds who participate in the process of schooling can traverse the path. Children can learn to observe carefully and to help each other reflect on classroom and community experiences. Determining the contributions the school is making implies generating information about learners' interactions with settings as they occur or shortly thereafter. Admittedly, no present action can be meaningful without consideration of the past and the future as well. We emphasize generating knowledge about what is happening *now* with the hope that plans for the future and what the school *can* do emerge.

To sketch a path is to propose direction, parameters, and procedures for traversing it. It is, at the same time, to leave room for personal options to fill in spaces and dotted lines, and to branch out to incorporate the ever-changing and surprising complexities of

Jessie Roderick *explores life through teaching, research, music, and crafts. In her work as a college professor she searches for ways to glimpse, encourage, and sustain the capricious in life in the classroom. She is committed to collaboration as one way of moving beyond what is to what might be. Collaborative research efforts have resulted in the development of observational and reflective techniques for describing what happens when learners interact with different settings. Currently, she is an associate professor at the University of Maryland. She is an active member of ASCD, the National Council of Teachers of English, and the World Council on Curriculum and Instruction.*

human interactions. Such personalized mapping is to be fully anticipated, examined, and appreciated, since the choices are determined by the traveler under the prevailing conditions of road, weather, time, space, and the like.

As stated earlier, the substantive focus of the path highlighted in this chapter is *involvement*—an individual's investment of self in interactions with persons, materials, or ideas. Although the specific direction the focus on involvement takes will vary with the traveler and her particular situation, guidelines for describing a person's involvement are offered. The nature of these parameters was determined to a large degree by research on involvement conducted by the author and her colleagues over a period of years.[2] Additional

[2] Jessie A. Roderick. *The Involvement Instrument.* Occasional Paper Fifteen. College Park, Maryland: Center for Young Children, University of Maryland, July 1975. Other pertinent Center for Young Children publications are: Jessie Roderick with Joan Moyer and Ruth Spodak, investigators. *Nonverbal Behavior of Young Children as It Relates to Their Decision Making: A Report of Research Findings.* Monograph 5, 1971; Jessie Roderick, principal investigator. *Identifying, Defining, Coding, and Rating Nonverbal Behaviors That Appear To Be Related to Involvement: Interim Report No. 2.* Occasional Paper Twelve, 1973; Jessie A. Roderick, Diane M. Lee, and Louise M. Berman. *Observation: Basis for Planning, Implementing, and Evaluating.* Occasional Paper Sixteen, 1975.

insights were obtained from ideas voiced in other chapters in this volume and literature on commitment, involvement, and knowledge-generation.

Traversing the Path

To become aware of options for shedding light on the uniqueness of the human being both as a creator and a creature of culture is a prime reason for traveling the path proposed in this chapter. Acting upon this awareness can contribute to the school's carrying out its responsibility for helping persons establish, in Phenix' words, ". . . a sense of direction and purpose in the human enterprise." [3]

A clearer understanding of self and others interacting with various settings helps establish direction and purpose in life. Teachers and other learners who wish to generate information that increases such understanding seek a broad, penetrating view of life and what it means to be human. As a result, they employ knowledge-generating techniques through which the *person* speaks. These techniques reveal the qualities of the person and help clarify how one thinks, feels, and acts. In essence, they provide indications of how and to what degree the learner opts for certain experiences and means of expression in his or her daily interactions. One such technique is observing and recording over a period of weeks what a learner does in selecting a project or activity and pursuing it to completion. Another technique involves a person's reflecting on and recording his experiences and feelings while interacting with someone from another culture or age group. This technique might consist of noting one's excitement and new learnings during a stay with a family in another country. Observing and reflecting help in gaining a clearer image of oneself and in making better decisions—decisions selected from among alternatives and based on fact as well as intuition.

Additional motivation for exploring the proposed path is the opportunity to build upon, revise, and adapt the ideas relative to what the schools are doing in the affective as set forth in this chapter. In so doing one might develop multi-dimensional ways of generating information, thereby achieving the best possible fit between personal qualities deemed important, procedures for clarifying these qualities, and efforts to determine the efficacy of these procedures.

Once motivated to take a journey or explore a path, a person must identify and select equipment, whether material, informational,

[3] Philip Phenix in Chapter 3 in this Yearbook.

or attitudinal, that facilitates successful travel along the path. The possession of certain personal qualities and the adoption of particular attitudes enhance the process of knowledge generation focusing on people interacting. However, individuals possessing certain personal qualities or attitudinal approaches to traversing the proposed path are not promised a journey free of conflict or ambiguity, but they are better able to cope with a path that has not been precharted in every detail.

Personal Qualities

Willingness to take risks. Among the personal qualities which enable one to travel the proposed path with confidence and with a toleration for, even appreciation of, the ambiguities encountered is the willingness to risk acting on incomplete knowledge. Facing up to the fact that we can't know everything even though we must act is basic to catching the essence of life that is in a constant state of flux and that refuses to be highly controlled. In trying to uncover the real in life it is necessary to move beyond the obvious and the everydayness of life. However, before significant progress in moving beyond the known or obvious can be made, attention and study must be focused on what is. For it is in the pursuit of learning about what *is* that possibilities emerge for going beyond the known to what might be.

Seeing persons in context. The willingness to recognize that efforts to know someone better do not necessarily strip the person of individuality or deny his or her privacy is another personal quality that facilitates one's traversing the path. Knowledge of the interplay between the person and the many elements of the environment is vital to knowing her or him well. The individual is not viewed as an entity apart from the settings in which he functions but rather as one who perceives richly and acts upon opportunities in the setting. This view of the interacting person implies a knowledge of the nature of settings which encourages the individual to act, to bring about change, and to move beyond what he or she already knows. In any event, it is the person who is highlighted, and all efforts are directed toward increased understanding of the person as a solitary and a social being. Knowing well also implies awareness of and skill in utilizing or at times even inventing procedures for generating knowledge which do not obliterate or bypass the person in the process.

Seeing persons as they are. If the proposed path to learning about others is to be traveled with any degree of success, the traveler must be willing to view persons as they *are* and not as what he might *like* them to be. Judgment is suspended while information is being obtained. The traveler must also see man as capable of self-reflection—of being able to look at what is within himself as well as how he responds to and acts upon what is without.[4]

Seeing persons as initiators. Individuals are also viewed as persons capable of taking initiative and *acting upon* rather than being acted upon thereby assuming a responding or reactive stance. In the former, one's actions are not controlled by external factors but by those within the person. The functioning of this internal locus of control is influenced by many factors including personal ones such as values, the individual's perception of his socioeconomic standing, and his perceptions of the concern and expectations of others. Aspects of the setting influencing the locus of control include how others view the individual and how they encourage self-responsibility and freedom to direct one's life. In another vein, L'Engle speaks of *participation with* as opposed to possessing someone or something in which case the person or thing and freedom diminish.[5] *Acting upon* is also *participating with* when one is aware and makes the decision to do so thoughtfully. *Acting upon* in this context is not done unthinkingly or unknowingly.

Seeing persons as communicators. The last personal quality selected for discussion is a willingness to view the individual as a communicator. A community is comprised of individuals who need one another and communicate with each other for the purpose of increasing knowledge and of gaining and offering strength and support. The person is a social being and thus many of his creative efforts are enhanced when they are collaborative and involve others in the community.[6] With collaboration and communication come a trust and acceptance of ourselves and others. When this happens, persons are more apt to make feelings as well as objective data part of their quest for knowledge of themselves and others.[7]

[4] Kaoru Yamamoto in Chapter 1 in this Yearbook.

[5] Madeleine L'Engle in Chapter 4 in this Yearbook.

[6] For a discussion of collaborative efforts in scientific fields, see: Lewis Thomas. *The Lives of a Cell: Notes of a Biology Watcher.* New York: The Viking Press, 1974.

[7] The idea of taking the risk of trusting one another and including feelings as part of data was proposed by Donald Michael at the Second General Assembly of the World Future Society session on "Human Values: Which Ones Must Change in the World of the Future and How," June 3, 1975. Washington, D.C.

Perspectives

A satisfying and productive journey along the path sketched in this chapter is partially a function of the traveler's perspectives on generating information about persons' interactions. Perspectives on knowledge generation are closely tied to personal qualities such as those just discussed. The perspectives below are among those recommended for the journey.

Describing observed interactions and helping persons reflect on interactions experienced are two attempts to clarify how a learner structures or makes meaning out of his interactions with the environment.[8] This process of clarifying reveals the multi-faceted, multi-valent nature of the person and settings. Knowledge generation is viewed as an opening-up process—one that uncovers and highlights the variety, complexity, unpredictability, and uniqueness of a person's interactions.

Knowledge-generating techniques that take into account the uniqueness of each person and her interactions in a variety of contexts need not cement or freeze our thinking but instead can reveal the range of possible interactions and the variety of ways they can be viewed. We can say on the basis of information obtained that a person can be X in one situation and Y in another. Likewise, we can say that X might be desirable in one situation and not in another. Life has a flow, a movement in and out, up and around. We are not bound nor should descriptive and reflective techniques bind us to an either/or mode of thinking. Forecasting and manipulating need not be the next step. On the contrary, the next step can be raising more questions and developing facilitative techniques for further exploration of life.

Recognizing the importance of viewing the learner in varied and specific settings prevents our obtaining and accepting a fragmented picture of how we see the learner and how the learner sees himself. Knowledge of the factors within contexts contributes to our knowing the person as an individual who selects from and builds upon those aspects of context that are necessary to his productive functioning. Such efforts to better understand the interplay between persons and settings further reveal the non-linearity of life. The linkages form in all directions and at times pile one on top of the other. Our view of generating knowledge about persons must be broad enough to

---

[8] For a discussion of the way persons look at the world, see: Kaoru Yamamoto. *Individuality: The Unique Learner.* Columbus, Ohio: Charles E. Merrill Publishing Company, 1975. pp. 1-21.

encompass the crisscross settings and the layer upon layer pileups which characterize human interactions. For when we hold such a view, we are able to tease out the complexities of human beings and to recognize the importance of encouraging the development and expression of them.

For the most part, persons who generate information try to employ objective procedures. On this path, objectivity is important but it is not the objectivity of detachment. Personal qualities of the observing and reflecting individual are determinants of why and how information is generated. These qualities also influence how results are communicated and the degree to which a person can stand back and view them. Coming to grips with and appreciating the human aspects of generating information causes persons to scrutinize what they say and think about what they see, hear, and feel. In the long run, this process enables persons to be more objective than if they pretended these factors did not exist.

Travelers who view evaluation in the manner just described recognize that attempts to generate information also help us identify what we don't know. There will always be the mystery of life—the wonderment which increases as our search for knowledge and understanding progresses. In fact, the ever-increasing awareness of the existence of the mysterious prompts us to accelerate our efforts to find out what we don't know.

Often the school presents to the young possibilities that are incongruent with the learner's intent. Travelers who view knowledge generation as proposed in this chapter are more apt to help persons realize their own possibilities instead of trying to make the young assume for their own the possibilities the school presents.[9] Efforts to make a learner like all other learners are minimized, and the person who doesn't meet others' expectations is not considered a failure. Individuals are encouraged to explore life in their own way, to define their unique styles, and to discover the values of access to this information.

Who Generates Information and Where?

Students, teachers, parents, specialists in the schools—in fact any person who contributes in some way to the nature and quality

---

[9] Dwayne Huebner. "The Contradiction Between the Recreative and the Established." In: James B. Macdonald and Esther Zaret, editors. *Schools in Search of Meaning.* Washington, D.C.: Association for Supervision and Curriculum Development, 1975. pp. 29-37.

of learning experiences for children and youth can generate information about what is happening in classroom settings. Children and youth can be taught to use their skills of perception in learning about themselves and others. They can reflect on their experiences and can observe their own interactions via videotape. They can also generate information with classmates by discussing and reflecting together and by observing one another. Persons who participate in planning for learning experiences can also participate in generating information about how and the degree to which their purposes were achieved. Through this process, individuals can progress in skills such as observing, listening, reflecting, suspending judgment until adequate evidence is obtained, interacting, and making future plans.

Where can information about persons interacting be obtained? Wherever learners see in settings opportunities for interacting with others, materials, and ideas that excite them. The art corner, the woodworking equipment set up in the hall, the chemistry lab, the library, the gym, or a conversation corner are places where individuals can be observed interacting. Any place that persons come together to make decisions about whom or to what they will invest their time and energies is appropriate for determining how personal goals are being carried out and the degree to which they have been accomplished.

Procedures

To observe and to talk with persons are natural ways to learn about others, the environment, and ourselves. These are also natural ways to ascertain what the school is doing in the affective. Witness the young child carefully examining a toy again and again or imitating adults and peers with whom she has contact. When used to satisfy the child's innate curiosity and desire to grow, these activities provide opportunities for others to generate knowledge about how the child interacts with her environment. Perceptual skills not dulled by the rush of life but instead sharpened and expanded can generate information that sheds light on the child's images and how she creates them.

The techniques or methodologies employed by travelers on our path should reflect the attitudes toward and perspectives on evaluation presented earlier. When such is the case, techniques of observing, discussing, and reflecting can generate knowledge that reveals the following about the learner: his uniqueness, the ways in which he changes over time and with situations, the unanticipated in his behavior, the complexity of his interactions with the environment, and how he feels about the way he perceives himself and his life experiences.

Techniques for generating information described above are numerous. They include interviewing, discussing, observing, reflecting (in writing and speech), and spontaneous conversations where there are no deliberate attempts to elicit a response. Interview and discussion-type techniques can include sentence and story completions, using materials to make up a story, placing oneself in a situation, responding to questions about how one might act in the situation, and responding to pictures and other stimuli.[10] Spontaneous discussions such as those that often occur during a group project might reveal how participants perceive themselves as members of a group. More specific comments relative to generating information using reflective and observational techniques follow.

Reflecting. Asking a person to reflect on her experiences can provide information concerning how she feels about the activity, what she perceives as exciting, important, or moving, and how she sees other participants. Reflecting on experiences can also help learners identify those aspects of an experience that should be continued, revised, or set aside even if only temporarily. Persons may be asked to reflect in response to written or spoken stimuli. In the latter, one person or a group may initiate the reflection.

Reflecting can be viewed as a learning experience from different perspectives. The person reflecting on an experience learns much about himself as he probes the nature of interactions he engages in and his reactions to and feelings about them. Seizing upon many opportunities to reflect moves an individual along the path to his becoming a reflective person on his own. In this process, persons may also come to respect and better understand the role that memory can play in not only analyzing life situations but in preserving their vividness.[11] A focused reflection on having viewed an exhibit of watercolor painting may sharpen memories about color

[10] Patricia Minuchin et al. *The Psychological Impact of School Experience: A Comparative Study of Nine-Year-Old Children in Contrasting Schools.* New York: Basic Books, Inc., 1969. pp. 163-81 and 458-73.

[11] Madeleine L'Engle in Chapter 4 in this Yearbook.

and technique which can later be used to produce a creative expression.

Observing. Observing a person engaged in an activity provides information about that individual *while* he/she is in the process of interacting. As a result, selected aspects of the *now* are clarified. In addition, a perspective on the past can be achieved when many *nows* recorded over time are examined. Greater clarification of the *now* is achieved when information about the various elements of the larger context accompany descriptions of individual actions. For when behaviors are viewed against a backdrop of information about others in the setting and how materials, time, and space are organized and utilized, the impact of the person on the setting and of the setting on the person becomes apparent.[12] Information about persons in the larger context can provide insight on how an individual appears to be affected by others who share experiences with him.[13]

Observations of persons interacting with the environment are often recorded in diary form. This way of describing what is observed produces a running account of actions and verbal utterances. Various forms of observational instruments consisting of categories or groups of behaviors can also be employed in recording observations. In this procedure, an abbreviated method of recording consisting of letters, numerals, or words is generally used. Persons traversing the path proposed in this chapter will select observational instruments or guidelines that capture the diversity, change, and spontaneity of behavior. Those persons will also select guidelines that generate information congruent with the proposed purposes of the interaction. An observational instrument focusing on learner decisions is hardly appropriate in a setting where someone other than the learner makes all the critical decisions.

A more complete picture of what a learner selects from settings and how he acts upon the selected aspects is obtained when a combination of knowledge-generating techniques is employed. In-

[12] For an examination of what has been termed the hidden curriculum, see: Philip Jackson. *Life in Classrooms.* New York: Holt, Rinehart and Winston, Inc., 1968.

[13] Richard J. Light. "Empirical Methods and Questions in Evaluation." In: Michael N. Apple *et al.*, editors. *Educational Evaluation: Analysis and Responsibility.* Berkeley, California: McCutchan Publishing Corporation, 1974. p. 129.

terviews, discussions, and reflections on experiences can provide checks on observational data. Likewise, information obtained by observing can serve as a check on information gained through self-report techniques. Since persons have different experiences at varying times under constantly changing conditions, judgments and inferences about persons interacting should be made only after many attempts to learn about individuals and to help them learn about themselves.[14]

The Involvement Instrument: An Example

The Involvement Instrument is offered as one way of generating information about persons interacting. It utilizes the path of observing and includes categories of Motion, Vision, Facial, Stance, Pause, Preciseness, and Physical Display of Emphasis.[15] The instrument was developed through the collaborative efforts of individuals from different walks of life at various stages in their professional and educational careers. The focus of the instrument is a person's nonverbal actions that appear to be indicators of involvement. Since nonverbal behaviors are generally considered spontaneous and not apt to be premeditated, information about these behaviors has the potential for providing insight into a person's involvement of self in an interaction. Although we cannot see the inner forces that motivate individuals, careful observation of overt actions coupled with attentive listening and our knowledge about persons in general can provide clues to inner processes or an individual's disposition to respond.

Information about the context in which an activity occurs is necessary for placing the recordings of actions subsumed in the several categories into a larger framework. For instance, the nature of the activity, the number of persons involved, and changes which occur in either or both help an observer account for a preponderance of Motions-unrelated-to-task or Visions-away-from-task. The Involvement Instrument Coding Sheet provides space for noting questions, additional information not called for by the category

[14] For descriptions of several classrooms, see: G. Alexander Moore. *Realities of the Urban Classroom: Observations in Elementary Schools.* Garden City, New York: Anchor Books, 1967.

[15] An abbreviated form of the Involvement Instrument, a sample coding sheet, and directions for using it are found at the end of this chapter.

descriptions, and suggestions for revisions. Although the form of the instrument presented at the end of this chapter was designed to observe individual learners over a period of time, it could be revised and used in other ways.

Guidelines and Use

How the Involvement Instrument is used depends on the type of information desired. Individuals may wish to obtain information about the range of nonverbal behaviors related to involvement evident in different classroom settings. When the instrument was used in industrial arts classes, the categories of Vision- and Motion-on-task, Physical Display of Emphasis, and Preciseness predominated. In contrast, as one would expect, there were few evidences of Physical Display of Emphasis and Preciseness in classrooms where students did not use manipulative materials or large equipment. This and similar information can cause persons to raise questions such as the following: Do elements within different settings encourage involvement to be displayed in different ways? Which aspects of setting facilitate an individual's becoming involved to the degree he desires? How might elements of setting be changed to invite more involvement?

It is not always necessary to use the Instrument in its entirety. For example, only the Facial, Motion, and Vision categories might be used to generate information about a student's carrying through on an activity he planned and his feelings about it. On the other hand, when the purpose of generating information is to observe individual children on an informal basis in a variety of activities, it is often appropriate to use all the categories. Since the category descriptions can be applied across age groups from infants to adults, it is necessary to include in the recordings a careful description of the larger context and the specific activities occurring within it.

In addition to the less formal ways of employing the Instrument described above, it may be used in more formalized research studies. For example, in a study with first-grade children the Involvement Instrument was used to determine whether a gradual increase in the complexity of a setting increases involvement as defined by the categories.[16] Three levels of language arts learning

---

[16] Louise Berman, Jessie Roderick, Shirley Browner, and Diane Lee. "A Study of the Impact of Specially Designed Settings on Children's Involvement: A Quality Improvement Project." Sponsored by the Maryland State Department of Education, The University of Maryland, and Rippling Woods School, Anne Arundel County, Maryland, 1976.

centers were developed and students were observed interacting at the centers. As students progressed from one level center to another, they were provided increased opportunities for personal input in the form of choices and elaboration. In this study verbal statements were also recorded and examined as possible indicators of involvement.

After behaviors observed in the different categories are recorded, a comparison of the number of tallies in the different categories can be made. Information resulting from this comparison can constitute a basis for discussing purposes, feelings, and possible ways to learn more about persons' interactions. Frequent observations followed by open discussions not only help in planning for future learning experiences, but also provide opportunity for individuals to become receptive to feedback and to utilize it in positive ways.

The need to generate information by using a combination of techniques was mentioned earlier in this section. Reflection and observation can complement each other as knowledge-generating techniques. Following is a set of questions designed to encourage a person to reflect on his involvement in an interaction. These questions can be used in conjunction with the Involvement Instrument.

What aspect of the activity was of most interest to you?

Can you identify the point at which you decided to continue the activity?

How often did you or did you wish you could return to, revise, or build upon the ideas explored in the activity?

Were you aware of other students' involvement in the activity? How did you know they were involved?

What was there about the activity that made you remain with it?

When did you seem to be exerting the most energy in the activity?

In what part of the activity did you feel particularly competent?

What would you change about the activity to make it more interesting to you?

What parts, if any, of this activity were like activities you engage in outside school?

Other questions such as the following might be asked to encourage a person to reflect on his involvement in general and not on a specific activity.

How do you know what is expected of you in school?

When do you generally want to stay with a task or change it?

Do you care about what is expected of you?

What important things would you like to become involved in?

When do you feel like laughing at yourself, at what you do?

Categories of the Involvement Instrument can be used as guidelines for developing other questions to prompt reflection.[17] In any case, the source of procedures or techniques for generating information about the person should be the person—what she says, acts, and feels. It is the person who is central to developing curricular designs, implementing them, and generating knowledge about what transpires during the implementation.

Involvement and Affect

Knowledge of humankind in general suggests that persons want to interact with others, with materials, and with ideas that have potential meaning for them as individuals. Educational literature is replete with exhortations to get students involved; to build upon their interests; and to encourage active participation in individual and group endeavors. However, what is often absent in the literature is the specificity required for selecting or designing settings that encourage involvement and for developing techniques to determine what happens when persons interact with these settings.

Since involvement is a process possessing many affective components, knowledge about this process can also provide information about what is happening in the affective in classroom settings. The literature on involvement and commitment as well as observations and testimonies related to classroom practices identify the affective and the process of becoming involved as critical curricular concerns. A comparison of selected aspects of affect discussed in this volume and others with the dimensions of involvement identified in the Involvement Instrument reveals similarities which can be helpful in increasing our knowledge about affect in classrooms.

[17] A description of a program in which children were encouraged to reflect on and discuss their feelings and experiences is found in: Arlene Uslander *et al. Their Universe: The Story of a Unique Sex Education Program for Kids.* New York: Delacorte Press, 1973.

What follows is a discussion of some possible parallels and relationships between involvement and affect. The similarities apparent to the author formed the basis for focusing on involvement and for presenting the Involvement Instrument as a means of describing what is happening in the realm of the affective in classroom settings.

In some writings involvement is viewed as an aspect of the affective as well as the affective an aspect of involvement. An example of the former is found in a study of emphases given cognitive and affective processes in selected classes. Involvement was one of the several affective criteria examined.[18] An example of the latter is found in an analytic scheme for assessing behavior in the classroom. One item of the scheme was involvement. Subsumed under involvement were work orientation, affect, and interaction. Affect was defined in terms of children's enjoying themselves, being passive or flat, restless or uneasy.[19]

An examination of chapters in this volume reveals possible relationships between affect and involvement. L'Engle's "all-rightness" or hope can be related to involvement in that hope can be a motivating force to become and to continue to be involved—to commit oneself in a particular direction. In another chapter, Yamamoto discusses the necessity for play. The opportunity to try on many different roles if desired and to explore roles in depth encourages involvement—an investment of self. To probe, to explore, to immerse oneself but also to stand back, to be detached for a time are part of the trying, questioning, scrutinizing, and immersing prerequisite to involvement. Opportunities to engage in these processes also prevent one from becoming involved without direction or discipline. Involvement for involvement's sake should also be part of the exploratory behavior that can precede or even verify one's decision to commit self.

It is also possible to consider some relationships between Phenix' levels of affect as discussed in his chapter and certain indicators of involvement included in the Involvement Instrument. Expressions of feelings of delight or pleasure suggesting present enjoyment or the immediate worth of an experience (Phenix' second level) might be noted in a relaxed muscle tone or in facial expressions such as a smile. Overt, observable indications of Phenix' third level, interest or intention, could include motion and vision

[18] Herbert J. Walberg and others. "Grade Level, Cognition, and Affect: A Cross Section of Classroom Perceptions." *Journal of Educational Psychology* 64 (2): 142-46; April 1973.

[19] Minuchin *et al., op. cit.,* p. 449.

related to the activity or interaction. Evidences of physical display of emphasis and preciseness observed in motions might also suggest interest which is being acted upon. A lack of response to distractions could also give clues as to the degree of interest a person has in an activity.

The fourth level of affect, critical reflection, appraisal, or judgment might be evidenced in a person's leaving an interaction, engaging in another activity or just musing and then returning to it but this time revising or even starting anew. Involving other persons in the process of changing or consulting persons during the overt break in the interaction might also suggest appraisal and critical reflection. Commitment to idealization, Phenix' final level of affect, might be observed in one's consistently returning to an activity and working to revise it.

The proposed relationships between affect, as discussed by various authors, and the Involvement Instrument can be viewed as a step in making affect more explicit. It is hoped that this beginning will encourage others to explore other relationships and devise procedures for explicating other processes, thereby clarifying what formal education is doing in the affective.

And What Next?

What can happen when teachers, students, peers, and other adults engaged in the process of schooling travel the proposed path and participate in generating knowledge about what happens when learners interact with settings? What can we do when we have at our fingertips information about the person in terms of the milieu in which he operates and the persons or materials he endows with affect or for which he shows concern, appreciation, interest, and value?

For one thing, we can become more skilled in making available to persons opportunities that present them with choices that appear worthy of their interest and energies. For when a range of such choices is available, the person is more apt to commit herself as opposed to dabbling or becoming committed without having examined alternatives. We can become more adept at helping persons determine an appropriate point of entry into an activity or series of engagements. What is comfortable, appropriate, or encouraging for an individual? We can increase our skill in identifying areas or times when it is important for some persons to have a rhythm of involvement and noninvolvement and when to be marginally or totally involved.

We can also become more knowledgeable about those with whom we collaborate in school settings. What is the curriculum coordinator concerned about? For whom or what does he show feeling? What questions is she probing? What kinds of interpersonal relations does he seek and cultivate? What methods of generating knowledge does this person prefer? These or similar questions can be raised about the resource teacher, the principal, the reading and math specialists, and the bus driver. The more we understand about our colleagues in these respects, the more we can contribute to providing a setting where they can engage wholeheartedly in interactions with those persons, ideas, and things which have meaning for them.

Our experience with generating knowledge about persons' involvements in interactions can also cause us to reexamine the procedures we employed and to revise where necessary. Did we oversimplify or does the information provide a picture of the complexity of personal interactions? Were we able to capture the feeling tone of what Stake would call the mystery of the experience? [20] What does our information tell us about the sometimes capricious and other times predictable actions of the individual? What does it suggest to us about the need not only to trust our intuition but also to use it more often? What does it tell us about time from the learner's perspective and about time from the perspective of the observer or listener? Answers to these and other questions enable each of us to know ourselves better and consequently make better decisions about our destiny.

Finally, what can and should happen as a result of having observed, reflected, and listened is an increase in communication among those persons who travel the path with us. We are a community of learners concerned with finding out about ourselves and others. Only when we share this knowledge with those around us in ever-widening circles can we progress in our efforts to help persons make commitments based on wise decisions. To travel the path alone is to travel the path with no conversation. Without communication or a sharing of meanings, the process of generating knowledge comes to a standstill—buried in one person's perceptions.

[20] Robert Stake, editor. *Evaluating the Arts in Education: A Responsive Approach.* Columbus, Ohio: Charles E. Merrill Publishing Company, 1975. p. 23.

INVOLVEMENT INSTRUMENT

(Abbreviated Form)*

CATEGORY DEFINITION AND DESCRIPTION	EXAMPLES
Context can be described in terms of the following elements in the setting:	
1. Age of the group or type of class	3-5 yr. olds; preschool
2. Teacher or leader role	Directive, non-directive, initiating or responsive behavior
3. Space—(a) placement of persons in the setting; (b) use of space by persons; and (c) size of space areas	Large open area; areas defined by furniture arrangement; persons in small clusters around the room
4. Prominent or unusual features of the setting	Visitor in the classroom; theme pervading all activities
5. Time framework—time of day; time scheduling	Snack time; free choice time; large block of time
6. Observable changes in any of the above	Group moves to outdoors or other room; teacher role changes
7. Other features specific to your research question	Special equipment, materials, furniture arrangement, or grouping of persons

An *Activity* exists when the following three criteria are met:	
1. Evidence exists of interaction between the observed person and another person(s) and/or materials;	Observed person working with puzzle

* Certain subcategories have been deleted. Persons wishing to use the complete Involvement Instrument are referred to: Jessie A. Roderick, *The Involvement Instrument.* Occasional Paper Fifteen. College Park, Maryland: Center for Young Children, University of Maryland, July 1975.

CATEGORY DEFINITION AND DESCRIPTION	EXAMPLES
2. Evidence exists to indicate that the observed person is giving priority to selected material(s)/person(s) from within the context;	Directs attention to puzzle even though other persons move in and out of puzzle area
3. Evidence exists of employment of parts of the body and/or senses.	Manipulating puzzle pieces with fingers and hands
An *Alternate Activity* is characterized by behavior that does not fit the *Activity* definition	Dancing alone, talking to oneself, running, meandering, etc.
Motion is defined as movements of the body as a whole and/or parts of the body. Note: *Motion* is recorded by using the sub-categories that follow. Each is identified by a subscript.	Crawl, throw an object, raise an arm
M_T—*Motion* on task or related to task (*Activity*)	Stirring (when *Activity* or task is cooking); turning the page (when *Activity* is reading)
M_{T_P}—*Motion* related to task with person(s)	Showing someone how to do a finger play or dancing with a partner
M_{T_M}—*Motion* related to task with material(s)	Typing on a typewriter
M_{T_B}—*Motion* related to task with both person(s) and material(s)	Constructing a collage in collaboration with other person(s) or showing picture to teacher or peer
M_A—*Motion* unrelated to task or *Activity*	Turning away from a task and picking up a book dropped by a passerby
Pause is defined as a person's temporary cessation of an *Activity* or a condition in which voluntary gross movements of the body stop. There is an expectation that the *Activity* or *Alternate Activity* will continue after the pause.	Stops running for a few seconds and then continues

CATEGORY DEFINITION AND DESCRIPTION	EXAMPLES
Vision is attention of the eyes as demonstrated by eye movement or eye position. Also included is head movement associated with eye position (head movement often facilitates or makes eye movement possible). Subscripts:	
V_T—Eyes focused on task (*Activity*); vision may be directed toward person(s) or material(s)	Looking at puzzle pieces when activity is putting puzzle together
V_A—Eyes directed away from task	Looking up or away from a task
V—Eye attention cannot be judged V_T or V_A	Looking around while dancing, rolling the eyes, widening of the eyes, etc.
Stance is defined as any change in whole body position	Sitting down, kneeling, standing up, or squatting which lasts more than a fleeting moment
Facial is defined as any change involving the total face or parts thereof not included in *Vision*. Mouth movements accompanying speech are also excluded.	Movement of the lips, tongue, nose, forehead; biting lips, turning down the lip
Preciseness is indicated by evidence of restrained, controlled body movements or withholding of force resulting from the following:	
1. Delicate or careful manipulation of material(s)	Placing small amounts of glue on a light fragile material
2. Careful or controlled interaction with person(s)	Guiding a person's hand in writing

Note: *Preciseness* refers to process not accuracy. Low, moderate, or high rating is designated by 1, 2, or 3

CATEGORY DEFINITION AND DESCRIPTION	EXAMPLES
Physical Display of Emphasis is defined as a display of force which may or may not be directed toward person(s) or material(s). It is a pushing out from the body as opposed to a holding back of force. Note: 1, 2, or 3 designates a low, moderate, or high rating.	Indicators include muscular contractions, colorations, tremors as found when grasping the handle of a hammer while pounding or clenching a fist
Comments are explanatory notes, reactions, or helpful suggestions. Also recorded are inferences about the *Vision* category.	Child is out of sight of observer. V_I—It appears that person looked away (inference).

DIRECTIONS FOR USING THE INVOLVEMENT CODING SHEET

STEP-BY-STEP DIRECTIONS

A. Before beginning to record, observe the setting and the person to be observed for approximately 5 to 15 minutes.

B. Provide the required information in the appropriate blanks at the top of the coding sheet.

C. Describe the *Context* in Column I.

D. Determine a time interval or coding signal. This can be a 10 second period, one minute period, or other. Use a watch with a second hand or a cassette audio tape on which time interval signals have been recorded.

E. In Column III describe the *Activity* in which the person being observed is engaged. Each time a new *Activity* is observed, describe it in Column III. If an *Alternate Activity* is observed, place brackets ([   ]) in the *Activity* column (Column III) and do not code in any other column. When the original *Activity* is resumed or a new *Activity* begun, describe it in Column III and code accompanying behaviors in the appropriate columns. It is important to record in the *Activity* column, along with a basic description of the *Activity,* who in addition to the observee is involved and who appears to be taking the initiative in directing the activity.

F. Record *Motions* (M), *Vision* (V), and *Pauses* (P) in Column IV with the appropriate coding symbol and accompanying subscript(s). Do not record REPEATED motions or more than one successive M_A, M_{T_M},

M_{T_P}, or M_{T_B} in one coding interval unless the *Motion* is interrupted by a P or an observed change in the *Motion* subscript. For example, if one M_{T_B} is FOLLOWED by a different M_{T_B}, only record one M_{T_B}. However, if an M_{T_B} is followed by a P, and then the same M_{T_B} occurs again, it would be recorded as follows: M_{T_B}

$\qquad\qquad$ P

$\qquad\qquad M_{T_B}$

The same rule holds for REPEATED *Visions* (V).

Record SIMULTANEOUS behaviors one next to the other in a horizontal line. For example, if *Vision-on-task* (V_T) occurred simultaneously with a *Motion-on-task* toward materials (M_{T_M}), the coding would appear as V_T, M_{T_M} (see first *Motion* block in Figure A). When a new *Motion* (M), *Vision* (V), and/or *Pause* (P) is observed, begin coding on a new horizontal line. Accordingly, there may be more than one horizontal line recorded in any ten-second interval. (See Coding block #11, Column IV in Figure A.)

When the subject's eyes cannot be seen directly, but from the head and body position and any other relevant cues, one can infer that the gaze is either on or off task, record the observation in Column IV and write V-I (I refers to inference) in the corresponding *Comment* column (Column IX).

If the observer desires, *Vision-on-task* (V_T) may be coded using additional subscripts to indicate *Vision-on-task-toward-material* (V_{T_M}) or *Vision-on-task-toward-person(s)* (V_{T_P}). Caution is advised in coding this information because it is highly judgmental.

G. Code *Stance* with a check ($\checkmark$) in Column V whenever a change in *Stance* is observed.

H. Code any change in *Facial* expression with a check ($\checkmark$) in Column VI.

I. Rate *Preciseness* of movements in Column VII using a 1, 2, or 3, to designate a low, moderate, or high rating respectively. (The rating judgment is made by comparing the subject's observed behavior with his own behavior over a period of time.)

J. In Column VIII rate *Physical Display of Emphasis* with either a 1, 2, or 3 to designate a low, moderate, or high rating. (The basis for rating is the observed person's behavior compared with his behavior over time.)

K. In Comments (Column IX), record any inferences made about *Vision*. Also write any additional comments, reactions, or helpful suggestions. If not able to code a behavior, make note of that fact in the *Comments* column. For example, if the person being observed is out of sight or if the observer's vision is blocked, note this in Column IX.

Sample entries—not a complete recording

FIGURE A
Coding Sheet
Nonverbal Indicators of Involvement

Date __5/14/76__   Time __10:05__   Subject # __64__   Observer __One__   In class ___ Video ___ Other ___ √ Booth

I	II	III	IV	V	VI	VII	VIII	IX
Context	Coding Signal	Activity	Motion $M,M_{T,A,M,B,P}$ Pause P Vision $V,V_{T,A}$	Stance (√)	Facial (√)	Preciseness 1, 2, 3	Physical Display of Emphasis 1, 2, 3	Comments
4- and 5-year old group Adults in facilitative role with minimal direction Children in various interest areas moving freely	5	Child painting at easel child-directed	$V_T\ M_{T_M}$			2	2	
	6	Solitary play Another child standing by watching	V_A		(√)			Furrowed brow and curled lip looked away (V-I)
	7	[ ]	—	—	—	—	—	—

	3	3
Doing detailed work on corner of paper		

9

Child is out of sight
—
—
—
—
—
—

10

V_T M_{T_P}, M_{T_M}

11

12

10

What the Schools Might Do: Some Alternatives for the Here and Now

William D. Hedges
Marian L. Martinello

Prefatory note: During the late 50's and early 60's, we each experienced student movements in different parts of the world. While working with the Ministry of Education in Korea, one of us observed students, faculty and other citizens participate in a revolt against the corruption in Syngman Rhee's government. People marched directly into the muzzles of heavy tank guns. They risked their lives for the right to speak out and demand to be heard. Their concerns, questions, and objectives emanated from their strong desire for a more humane, egalitarian, and open society. Similar concerns were being expressed in the United States where the other author was caught up in the surge of humanism among students on East and West Coasts. Value questions were raised in ever more probing ways and questions of selfhood and relationships with others caused some observers of the ferment of those days to examine their capacity for humaneness. Some years later we wonder where much of that energy and strong sense of direction have gone. People seem too willing to conform to societal norms which are inconsistent with the values of liberated people. We hear the cry of disillusionment; we sense an erosion of idealism; we perceive an increasing willingness to become resigned to "reality" and we wonder: What has gone wrong? Where are we headed? What might the schools do?

∾

No matter what a person's social status, material wealth, or trappings of success, if that person remains frustrated by questions of selfhood, how meaningful is his or her life? No matter how many years of schooling or the number of degrees acquired, the person who does not perceive living as *good* has experienced an education of little consequence.

What might the school have done for those who have not found identity and community? More important: What might the school do to aid those who are yet to come in their continuing quest to BE?

It is the school's philosophy which gives education wholeness, direction and purpose. The values and assumptions that comprise a philosophy of education provide the premises for practices which have integrity, consistency, and meaning for teacher and learner.

In a culturally pluralistic society such as ours, there are many sets of values. But for a society to survive there must be a common set of values as well. We believe that the core values of a diverse and dynamic democracy include respect for and expectation of each person's right: (a) to choose one's own values, (b) to endeavor to live by them, and (c) to assume responsibility for contributing to the development of the self, one's social group, and to the broader culture of which one is a part. These values have to do with being human and humane.

This common core of values advances an image of the person as comfortable with change as the only constant in a dynamic world and, therefore:

1. Willing to change himself and able to bring about change in his environment

2. Capable of perceiving from many different perspectives: himself, others, the phenomena of his world

3. Having a strong sense of identity constituted of self-acceptance, self-esteem, and commitment to self-determined life purposes

4. Competent and therefore self-confident in areas of chosen activity

5. Autonomous and inclined to invest himself authentically and intensely in endeavors of his choice, and in others with trust, empathy, compassion, and understanding

William D. Hedges, *former secondary school teacher of mathematics and science, is Professor of Education at the University of Florida in Gainesville. Past president of the Society of Professors of Education, Professor Hedges is the author of two books, some one hundred articles and a number of research publications. He has been a member of the faculty at the Universities of Virginia and Missouri and has taught summers at Washington University and New York University. His overseas experience consists of two years in Korea through George Peabody College for Teachers, his alma mater.*

6. Capable of suspending judgment in weighing alternatives; willing to risk once goals are decided upon

7. Feeling without apology and with understanding of the noncognitive dimensions of being

8. Inquiring, analyzing, and synthesizing to explore and assess problems and deal with their complexity

9. Evaluating to direct his own growth and offer feedback to those with whom he interacts

10. Free to be himself and capable of having an impact on others through his integrity of being.

The reader will recognize that this view of humankind requires the educative process to free people to be themselves. It values autonomy and independence as well as concern for others and interdependence. It decries stereotypes which societies can press upon their people, and the imposition of constraints and conventions through roles which can retard the individual's growth. It calls for the development of persons who have the courage, capability, and motivation to endeavor to change what they do not like about themselves, their lives, their cultures, their world.

Assumptions Give Directions for Practice

In accordance with the foregoing view of humankind the following assumptions are made about learners and the processes of learning:

1. Direct experience provides the impetus and substance from which learners make their personal meanings.

2. Experience contributes best to continued learning when it promotes the development of thinking and feeling processes.

3. The curriculum which enables learners to make associations and perceive interrelationships among the disciplines of knowledge and their component skills is interdisciplinary, integrated, and organized around themes of interest to learners.

4. Effective evaluation is an ongoing process, more formative than summative in nature; it concentrates on growth from benchline data rather than on idiographic comparisons.

5. For maximum learning, each person must be valued for himself with his uniqueness recognized and respected.

6. Autonomy and cooperation in learning are encouraged when learners assume responsibility for the teaching and learning of self and others.

Assumptions provide directions for practice. In the sections that follow, we attempt to clarify the meanings of our premises for the processes of educating, thereby suggesting *some alternatives for the schools.* Our purposes are to share our perspective on education with our readers, invite them to examine the match of our assumptions with our recommended practices, and to encourage them to do the same with their own perspectives.

Developing Personal Meanings

During the first decade of this century, Dewey advanced the idea that education and the process of living are synonymous—or should be.[1] "Live and Learn" was the adage. It refers to the importance of experience in providing people with the means of making their own meanings, that is, of learning.

Our meanings are made through our firsthand concrete experiences with the stuff and people of our worlds. We know that direct interaction with our environments enlarges our awareness of what

---

[1] John Dewey. *Experience and Education.* Kappa Delta Pi, 1938. New York: Collier Books, 1968.

Marian Letizia Martinello *was born into an Italian-American community in New York City in 1935. The internal conflicts she experienced with regard to ethnic identity vs. assimilation into the dominant culture influenced her later choice of education as a profession. She earned bachelor's and master's degrees at Queens College of CUNY and taught in public schools in New York and in Berkeley, California where she worked with children of varied minority groups. After serving as a laboratory school teacher for the University of California, she taught at Queens College while completing doctoral work at Teachers College, Columbia University. In 1970 she joined the faculty of the University of Florida where she worked extensively with teachers and black children from rural backgrounds. Currently a member of the Division of Education of the University of Texas at San Antonio, Dr. Martinello is involved in programs for the education of teachers for multicultural communities and in program development for the education of Mexican American children.*

there is to learn, what we have learned, what we need to learn, and what we want to learn. But the school has tended to stress vicarious experiences, that is, those experiences which are translated for the learner before he has a chance to have his own. The tendency has grown to teach for pieced learnings rather than whole meanings. Where this has been done, students have learned to rely on teachers and texts, on the translators and the translations, more than on themselves for their learnings. They thus became dependent learners with limited perceptions and borrowed meanings; they became increasingly closed to new direct experience and distrustful of their thoughts, feelings, and abilities to learn for themselves.

One alternative is to change the nature of opportunities for experiences the school offers from vicarious and superficial to direct and probing for the development of learnings which have, for the learner, present purposes rather than largely future functions. For example, if the school proposes to develop literacy and computation skills, it would do well to offer learners opportunities to:

1. Use language to communicate their personal experiences, thoughts, and feelings to others rather than to complete prescribed exercises which are essentially unrelated to their reasons for wanting to use language;

2. Read to explore their questions and problems or their expressed and emerging interests rather than plod through materials which have little relation to their interests or backgrounds;

3. Use and manipulate numbers within personally relevant contexts rather than complete workbook pages without comprehension of their purpose.

If the school intends to teach learners about their environments, it would do well to engage them with the substance of those environments in ways which promote intimacy with what is to be learned. It must see its responsibility for developing interests, encouraging depth of study, promoting reflection on experience for its reconstruction, and exposing learners to varied perspectives from which to view themselves and their environments.[2]

Direct experience promotes involvement. Involvement generates interest, the quest to know and find out. Interest requests new experiences and further involvement. And so, personal meanings are sought and made.

Education and the Good Life

Literacy is not enough; more is needed to live a personally satisfying life. People grow from their myriad experiences by thinking and feeling at increasingly higher levels of sophistication. As the ability to perform each human process is developed, the person becomes an increasingly autonomous learner. He becomes more open to new experience and better able to make connections between past and present experiences, produce change within himself, and perhaps, bring about change in the environment.

Consider the curriculum of daily life. In addition to reading, writing, and computing, there are decisions to be made, risks to be taken, values to be lived by, feelings to be expressed, thoughts to be received, pondered, and communicated. Each of us attempts these

[2] See chapter by Jessie Roderick on studying settings.

things every day; even the most literate among us experience difficulty in doing them well.

The single most valuable contribution the school can make to each person is the development of his or her abilities to make sense out of life and enjoy its richness. We awaken each morning to a personal wealth of twenty-four hours yet unspent. The school might teach us how to spend them well. They cannot be spent well if individuals are constantly striving to live up to others' expectations and views of what they should do or be. They cannot be spent well if external norms become more important than personally satisfying values.

The school has tended to acculturate for constraining rather than liberating the student's person. Sometimes openly, most times tacitly, learners in the United States have been taught that they should aspire to wealth, power, and status defined rather narrowly in terms of money and material possessions, control over others without reciprocity, and the acknowledgment by others that one has risen above them.[3] Learners have been exposed to these values by much of what was said, done, and required in their schooling. Some adopted the values, strove to achieve the implied goals, and succeeded. Others failed. Some withdrew. Some rebelled. It may be that those who succeeded may not be living their days as well as those who rebelled. By seeking the "wealth" derived from many and varied experiences, the "power" of fate-control, and the "status" derived from feeling good about oneself, one's ways of being and the personal direction of one's growth, the divergent ones, as Hampden-Turner [4] suggests, may be living rewarding lives despite their schooling. The school might have made their pursuit of the good life less painful. It *can* do so for future generations.

An alternative for the school is to educate learners in, for example: *perceiving* from many and varied perspectives; *communicating* thoughts and feelings in reciprocally open, honest, and constructive ways; *loving* by spending oneself in trusting, empathic, and mutually enhancing relationships; *problem solving* and *decision making* which consider varied alternatives and their consequences; *creating* for the generation of innovative possibilities in all facets of human thought, feeling, and action; and *valuing* to continually

[3] Marian L. Martinello and George M. Schuncke. "Wealth, Power and Status as the Hidden Goals of American Education." Unpublished paper, College of Education, University of Florida, Gainesville, 1975.

[4] Richard Hampden-Turner. *Radical Man.* Cambridge, Massachusetts: Schenkman Publishing Co., 1970.

determine one's own livable code of ethics.[5] During each school day, the processes of human living and being come into play. Too often, the shared and explored values, problems, decisions, relationships, communications, and perceptions are determined by and considered the exclusive province of the teacher. The school can and must help learners develop their abilities to perform these processes, thereby teaching them to do more than memorize others' meanings and unthinkingly adopt others' values. Young as well as older students may be encouraged to raise questions about each new experience merely by being invited to do so. Their questions can lead to new directions for study. As problems arise, they can be asked to work at exploring and resolving them. When decisions must be made, they can be asked to participate in making them. When questions of risk taking and valuing arise, they can be invited to think about what is just and good for themselves and their peers. When feelings come to the fore, they can be encouraged to express them, understand them, and create from them.

The point we wish to make is that curriculum must be viewed as designed for learning goals which seek more than proficiency in the 3 R's or adoption of all that is traditionally held sacred. It must offer learners opportunities to learn to direct the course of their own lives. In the practicing, they will learn to live their days well and better than most of us can honestly claim to be doing.

This alternative for education is far less easily pursued than that which the school has chosen in the past. It is not difficult to find teachers who are literate and knowledgeable of the traditional goals. To find those who are sophisticated in the processing capabilities and who are models of the image of humankind as profiled at the start of this chapter will require dramatic changes in criteria for teacher education and selection. We might start by attracting some rebels to our ranks.

Learners' Interests and the Curriculum

Reflect for a moment on those learning experiences of greatest significance to you. What made them memorable?

Impact. Scrutiny. Recollection. Renewal. These have been advanced as qualities of aesthetic experience.[6] They may also be

---

[5] Louise M. Berman. *New Priorities in the Curriculum.* Columbus, Ohio: Charles E. Merrill Publishing Company, 1968.

[6] Kenneth Clark. *Looking at Pictures.* New York: Holt, Rinehart, and Winston, 1960.

considered qualities of memorable learning experiences—those which have made the process of learning enjoyable as well as productive.

A learning experience which has *impact* on the learner captures his attention. It causes him to do a double take, to come back for another look, because he was so taken by the first encounter.

Scrutiny means depth of study. It is evident in experiences which encourage the learner to probe, explore, examine, and deepen his understandings of what he is studying.

Recollection entails the reconstruction of experience. It is reflection focused on finding the fit between goals and achievements, past learnings and new meanings, and the directions these insights offer for additional experiences.

Renewal comes from increased awareness of the array of possibilities for examining any subject of study and consciously perceiving from different perspectives. The experience which renews the learner broadens his knowledge of alternative ways of perceiving himself and the environment.

We submit that impact, scrutiny, recollection, and renewal are evident in all experiences of significance to learners at any age. Unfortunately, much of students' schooling has not captured and maintained their interest, promoted their desire to study beyond established requirements for demonstrating achievement, encouraged their conscious reconstruction of experience or reflection on personal growth, or enhanced their perceptual abilities and, therefore, enlarged their insights. One indicting piece of evidence is the paucity of school experiences each of us can recall as memorable.

On analysis, it seems that the school has erred in not giving sufficient attention to the interaction of cognitive and affective goals of education. Receiving and responding behaviors are requisites of all learnings. According to Krathwohl, Bloom, and Masia, these learnings are concerned with awareness and attention, appreciation, enjoyment, and satisfaction—*interest.*[7]

An alternative for the school is to use the interests learners bring with them as topics of serious study and generate enthusiasms for new ones, building, in the process, interdisciplinary and integrated curricula. Basic skills as well as the processing capabilities referred to in the foregoing section can be developed by teaching

[7] D. R. Krathwohl, B. Bloom, and B. Masia, editors. *Taxonomy of Educational Objectives: The Classification of Educational Goals, Handbook II: Affective Domain.* New York: David McKay Publishing Co., 1964.

from themes of interest. Test the assumption. Take a topic of personal interest and consider its possibilities for learnings in each and all of the traditional curriculum areas. For process learnings, consider the possibilities of that theme for the development of capabilities in communicating, perceiving, decision making, problem solving, valuing, and creating.

Consider, for instance, the learning experiences which might arise from learners' interest in stamps. Possibilities come to mind for oral and written language development as through the study and procurement of first day covers; of computative activities relative to stamp values and the currency of different nations as reflected in their postage; of aesthetic awareness and expression in the examination, appreciation, and creation of stamp designs; of inquiry into stamp origins, their historical and cultural significance and their use. One activity leads to another to promote an integrated approach to learning. When this occurs, in-school learning more closely approximates the natural interplay of cognition and affect in nonformal learning situations. Education then takes on a richness and depth for the learner because he sees the value of learnings both he and his teacher seek for his acquisition.

We are not suggesting that curriculum be developed in a capricious way, subject to the whims of the moment or the few. Rather, we believe that learnings are more readily sought and acquired and remembered when they are desired by learners. Building and fanning such desire is a very real option for the school. It is not as risky as those routes the school has taken in the past. But it is far more complex and demanding. Therein lies its professional challenge.

Evaluation To Promote Growth

Historically, schooling has served a number of functions.[8] A primary function has been to weed out those who were not to be permitted to proceed to the next, more advanced level. Although there were numerous reasons for this selection process, two of the most significant were: (a) nations in their early stages of development did not have the economic base to support mass education and (b) only a smaller and smaller percentage of the populace were actually needed by the society at each succeeding level of education.

---

[8] Benjamin S. Bloom, J. Thomas Hastings, and George F. Madaus. *Handbook on Formative and Summative Evaluation of Student Learning.* New York: McGraw-Hill Book Co., 1971.

It followed that if a major press of primary education was to eliminate numbers of students, then procedures such as examinations had to be developed and instituted around a defined and graded set of learning tasks at the respective levels. As a result, much of the time, energies, and thinking of teachers and administrators were given to the grading and classifying of students. It is understandable that in the process, our very thinking and feeling about the nature and purpose of schooling were subtly but strongly shaped.

Whether and how the sorting and labeling of learners affected them was not (and frequently still is not) a major concern of the educator. This too is understandable because the system has worked well in that it has retained a high percentage of those students who could and did succeed in school at the higher levels. At the same time, it has provided data other than mere personal opinion for eliminating the others.

Today, as more nations are developing increasingly complex economic and social systems, there is a growing awareness of the necessity for continuing education for all, whatever their status in the labor force or in the broader society. It is also recognized by leaders in these developing countries that schooling can be an effective instrument for indoctrination. Coupled with the above two forces is the strong press by the masses for upward mobility through schooling as they learn about other peoples of the world through the mass media of radio and television.

We note, therefore, as we look about, that an increasingly large proportion of the budgets of nations is being devoted to education and that this is more pronounced, as a general rule, in those nations which are the most developed economically. Education in the United States is an illustration of this phenomenon, that is, mass education through the secondary level is virtually a requirement and study at the community college level is moving in that direction. At the same time, it is fascinating but tragic to observe how, in our society, the narrow interpretation of the evaluative process continues to be evidenced in the devising of instruments and the securing of data to enable and justify the elimination of students. This continues even though it is no longer nearly as relevant to our actual goals as it was at one time and neither is it relevant to our desired goals, that is, universal continuing education for a democratic society. Unfortunately, our thinking has so tenaciously held to a selection function for education that evaluation has become an emotion-laden term.

It is only relatively recently that the effects on students of this categorization and labeling through summative or terminal evaluative procedures have been studied.[9] The impact on the individual's perception of self as competent or incompetent, worthy or unworthy, desirable or undesirable is only beginning to emerge; as yet, it is far from being widely recognized. However, as these insights appear, efforts are also appearing which are designed to change the operational function of evaluation from the classifying and labeling of students toward the securing of data needed to facilitate their learning.

The school might endeavor to change the concept of evaluation *from* that of testing to exclude people from school, through the judging of achievement in static terms of a classificatory nature, *to* that of obtaining and using data for continually modifying the nature of instruction and learning. What is needed are systematic means for monitoring what is happening to learners and changing techniques and procedures when these are seen to be antithetical to the desired goal of individual growth and development. As this occurs, such "in process" or formative assessment makes possible the reduction, if not the elimination, of the aversive effects of the examining process. Evaluation should provide helpful feedback crucial to continued effective learning.

Valuing the Learner's Person

In the 30's Boyd Bode wrote the timely and propitious *Progressive Education at the Crossroad*. Almost a half century later, it would not be untimely for a book to be written entitled *Public Education at the Crossroad*. The major issue with which this book would deal would be whether the essential function of the school is to de-emphasize individuality or to nurture and enhance it.

In much of the world the press is on for education to be employed as an instrument for molding people to the prescriptions of particular ways of thinking and feeling. This was evident in Germany during the 30's and is strikingly apparent today in China. The leaders of emerging nations reach quickly for control of the school, recognizing it as a powerful instrument for shaping the minds and hearts of people.

With the tremendous advance in technology, especially the development of radio, screen, and television, the means for reaching

    [9] Nicholas Hobbs. *The Futures of Children*. San Francisco: Bass Publishers, 1975.

people effectively has multiplied the potential for de-emphasizing the uniqueness, the individuality of man. Morris and Tesconi [10] view our technological culture as dehumanizing, denying the affective part of man, particularly as regards the human need for self-esteem through the assertion of individuality.

We believe that for maximum learning and for maximum richness of living, each person must be valued for himself with his uniqueness recognized and not only respected, but revered: *I am a self and you are a self and I don't want to be made to feel guilty if I am not like you nor should you be made to feel guilty if you are unlike me.*

There is an alternative for the school: It can assume a function very different from that of systematically extinguishing variety, reducing difference, and discouraging uniqueness. The school must assume, as one of its primary functions, the nurturing of variety, the emphasizing of difference, the encouraging of a sense of identity, a sense of self in each student. No longer should the school say to the immigrant, the black, or the poor white: "You are only of worth, you can only feel good about yourself . . . if you learn to look, behave, and think and feel in prescribed ways." When the school says this to children, then as adults they are compelled to expend huge amounts of energy in a struggle to BE themselves. Even when this is achieved, there frequently is still a residual and pervading sense of guilt.

Dewey wrote of the school's assimilative function; he was concerned about developing a sense of community and cooperation among people. He would not have subscribed to dehumanization; he would have been appalled at the subtle and not so subtle ways in which the school has stamped out difference under the banner of developing one people with a strong sense of nationhood. Morris and Tesconi state:

> . . . we have taken Dewey's rather moderate view of the school's assimilative function and made it a sort of moral imperative. We ignore the fact that assimilation destroys differences. Moreover, continuance of the "melting pot" ideology leads to the type of homogeneity necessary to bureautechnocracy and contributes to the decline of *person*. The carry-over of the "melting pot" ideology—from a period when it *may* have been *partially* defensible to an era which already suffers too much homogenization—is misguided and even dangerous. It has already led to a situation in education wherein we cannot tolerate difference in language or

---

[10] Van Cleve Morris and Charles A. Tesconi. *The Anti-Man Culture.* Urbana: University of Illinois Press, 1972.

even language styles, culture, habits, thought patterns, behaviors, and personalities. For example, our talk about achievement in school *suggests* a concern with individuality. If we reward achievement per se, then by definition we appear to be thinking in terms of the individual. But we do not reward achievement as such; rather, we reward the achievement (largely teacher perceived) of certain character types with which the teacher can deal.[11]

The race will be a close one insofar as the alternative chosen by the school. Every time you or I or some other is so shaped and trained that we give up our sense of selfhood in some small or major way, then we are that much more ready to assist in the elimination of difference, of selfness, in some other. The converse is equally true: If I am a real identity, then I will assist you in becoming you.

In short, can the school choose between the need to cultivate the cooperative, social aspect of education and, in doing so, avoid the pitfall of reducing or eliminating the uniqueness of the individual? This leads us to our last major alternative, that is, the balance between responsibility for one's self and responsibility for others.

The School and Socialization

In the 60's one of the authors wrote as follows:

Historically the school has taught the three R's and it has left much of the process of socialization and the development of values—at least officially—to the home, church, and community. It is conceivable that we may someday see the home formally assuming the student's intellectual education, with the school becoming primarily a center for socialization.[12]

A major theme throughout this chapter has concerned the legitimization of the school's role as a purveyor and developer of values. This section is designed to bring the various elements of that thesis sharply into focus.

One reason that children traveled to a school was the need for them to gather in the physical proximity of a teacher, that is, a conveyor of knowledge and skills. Trudging to the country school and, in recent decades, riding the school bus have continued this gathering of children together with a teacher.

However, this need to place children within hearing and seeing distance of the information source at a central location is disap-

[11] *Ibid.*, p. 143.

[12] William D. Hedges. "Will We Recognize Tomorrow's Elementary School?" *NEA Journal* 56: 9-12; December 1967.

pearing. The information is now at our finger tips via the radio, television, and most recently the computer-based instructional terminal and interactive television located in the home. So, the question is: Why send children to school? The response will increasingly be: There is today less reason than formerly to send children to school—if the function of the school is primarily that of transmitting information and developing literacy skills. These can be acquired at individually guided rates and routes via computer controlled instructional programs centered in the home. But as we have argued in the foregoing sections, education is not limited to basic skills and information acquisition. With Joyce, we believe that education has at least three particularly important dimensions: intellectual, social, and personal.[13] We have discussed the school's role in creating a citizenry of self-motivating, self-starting, self-instructing, perpetual learners. The desired graduates are both teachers and students, persons who work at becoming increasingly sophisticated in thinking and feeling, who understand themselves and can direct the course of their lives with a sense of satisfaction in doing so, persons who perceive their responsibilities to and feel community with their fellow human beings.

A purpose of education is social: learning how to relate to, share with, learn from, care about, and be sensitive toward others. Conceived as a center where people learn to experience one another, thereby enlarging their perceptions and their abilities to interact with and relate to others, the school becomes an institution, within the total learning laboratory of its community, which is instrumental in improving the social life of that community. Children and adults who assume responsibility for teaching one another will acquire a sense of belonging and contributing while strengthening their command of skills used and knowledge communicated. Teachers who are sensitive to the dynamics of interpersonal interaction provide the guidance and feedback necessary for this to occur in all facets of school activity.

We believe that the alternatives we have suggested for the school have significance for improving the quality of education. The image of humankind which we have proffered is applicable, indeed, desirable for all to aspire to, but paths to its attainment may differ. Admittedly, our biases are evident in all our recommendations. Though we feel entitled to our biases, we also recognize

[13] Bruce Joyce. *New Strategies in Social Education*. Chicago: Science Research Associates, 1972.

the rights of persons who value differently to shape their schools to better match their assumptions about teaching and learning. So, we suggest that the public school be reconceived as *schools* offering alternative approaches to education drawn from different philosophical bases.

Alternative Schools

A critically important task for all of us concerned with education is to identify an array of possibilities which will enable a number of the value-based alternatives people want in the school but which either are not now available or are only accessible to minute percentages of the populace. With such an identification, we might then initiate action to bring these alternatives into existence or to increase their prevalence.

We will not belabor the point that there are too few alternatives currently available to students and teachers. This is well documented in the critiques of education. What we *are* suggesting for education is similar, in some respects, to what we have had in this country in religion for many generations, that is, a diversity of environments which match the diversity in expectations, needs, feelings, attitudes, and opinions of their clients. In so suggesting, we are also recognizing that educational principles and practices are based on faith, on feelings, on intuition and preference as well as reason.

There are data to suggest that people can and do learn in school, but much of what they learn, if we pause to think about it, is not what we would have chosen for them. For example, all learners search eagerly for evidence of their self-worth. Schools, as presently designed, deny evidence of adequacy to many through denying opportunities for successful learning experiences. This suggests a need either that the school change through increasing the heterogeneity of its offerings or, as some have suggested, that it assume a coordinating role that will enable its learners to achieve success experiences in other community institutions. It is not defensible to continue to support an institution which enables only a few to succeed, while so many others seem inevitably to fail.

The fact that parents not only have differing expectations about the purposes of the school but are becoming more vocal in their expressions of these differences is encouraging. It is encouraging because as parents increasingly insist on becoming involved in the decision-making processes, it is probable that they will push for opportunities for experiences in the school and community that will help their children toward successful achievement. It is important for the school not only to recognize this reality of the need for increased parental involvement in decision making, but also to view it as desirable. We have tended to keep parents at arm's length and in a submissive posture. If we can come to understand that when we share the decision making we also share the responsibility for the results, perhaps some of our defensiveness can be overcome. If we cannot support such sharing we are likely to see a continuing disenchantment by groups of parents resulting, in some cases, in the establishment of alternative private schools.

To consider the needs and values of clients without reference to those of their consultants is to deny the professional his identity. Like parents and learners, teachers have preferences and priorities for the process of education. Public school situations often require teachers to be servants—to do the bidding of others without reference to their own wishes. The choice they have is limited to remaining in a public school teaching position or leaving. Those who remain learn to "play the game," to survive in an institution that prizes conformity and conservation of the values of the culture-in-dominance. To the degree that teachers do this, to the degree that they adopt a set of values that the school prescribes without considering those they might wish to hold and influence their behaviors as educators, they are denying their professional identities.

There may be a strong link between faddism in education and some teachers' inadequately defined and unclarified assumptions about knowledge and knowing, learners and learning. The professional practices from a philosophical framework which teachers develop as they practice and which is influenced by the ways they find themselves behaving most comfortably. They have their own set of expectations for their behavior, and continually check their behavior against the values to which they subscribe. By contrast, the functionary behaves in accordance with the expectations of others and, thus, rarely assumes responsibility for maintaining a correspondence between his behaviors and the values to which he is expected to subscribe. And so, he is faulted for not practicing what he preaches. The point is that he has not made the connection between belief and behavior because he has not felt the need or had the opportunity to determine what assumptions he holds about human development, learning, and teaching.

Determining what one believes as an educator is difficult. It requires thinking through one's values, testing the meanings of those values for practice, and associating with those who understand enough to give constructive feedback, who agree enough to provide reinforcement, and who, because they are going through the same process, are able to offer support born of empathy.

It is not easy for a teacher to test professional assumptions in situations where those assumptions are not shared or understood or considered legitimate. In schools in which teachers associate and collaborate because they share a common philosophy, sets of learning goals, and a preferred methodology, the professional staffs enjoy the opportunity—indeed, the necessity—of improving the practice of their shared philosophy. Such schools can thrive on the *esprit de corps* which teachers, administrators, and parents of similar philosophical bent and bias can develop. The challenge of contradictory viewpoints on education is offered by the coexistence of schools which do not apologize for what they value but allow their values to stand out in high relief for the scrutiny of proponents and antagonists. This is possible because professional staffs and clients, brought together on the basis of agreement with the premises from which they work and think about education, can prevent the dissipation of energies over hostilities which emerge among people of different perspectives when they fail to understand one another's viewpoints or acknowledge the possibility that viewpoints other than their own are worth entertaining.

Like parents, teachers want to improve the quality of education they offer students. To improve something, one must consider possibilities for change. The teacher cannot feel free to test and evaluate ideas for change toward improving his teaching and the learning of his students unless he enjoys some degree of professional autonomy—autonomy made explicit, encouraged and protected, and reinforced over time. Teachers do not usually believe they enjoy autonomy to test their own ideas because they feel the constraints of bureaucratic rules that appear to be inconsistent with their purposes, and worse, their philosophies as well.

The school has a responsibility to offer teachers opportunities to be *scholar-teachers,* professionals who inquire into their work and contribute to their profession's body of knowledge, as Schaefer defines the term.[14] But inquiry entails risk and risk can most effectively be tolerated in an atmosphere of trust and support. In schools where the expectations of the professional staff and clients are

---

[14] Robert J. Schaefer. *The School as a Center of Inquiry.* New York: Harper & Row, 1967.

similar, arising from a shared conceptual framework for viewing the educative process, teachers are most likely to risk trial of different ways of working with learners and seek evaluation of what they are doing in terms of their school's educational orientation and commitments. Accordingly, the inquiry and its associated evaluation can be more open, more honest, and more likely to provide guidelines for better accomplishing what all parties agree the school purports to accomplish.

Inasmuch as our culture requires people to make decisions that will influence the qualities and characteristics of their life styles, their work, their government, their economy, their culture and society, we submit that they have a *right* to decide. That right should be recognized and protected by the schools. It is best protected when opportunities to participate in decision making are offered clients and professionals alike. A way to encourage decision making for the guidance of learning is for the schools to offer alternatives—from alternative learning activities to alternative educational programs.

We hope the reader will examine the premises for quality education that we have offered here with an eye to clarifying his or her own. The intent is to encourage the identification of alternatives for educational programs which have solid philosophical bases as well as offer clients and professionals rich opportunities to choose wisely for themselves.

11

Curriculum Leadership: That All May Feel, Value, and Grow

Louise M. Berman

*G*ood times! Hard times! War! Peace! All manner of changes take place within communities, within cities, within nations, within the world! Yet despite the shifts, complexities, and uncertainties which may characterize much of modern living, the need persists for educating children and youth—indeed all persons!

Two groups of questions must be considered when we ponder the place of education in a democratic society. The first area of concern has to do with the differences of background, outlook, viewpoints, desires, and goals persons responsible for the nurturing of children and youth in the ways of the culture bring to their tasks. These differences can add richness to living and schooling.

A second group of concerns has to do with finding and developing commonalities in thinking and behaving that might be useful as educational leaders go about their work. Commonalities are necessary in societies which prize caring, collaboration, and mutuality.

Diversity and *commonness*—these qualities are characteristic of a democracy. These are qualities that must be considered when planning for schooling. ·These are qualities that must be integral to concerns about educational leadership. Thus the themes of diversity and commonness are foundational to this chapter.

Curriculum Leadership: Diversity of Background

Persons act in light of what at the moment seems to be the most sensible way of acting. They behave in terms of facts as they perceive them, not as others see them.[1] Individuals who become principals, curriculum directors, teachers, supervisors, or teacher aides see life as they have perceived it, participated in it, and abstracted from it.

Yet life today and in the recent past is and has been characterized by increasing diversity of ideology and experiences. Thus, individuals stepping into positions where they assume responsibility for the nurturing of persons in a variety of educational programs are apt to bring unusual blends of experiences. The home, the school, and the culture in general are contexts from which lasting perceptions are derived. Perceptions relative to life, death, happiness, anxiety, and self-understanding have been generated by the settings through which persons pass en route to assuming positions of leadership. These perceptions, stored as memories, may influence the nature of future leadership.

Influences of the Home

If attention is given to the perceptions that persons bring to their tasks, we cannot neglect the strong impact of homes. Sociologists have characterized the orientations of homes in various ways. It is not our intent to attempt a detailed analysis but rather to mention that various types of homes can have very different webs of interrelationships, priorities, and complexities evident in them.[2]

[1] Arthur Combs and Donald W. Snygg. *Individual Behavior: A Perceptual Approach to Behavior.* Revised edition. New York: Harper & Brothers, Publishers, 1959. p. 17.

[2] Much literature exists on the many types of homes found in the United States and other parts of the world. One can consider the effect of urban or rural living upon the home. Or the home can be examined from psychological, sociological, or mental health stances. See: R. D. Laing and A. Esterson. *Sanity, Madness, and the Family.* Second edition. New York: Basic Books, Inc., Publishers, 1971. Examples of literature from which one can derive insights about the impact of the home, especially upon the adolescent include: Glen H. Elder, Jr. "Adolescent Socialization and Development." In: Edgar F. Borgatta and William W. Lambert, editors. *Handbook of Personality Theory and Research.* Chicago: Rand McNally and Company, 1968. pp. 239-364; Erik H. Erikson. *Identity: Youth and Crisis.* New York: W. W. Norton & Company, Inc., 1968; Hans Gerth and C. Wright Mills. *Character and Social Structure: The Psychology of Social Institutions.* New York: Harcourt, Brace, & World, Inc.,

Keenly aware of the awesomeness and potential grandeur of the person, **Louise M. Berman** is especially interested in what can be done so that persons have opportunities to live quality lives. Currently she is a professor at the University of Maryland, College Park. Among her professional activities have been serving as Associate Secretary of ASCD, as a member of its Board of Directors, and on certain other ASCD committees and commissions. Because of her interest in persons representing diversity of backgrounds, she is also active in the World Council on Curriculum and Instruction. She has written a number of articles and books and has co-authored Curriculum: Teaching the How, What, and Why of Living (Charles E. Merrill Publishing Company, 1977) with Jessie Roderick.

For example, certain homes are characterized by participation of all family members in the decision-making process, lack of stated standards of "rightness" and "wrongness,"[3] absence of binding relationships among family members, and a future rather than a past or present time orientation. Intellectual maturity, emotional stamina, and possession of relevant information—essential ingredi-

---

1953; William Glasser. The Identity Society. New York: Harper & Row, Inc., 1971; Julius Segal, editor. The Mental Health of the Child: Program Reports of the National Institute of Mental Health. Rockville, Maryland: National Institute of Mental Health, 1971; Kaoru Yamamoto. "Man in Urban America." In: Edwin L. Herr, editor. Vocational Guidance and Human Development. Boston: Houghton Mifflin Company, 1974. pp. 83-108. The fact that setting alone does not determine one's basic attitudes and values is discussed in: William McCord and others. Life Styles in the Black Ghetto. New York: W. W. Norton & Company, Inc., 1969. McCord and his co-authors discuss such life styles as "The Stoic," "The Defeated," "The Achiever," and "The Revolutionary."

[3] See Madeleine L'Engle's chapter in this book for a further discussion of values. For an analysis of different ways of dealing with values, see: Douglas P. Superka and others. Values Education Sourcebook. Boulder: Social Science Education Consortium. ERIC Clearinghouse for Social Studies/Social Education, 1976.

ents to quality living and decision making may or may not be highlighted as family members engage in the complexities of living.

In other homes, one may find stated standards of correctness. The young may be given only limited powers of decision, for members of families are arranged in hierarchical rather than egalitarian fashion. Relationships among family members may be seen as binding. Although loyalty may exist to establishments which are a source of income, a sense of community is frequently obtained from familial and other obligatory ties rather than from voluntary arrangements.

Possibly emerging from the above ideology, one may find a third way of living on the part of some individuals. Homes in the traditional sense may not be evident, but rather individuals with highly idiosyncratic life styles may group themselves together on voluntary bases.[4] These "families" can hardly be characterized since commonalities among them may be difficult to find. Public evaluative criteria scarcely apply to them. Perhaps, however, the major distinguishing feature of persons in these cultures is the distaste for the *status quo*. The members of the "families" may seek to withdraw from the larger world or they may seek to change it, sometimes in dramatic ways rather than through procedures of planned change.

Virtually limitless permutations and combinations of these backgrounds of home experience exist. From the great variety of subcultures evident in homes and families comes our educational leadership.

Influence of the School

Although a democratic society should make possible diversity in the schools, it is not until the past decade that one finds a prevalence of heterogeneity of practices. For example, during the 60's many children and youth who are now curriculum leaders may have been undergoing social studies, mathematics, English, science, or other curricula which were erected upon understanding of each discipline. The schools, building upon the work of the giants in the

[4] Midge Decter. *Liberal Parents, Radical Children.* New York: Basic Books, 1975. Also see: Robert Houriet. *Getting Back Together.* New York: Coward, McCann & Geoghegan, Inc., 1971. For a study of a commune which is now in its third generation, see: Benjamin Zablocki. *The Joyful Community.* Baltimore: Penguin Books, Inc., 1971. Another type of commune experience is discussed by William Irwin Thompson. "Lindisfarne: Education for a Planetary Culture." In: Robert R. Leeper, editor. *Emerging Moral Dimensions in Society: Implications for Schooling.* Washington, D.C.: Association for Supervision and Curriculum Development, 1975. pp. 43-67.

various disciplines, sought to make miniature biologists, or historians, or mathematicians of their students. The interests of the learner or the intrinsic worth of the subject for the learner were of secondary significance. Students learned skills of inquiry, but ordinarily within narrowly confined frameworks of the particular disciplines of the particular time. Critical issues of living frequently were left untouched by the schools.

Dissatisfied with a narrow approach to the disciplines, some persons sought to group them into larger categories, designed to enhance meaning[5] or to develop entries to the disciplines based upon the psychological orientations of learners.[6] Requiring critical philosophical and epistemological expertise, many of the redirected considerations of the disciplines went basically unheeded when it came to classroom practice.

Alternative forms of colleges, universities, secondary, middle, elementary, and nursery schools provided another option for children and young persons. Parents, students, and community members hastened into the schools to make decisions formerly reserved primarily for professional personnel. Some people even spoke of closing schools and returning to the apprenticeship patterns characteristic of previous generations.[7] School curricula in certain instances were determined primarily on-the-spot with little formal evaluation conducted.

Other cultures left their marks upon the schools of this country. Among the curricular orientations transplanted to American soil, not least in the felt impact, was the British Primary School with its emphasis upon the individual and the necessity of planning environments in which children can develop in their own ways. Many school districts consequently changed their architectural designs, yet the potential effects of planned environments upon the development of competence in children have remained basically an unexplored area.[8]

[5] Philip Phenix. *Realms of Meaning: A Philosophy of the Curriculum for General Education.* New York: McGraw-Hill Book Company, 1964.

[6] L. Craig Wilson. *The Open Access Curriculum.* Boston: Allyn and Bacon, 1971.

[7] Ivan Illich. *Deschooling Society.* In: Ruth Nanda Anshen, editor. *World Perspectives,* Volume Forty-four. New York: Harper & Row, Publishers, 1971.

[8] See: Constance Perin. *With Man in Mind: An Interdisciplinary Prospectus for Environmental Design.* Cambridge, Massachusetts: The MIT Press, 1970, for an elaboration of the concept of environment as building competence.

Concurrent with the multiple strands developing relative to schooling was a trend on the part of many individuals to keep schools basically as they were with perhaps some minor modifications. Some textbooks might have "multiethnic" pictures and vocabulary; some desks might be unscrewed from the floors and placed in open space; some paraprofessionals might enter the classroom to assist the teacher; some tests might be checked for cultural bias. Basically, however, the intent, curriculum plan, and structure of the schools have undergone only minor changes. Consequently, the effect of formal instruction upon the student was probably only insignificantly different from that of preceding generations.

Out of these various orientations to schooling and curriculum have emerged persons who currently assume leadership positions in our schools.

Influences of the Culture

Another potential area of high impact experiences is the culture. As pointed out by Webb in his chapter, many of the young people of the 60's felt a sense of powerlessness and alienation. Only through rebellion, it seemed, could the young shatter the chains which rendered them incapable of exerting positive force. The wars of the time seemed senseless to them and failed to evoke on the part of many any positive feelings or action. Many curriculum workers-to-be developed feelings of cynicism.[9] The cynicism was frequently followed by pangs of anxiety and disquietude. A less than hopeful view of life created a seedbed in which might flourish pessimistic views of life, persons, and schooling.

On the other hand, the culture of more recent years has seen a return to the apathy of the 50's and a feeling on the part of some that the critical need is to carve out a niche in which one can be relatively assured of some form of financial security. Boredom but steadiness, interest in mobilizing for economic welfare, but lack of imagination in the realm of the spirit, have characterized many persons. Many of these individuals are and will be curriculum leaders.

[9] See Rodman Webb's chapter in this book for a fuller discussion of the point. Also see: Jacques Ellul. *Hope in Time of Abandonment.* C. Edward Hopkin, translator. New York: The Seabury Press, 1973; Floyd Matson. *The Broken Image: Man, Science, and Society.* New York: George Braziller, 1964; Charles A. Reich. *The Greening of America.* New York: Random House, Inc., 1970; Theodore Roszak. *Where the Wasteland Ends: Politics and Transcendence in Post-industrial Society.* Garden City, New York: Anchor Books, Doubleday & Company, Inc., 1973.

In any culture one usually finds a dedicated few who are anxious to contribute to the common good and who will assume responsibility for the welfare of others. Such persons may be found as active participants in community groups or in organizations such as Common Cause where they seem to feel that their efforts will make a difference.

Interaction with the environment helps shape a person. The curriculum workers of tomorrow are persons who have been influenced in varying ways by their settings.

Sources of Insight for Curriculum Workers

If diversity is prized in families, homes, and the culture in general, those persons who assume tasks of curriculum leadership in the schools may come with a variety of perspectives. The task of the school, then, is to foster diversity but within a framework containing some common understandings.

In searching for sources which might provide common and valuable foundations for curriculum workers, a number of sources were considered. Because literature on play seemed to combine exciting ideas from a variety of fields and to provide insights useful in considering the potential impact of the curriculum worker on schooling, play is used as a basis for reexamining curriculum leadership.

At first glance, play may appear to be a shallow concept upon which to build certain pervasive and pervading ideas about educational leadership. However, play has within it notions of toying with ideas, of gaining self-mastery, of disciplining one's self to carry out a critical task, of transcending the what-is to reach for what might be. Play has been described as "playful renewal," "the joy of self-expression," and "the mastery of complex life situations." [10] In talking about play as it pertains to the curriculum, Phenix has said that "play may turn out to be the most important feature of the curriculum." [11]

In certain periods of history, and these times seem to be among them, many persons tend to highlight utilitarian ends to the neglect of elements of the human spirit. The intrinsic satisfactions and

[10] Erik II. Erikson. "Play and Actuality." In: Maria W. Piers, editor. *Play and Development.* New York: W. W. Norton & Company, Inc., 1972. p. 131.

[11] Philip Phenix. "The Play Element in Education." *Educational Forum* 29: 297-306; March 1965. Copyright © 1965 by Kappa Delta Pi.

aesthetic qualities of life that give energy and vision to living may be ignored.[12] It is at such times that curriculum workers may need to look to play for new and rewarding insights.

Curriculum workers have traditionally given attention to *homo sapiens,* man the knower, and *homo faber,* man the maker. However, schools can be richer if they give consideration to *homo ludens,* man the player.[13] Let us consider the curriculum worker as *homo ludens* as we search for boldness, freshness, imagination, and integration in the lives of curriculum workers and ultimately in the lives of all whom the schools touch.

The Curriculum Worker as Player

Play has been defined as "what a person does when he can choose the arbitrariness of the constraints within which he will act or imagine." [14] For the remainder of this paper, the curriculum worker, whatever the title, is seen as a player. Obviously some objections may be raised, for schools are seen in large part as places to work. However we are less concerned here with the ethologist's distinctions between play and non-play [15] than with the features of play that can provide some useful perspectives on schooling. Aspects of play given consideration are: (a) enjoying, (b) transcending, (c) questing, (d) mastering, (e) renewing, and (f) expressing. These concepts are seen as possessing fruitful leads for the curriculum worker; therefore each concept is discussed rather generally and then more specifically in terms of the curriculum worker.

Playing as Enjoying

If one watches the play of children, one realizes that enjoyment must accompany their play or they turn to other types of activity. What characterizes a play activity that seems to bring enjoyment? First, the activity is ordinarily carried out spontaneously and autonomously. Second, the player determines the activity's initiation, its rhythm, its direction, and its termination. Third, the activity, lacking routinization or mechanization, brings a sense of exhilaration to the player.

[12] See: Ortega y Gasset. *The Revolt of the Masses.* Authorized translation from the Spanish. New York: W. W. Norton & Company, Inc., 1932.

[13] Johan Huizinga. *Homo Ludens: A Study of the Play Element in Culture.* Boston: The Beacon Press, 1950. Foreword.

[14] Brian Sutton-Smith. "Play as a Transformational Set." *Journal of Health, Physical Education, and Recreation.* 43: 32-34; June 1972.

[15] Michael J. Ellis. *Why People Play.* Englewood Cliffs, New Jersey: Prentice-Hall, Inc., 1973. pp. 17, 18.

On these points, Murphy says, "that play . . . is most playful, when it is spontaneous, evolving from an integration of impulse and ideas and providing expression, release, sometimes climax, often mastery, with a degree of exhilaration, and refreshment. Good play leaves one feeling good, happy, alive." [16]

Play is seen *as* an end; work is activity *for* an end. Therefore adding to the enjoyment of play can be its seeming purposelessness in terms of completing an activity *for* an end.[17] Play provides a setting in which moments of ecstasy [18] and intense involvement occur. In other words, play can unfetter players from the demands of work or duty and help them transcend the here and now. This point is discussed in more detail in the section "Playing as Transcending."

Play is a heightened experience in which the key factor is the enjoyment it brings rather than the task it accomplishes. If we examine the concept of enjoyment from the stance of the curriculum worker as player, certain ideas bearing consideration emerge.

"Glint-in-the-eye behavior." [19] Curriculum workers *as workers,* frequently take themselves and others so seriously that delight, sense of humor, and a liking for persons or tasks are not evident. They may lack "glint-in-the-eye behavior." Curriculum workers *as players* are truly enthusiastic, even ecstatic, about their opportunities to work for and with others, about their freedom to create new and novel situations. Their behavior shows a spark, a vitality, a sense of newness and freshness. In addition, the curriculum worker as player seeks to understand those with whom he works so that he can assist in creating settings where others exhibit "glint-in-the-eye behavior."

Opportunities for voluntary activities. Curriculum workers as players enjoy their activities in part because they have participated

[16] Lois Barclay Murphy. "Infants' Play and Cognitive Development." In: Maria W. Piers, editor. *Play and Development.* New York: W. W. Norton & Company, Inc., 1972. pp. 120, 121.

[17] For further ideas relative to play being the end rather than the means to the end see in addition to Kaoru Yamamoto's chapter in this book: Horace Bushnell. *An Oration Delivered Before the Society of Phi Beta Kappa at Cambridge.* Cambridge: George Nichols, 1848. p. 8; and, Mary Reilly, editor. *Play as Exploratory Learning: Studies of Curiosity Behavior.* Beverly Hills, California: Sage Publications, 1974. p. 87.

[18] See Madeleine L'Engle's chapter in this book for comments on ecstasy.

[19] Michael J. Ellis, *op. cit.,* p. 21.

in selecting them. Because enjoyment is so important, persons may volunteer to explore, examine, toy with an idea. They may throw the idea out after initial examination or they may select to do something worthwhile with it. The need for efficiency can bury an individual's strengths. These strengths or evidences of personal power may become evident when persons on a voluntary basis can engage in activities which excite them.

Bushnell says, "We play because we have in us a fund of life that wants to expend itself." [20] Once teachers and others in the school system feel that their own energizing powers are cut off from renewing the setting of which they are a part, they may find boredom and lethargy setting in. Fun-loving and exciting persons at the helm can help stimulate a re-creative and voluntary spirit in all. Enjoyment is critical to the curriculum worker as player if freshness of person and zest of ideas are cherished. More opportunities for voluntary involvement may bring more enjoyment to those engaged in schooling.

Playing as Transcending

A peculiarly human quality is the desire to look beyond *what is* to *what can be.* Considering the development of a new skill, looking at one's attitudes in terms of which ones should endure and which ones should change, pondering various ways of valuing and the meaning of them for one's own personal code of ethics, fantasizing about what might be—these are all ways of transcending the present.

That a person can transcend the present is possible because an individual can experience privately or intraorganically his own actions. A person feels and these feelings may not be seen or felt by anyone else. However, because an individual can symbolize, he or she can make some sense out of the world. The nature of the symbolic assumes points of reference, and connections between symbols and objects. Thus one's inner world can achieve some semblance of order. [21]

[20] Horace Bushnell, *op. cit.*, pp. 8, 9.

[21] For a discussion of feelings and symbols see the work of Susanne K. Langer. *Mind: An Essay on Human Feeling.* Volume I. Baltimore: The Johns Hopkins Press, 1967. pp. 3-32; *Philosophy in a New Key: A Study in the Symbolism of Reason, Rite, and Art.* New York: Mentor Books, 1942, 1951; *Philosophical Sketches.* New York: Mentor Books, 1962. pp. 53-61. Also see: Hugh Dalziel Duncan. *Symbols in Society.* New York: Oxford University Press, 1968; and Erich Kahler. "The Nature of the Symbol." In: Rollo May, editor. *Symbolism in Religion and Literature.* New York: George Braziller, 1960. pp. 50-73.

But in order to transcend, order is not enough. There must be communication of one's inner reality with others. Private meanings must become public and as communication is opened and shared, a transcending of the mundane, the fragmented, and the unworthwhile can occur.

That play can take us beyond the fragmentation of daily living to more transcendent qualities is obvious if we observe persons engaged in play which leads to greater mastery of one's self or a skill connected with a self-imposed constraint. To gain further insight into the transcending qualities of play, attention is directed briefly to concepts of myth, the aesthetic, and collaboration.

Myth. Myth is frequently described as a belief that is unverifiable. At least a partial truth is found in myth; and because of the potential for belief, myth, like play, can contribute to a person's system of meanings. Myth also resembles play in that frequently it utilizes symbols of significance to a group of persons. Myth has powers to evoke thinking, to stimulate further pursuit of meanings. The importance of myth in play and individual development is ably discussed by L'Engle,[22] Huizinga,[23] Reilly,[24] and Clark.[25] Exposure to myth enables a person to realize what is within his control and what is outside his domain. Myth also provides opportunities for the person to develop coherence in the perception of reality and the part that he as a complex, interrelated and intricate being can play in the society he envisions.

Obviously the curriculum worker needs new images of what might be if he in concert with others is to shift the focus of the institution of which he is part. Myth can provide such images. In addition, myth gives new insights which might change how persons pattern their world. New orders or patterns are necessary if educators are to possess the creative framework for relevant forms of schooling.

The aesthetic. The curriculum worker who is anxious to transcend the mundane needs to search out for himself those areas of living which he finds aesthetically pleasing in order to design sacred aspirations and to implement courageous acts. Transcending the

---

[22] See Madeleine L'Engle's chapter in this publication.

[23] Johan Huizinga, *op. cit.*, pp. 4, 5.

[24] Mary Reilly, editor, *op. cit.*, pp. 99-101.

[25] For a discussion of institutional myth and its vitalizing power, see: Burton R. Clark. *The Distinctive College: Antioch, Reed, and Swarthmore.* Chicago: Aldine Publishing Company, 1970.

mundane can take place in one's personal life as one listens to a great piece of music, investigates the intricacies of a fine relationship, or develops prowess in some new sport.

Professionally, the curriculum worker can build the transcendent into his life when he attempts to bring together a group of diverse persons to focus upon a common problem, or when he makes it possible for colleagues to explore new curriculum designs within settings that are conducive to reflection and generation of new ideas.

The curriculum worker can help others in their search for transcendence by knowing what seems to cause those with whom he works to lead less than glowing lives and by seeking to remove impediments from their existence. For example, for one person the curriculum worker may need to give assistance on jobs which are very detailed. For another, assisting in transcendence may mean bringing a challenging book. For a third, it may mean introducing him to a like-minded person for the exchange of ideas. For a fourth, it may mean providing objective systematic feedback about his classroom behavior so that he may change as he sees fit. The facilitators of and obstacles to transcendence vary from person to person, but the transcending curriculum worker can assist others in their endeavors to find this critical quality of living.

Collaboration. At times persons interested in transcending need to be able to stay simultaneously in an experience and yet out of it, sometimes referred to as "as if" behavior.[26] This form of transcending involves seeing not only one's own experience but also that of others. At other times transcending may involve reaching out to others in an effort to share their common humanity—to be one with others. When persons exhibit "as if" behavior or when they share in fulfilling of common purposes, collaboration may ensue.

Collaboration may take place when persons bring their respective competences to bear upon a research problem; when staff members plan together for a heightened experience for an uninvolved child; when persons think together, dream together, and plan ahead for future events. Collaboration may become the rule rather than the exception of a group of persons, thus enhancing their individual ways of feeling, valuing, and growing.

Another way of collaborating is through a study of the rituals that may have developed in the setting of which one is part. For

[26] For additional discussion see Kaoru Yamamoto's chapter in this book and also Mary Reilly, editor, *op. cit.*, p. 101.

example, one might use ecological procedures to study what the rituals of the school are and then to examine which of the rituals are constructive and which are destructive.[27] Families can study the rituals surrounding holidays or birthdays. Professional personnel might want to study coffee breaks, conversations in lunch rooms, forms of greetings, the types and content of written memos, utilization of certain procedures in bringing about curriculum change or in producing curriculum materials. Rituals are dependable, common aspects which can serve as stabilizing and unifying—but hopefully not deadening—factors in situations where collaboration is prized.

Curriculum workers as players need to plan for those practices which invite attention to myth, focus on the aesthetic and a desire for collaboration. Such practices encourage the pooling of mutual resources in the search for answers to baffling dilemmas.

Playing as Questing

Transcending involves *looking* beyond; questing involves pushing beyond. Transcending may involve passive reflection, looking back, up, or ahead; questing involves active futuristic searching and planning. Transcending may or may not be intentional; questing always involves willful, intentional, knowing behavior. Questing is like play in that it involves challenge, pursuit, digging, applying, knowing—all components of play.

Playing as knowledge seeking. Characteristic of many forms of play is the need to seek knowledge. Consider the tennis player, the football player, the bridge player, or any kind of player to whom knowledge and skill are important. Although play is seen by some as escape from the real world where knowledge is essential, persons who engage in many forms of play are extremely knowledgeable in their area of activity.

Persons search for knowledge when they are aroused by something in the environment and then rearrange old ideas or engage in new syntheses. Certain human functions or processes may trigger knowledge seeking with a person. For example, when a person tries

[27] See Jessie Roderick's chapter in this book for ideas about ecological research. Also see: Seymour B. Sarason. *The Culture of the School and the Problem of Change.* Boston: Allyn and Bacon, Inc., 1971. For a study of the problem of accommodation to change without the loss of continuity see: Benson R. Snyder, M.D. *The Hidden Curriculum.* New York: Alfred A. Knopf, 1971. The problem of ritual within a setting in which rituals have little meaning for the participants is discussed in: Elizabeth M. Eddy. *Walk the White Line: A Profile of Urban Education.* Garden City, New York: Anchor Books, Doubleday & Company, Inc., 1967.

to communicate a concept to another individual or to make a difficult decision, that person may come to see the imperfections of his or her knowledge in a given area or field. The person may then engage in a search for new or more relevant knowledge.

The notion that the environment has and can have many arousing features has many implications for the curriculum worker as player. First, curriculum workers should not ignore stimuli which are "novel, complex, or dissonant." [28] Events might vary from the request for assistance from a teacher wanting to try new evaluative techniques in social studies to a request from a community group desiring programs for the elderly in school buildings. Events might include the suggestion from a teacher that a totally new program be developed in which greater emphasis is placed upon assisting persons in gaining competence in dealing with moral issues to a request for more cognitively oriented materials in reading. When sparked, curriculum workers should garner their resources as they search for responses to the arousal event. At the same time curriculum workers should see as part of their professional repertoire the ability to ignite settings so that teachers and others involved in the educational enterprise have an opportunity to grow through arousing features. Considering the many value-laden questions plaguing our nation, the wise curriculum worker may try to ignite fires which cause teachers to immerse themselves in ideas critical to the development and perpetuation of a just society.

Second, curriculum workers as players need to realize that arousing features for one person may not have the same effect upon another; therefore curriculum workers as they come to know persons must learn what is apt to be stimulating for the various persons with whom they work. For example, some people become vibrant and excited when they are given released time to become a resource person in a given area. Other individuals may thrive on the opportunity to mobilize persons to carry out a task the group deems important.

Third, curriculum workers need to be sensitive to the effect of physical settings upon those who must inhabit them.[29] As curriculum workers exert influence on the plans of buildings, they need to consider whether a building which lets the outside in stimulates an interest in questing. Does the necessity of individuals to move

[28] Michael J. Ellis, *op. cit.*, p. 136.

[29] For a discussion of the interaction of persons and settings, see: Rudolf H. Moos. *The Human Context: Environmental Determinants of Behavior.* New York: John Wiley & Sons, 1976.

about in a small or large space deter or facilitate their desires for questing? What kinds of physical settings seem to foster joy? flexibility of thinking and acting? sense of humor? To what degree does the setting provide the individual with arousing features? [30]

Fourth, if the search for new ideas and new insights is important, then curriculum workers need to encourage all who use the setting to assume responsibility to see that it contains freshness, newness for those who inhabit the setting. Providing for vitality of context can cause people to delve into new and fresh considerations with excitement.

Questing and anxiety. If a person is to quest he or she must have learned how to manage anxieties; otherwise, the individual is apt to return continuously to the familiar. "Theories of play developed by Piaget and by psychoanalytic theorists have suggested that when a child is anxious he will prefer to play with toys on the basis of the relevance to the source of his anxiety, whereas when a child is not anxious he will prefer to play with toys on the basis of their novelty." [31] If we make some inferences from research on children's play, we can suggest that if we are concerned about seeing play behavior, we must watch the level of anxiety a person brings to task performance.

The individual who is overly concerned about himself or his tasks is not apt to bring much excitement to the job. A means of dealing with anxiety either through peer interaction or access to a faculty counselor where anxiety is openly examined is necessary if anxiety is not to stand in the way of creative movement in the school. [32]

Playing as Mastering

Enjoying, transcending, and questing are all important to the process of playing. Yet frequently playing does involve mastering.

---

[30] J. B. Gilmore. "Summary of Play Research." *Journal of Health, Physical Education, Recreation* 43: 29-31; June 1972.

[31] See: Brian Sutton-Smith. "The Role of Play in Cognitive Development." *Young Children* 22: 361-70; September 1967. Copyright © 1967 by the National Association for the Education of Young Children; or R. E. Herron and Brian Sutton-Smith. *Child's Play.* New York: John Wiley & Sons, Inc., 1971. pp. 252-66.

[32] For discussions of the anxiety of teachers and the need for self-understanding see work of Arthur T. Jersild such as: *In Search of Self: An Exploration of the Role of the School in Promoting Self-Understanding.* New York: Bureau of Publications, Teachers College, Columbia University, 1952; and *When Teachers Face Themselves.* New York: Bureau of Publications, Teachers College, Columbia University, 1955.

Think about the person who is constantly seeking greater self-understanding, more self-awareness, or increased personal discipline in daily living. This person is engaged in the art of growing and thus mastering the complexities of life which every human being faces, avoiding "the tyranny of the mediocre." [33]

Yamamoto, in an earlier chapter, describes play as a situation in which the actor is in command—is the master. In the next few paragraphs play as mastery is discussed in terms of achieving a balance between openness and closure in one's activities, understanding wholes, gaining knowledge of rules and skills in techniques, and utilizing resources effectively.

Openness and closure. Playing frequently has a rhythm. When a player masters a pertinent skill, he or she may bring closure to acquiring a given competence, but having achieved a certain level of mastery, opens up for the self new arenas in which exist skills begging to be mastered. The child who builds something to her satisfaction with large blocks may move on to more intricate kinds of constructions utilizing smaller blocks. The tennis player who is temporarily satisfied with his forehand may bring momentary closure to improving skill in that area while he works on his backhand. The temporary feelings of closure accompanied by new challenges needing attention are important features of play.

The curriculum worker as player can establish a rhythm of closure and openness in his/her own life and can provide a setting where others have the opportunity to feel the satisfaction that can come with closure while simultaneously feeling the freshness that can accompany delving into a new area. For example, instead of establishing all long-term committees, curriculum workers can set up *ad hoc* groups that have a specific charge to be carried out in a stipulated period of time. When they bring closure to their tasks, however, these groups should have the option of helping in establishing a new *ad hoc* committee to explore perspectives and insights growing out of previous work. A rhythm of opening and closing can provide a balance of newness and fulfillment—frequent outcomes.

Understanding wholes. In certain kinds of play it is not enough to understand some of the parts. One must understand and fre-

[33] Cornelis Verhoeven. *The Philosophy of Wonder: An Introduction and Incitement to Philosophy.* Mary Foran, translator. New York: The Macmillan Company, 1972.

quently master the whole if the parts are to make sense. In dramatic play, children frequently assign roles to their peers in order to create a "family." Each child, however, enters not only into his or her own role but also into the total situation which the group has created. In a football game a person needs some understanding of and mastery of various tasks of team members in order to fully comprehend his own tasks and carry them out well.

The curriculum worker as player needs an idea of the total system within which he is working, some comprehension of the interrelationship of the parts, and mastery of various tasks that need to be carried out within the system. Likewise the curriculum worker needs to ensure that those who work with him/her also have the opportunity to see and know the total operation of which they are part. It is not enough for an art teacher to be skilled in techniques of teaching painting or for a teacher of mathematics to know the latest skills of inquiry in his/her field. Rather each teacher needs to know the components of that field and others within the school or school system. Only when such mastery of the total setting is achieved can collaborative effort emerge on specific issues crosscutting the curriculum.[34]

Mastery of techniques and roles. Hand in hand with getting a grasp of the total situation, persons need to gain mastery of the techniques and rules governing their own specializations. To master any idea, concept, or skill is ordinarily a struggle—a struggle with certain rules.[35] In group games, competitive games, cooperative games, practice play, and unstructured play, the need for rules and procedures is usually present.[36]

In schools the need to know procedures and rules is obvious. How many experienced and not so experienced teachers have had problems with children and their parents because they have not been aware of the codes of behavior or rules tacitly governing the behavior of the students they teach? How much could be learned if teachers were to videotape their classrooms in order to see con-

[34] One school of curricular thought advocates emphasis on "structure of the disciplines" as a means of schooling. Much of the literature of the 60's was based upon this viewpoint. One example is: G. W. Ford and Lawrence Pugno. *The Structure of Knowledge and the Curriculum.* Chicago: Rand McNally & Company, 1964. This book contains chapters by Joseph J. Schwab, L. H. Lange, Graham C. Wilson, and Michael Scriven.

[35] Johan Huizinga, *op. cit.,* pp. 40, 41. Also see: Rivka R. Eifermann. "Social Play in Childhood." In: R. G. Herron and Brian Sutton-Smith, *op. cit.,* pp. 270-97, 287-88.

[36] *Ibid.*

gruities and incongruities between rules which they think are operating and those that are actually operating!

How much more effectively and quickly might curriculum change come about if proposals for change indicated a clear understanding of the procedures, techniques, and knowledges within the field in which change is being contemplated. The wise curriculum worker will assist in providing a setting where all who live and work in it can be aware of procedures, rules, and techniques, thus cutting down on anxiety, apprehension, and apathy.

People, time, space, materials. Players ordinarily play within constraints of time and space and utilize certain materials. The pool player plays within the constraints of a table, the performing musician needs a responsive piano and a sympathetic audience, the host selects guests congenial to the tone and setting of a gathering.

In schools, the resources are people, time, space, and materials. If we consider people, there are many skills that need to be mastered. In an earlier chapter Yamamoto indicates that persons need to learn to work with themselves, with peers within the group, and with other groups. Knox's Play Scale indicates that participation with persons develops in the following manner:

1. egocentricity and attention demand;
2. interaction with one person, the mother figure;
3. interest in others, primarily through observation;
4. association but not true interaction with peers;
5. cooperation and true interaction with others.[37]

If we are concerned that persons achieve flexibility and skill in working with people, the curriculum worker needs to help establish a setting in which persons are comfortable either to work alone or in concert with others depending upon the nature of the task. Persons need to develop a repertoire of skills related to working with others if the schools are to use adequately the wealth of human resources—both professional and lay—ordinarily found in the school community.

Time and space are usually limited in school settings. Phenix says, "It is because of the need for limitation that the educational system is subdivided by clearly marked boundaries: in time, by class periods, sessions, courses, and grade and degree levels; in space, by classrooms, subjects, departments, divisions, schools, and

---

[37] Susan Knox. "A Play Scale." In: Mary Reilly, editor, *op. cit.*, p. 250.

colleges. Whatever their drawbacks, these demarcations in time and space are necessary to the successful management of teaching and learning." [38]

In less clearly marked ways time and space receive attention in classrooms, as children and teachers attempt to live within the limitations their contexts impose upon them. The active child needing much exercise may find the constraints of the classroom very limiting. The wise curriculum worker is able to help teachers reach beyond the classroom in terms of space. In addition, he/she can help teachers adapt their schedules in some degree to the individual time perspectives of the students.

By learning to observe carefully how children and young people of all ages utilize materials the curriculum worker can plan more fully for their use in creative and meaningful ways.

Playing as Renewing

Persons who take time for play are frequently persons who cherish self-renewal. Playing is a renewing kind of activity, for it frequently involves the confrontation of experience and its consolidation. In addition, play means dealing with complexity and change and developing a community of relationships.

Consolidation of experience. All individuals daily take in new experiences. Frequently, persons become confused because they lack the skills to make sense of the diverse bits of information they accumulate. If, however, people have the opportunity to confront experience as in play and mull it over, they may arrive at new syntheses.[39]

Curriculum workers as players, desiring that those with whom they work consolidate their experiences into new and more meaningful wholes, need to provide settings in which persons can ruminate, reflect, and rest without the necessity of fulfilling some stated purpose. If we cherish consolidation there need to be times in schooling when individuals can gather in a relaxed manner to talk, to think, to deal with trivia, so to speak. In reflection, new solutions to old problems may be found or questions needing answering may appear on the horizon.

[38] Philip Phenix, "The Play Element in Education," in: Ronald Hyman, editor, *op. cit.*, p. 305.

[39] Millie Almy. "Spontaneous Play: An Avenue for Intellectual Development." *Young Children* 23: 276; May 1967.

Change. Unless individuals can deal with complexity, dissonance, and change, society stands to suffer.[40] Educational leaders must be concerned about problems of change or schools will become ordinary places with ordinary programs. Persons who give attention to renewing kinds of experiences may find that schools become extraordinary places with extraordinary programs. Phenix says, "When everybody has to go to school, the experience readily loses its special charm. The 'common school' becomes commonplace. The everyday easily lapses into the humdrum and the routine." [41]

In order to avoid the gripping power of routine and the potential for mechanization, more attention must be given to change.

Play is concerned with the development of capacity to deal with change. It is a personal process in that what is new, complex, or dissonant can only be so in relation to the previous experience of the individual. This conception of play and its place in our evolution past and present, both collectively and individually, calls for a differing leadership style. It is not play if the course of the behavior is determined entirely by a leader. Play comes from the individual exercise of options among opportunities to complexify a private world. The creative response to a setting is highly desirable and cannot by definition be foreseen by the leader or player; hierarchical management of this area of behavior is not effective. More subtle leadership is called for. It will consist of concerted efforts to constructively increase the options open to clients so that end points in a stream of behavior become increasingly difficult to predict. The process will involve a dynamic situation where a manager or facilitator is continuously thinking ahead to open new paths for behavior among his clients so that they progress toward increasing heterogeneity or individuality.[42]

If we are concerned about utilizing insights from play as vehicles for change, then the assumption is that we are more concerned about individuality than homogeneity, more interested in evoking flair than mundaneness.

Play anticipates life and as a result the person at play constantly exhibits "novel behaviors, novel combinations, and novel consequences." [43] It is an anticipatory set of mind which curriculum

[40] For a discussion of the necessity of individuals being attuned to change and creativity, see: John W. Gardner. *Self-Renewal: The Individual and the Innovative Society.* New York: Harper & Row, Publishers, 1964.

[41] Philip Phenix, "The Play Element in Education," in: Ronald Hyman, editor, *op. cit.,* p. 303.

[42] M. J. Ellis. "Play: Practice and Research in the 1970's." *Journal of Health, Physical Education, Recreation* 43: 30, 31; June 1972.

[43] Brian Sutton-Smith, "Play as a Transformational Set," *Journal of Health, Physical Education, Recreation, op. cit.,* p. 32.

workers must try to create with those with whom they work if the schools are to be vehicles of change for the persons within them and for the society in general. Curriculum workers must also be aware of the moral dilemmas inherent in the change process so that change is selective and wise rather than random or inappropriate.

Community of relationships. Certain forms of play may be solitary kinds of activities. Frequently though, persons who enjoy various types of play activities find camaraderie in clubs or organizations in which interest in the area is the key to membership. Consider persons who enjoy sailing and join yacht clubs, chess players who join chess clubs, needlework "bugs" who work together to create, to design, or to display their wares, hikers who join with other like-minded persons to wander on unexplored trails. An excitement and enthusiasm ordinarily pervades the voluntary groups based upon some form of play.

If we apply what we see in voluntary play groups to the functions of the curriculum worker, then attention needs to be given to several areas. First, school settings need to provide opportunities for individuals to be real persons—persons who can express their feelings, their anxieties, their stresses as well as their knowledge. The curriculum worker needs to provide differentiated opportunities for all, ranging from those who are extravagantly excited about an idea to those who feel only moderately interested in it. The curriculum worker needs to be able to express calmness, irritation, joy, anticipation, weariness, and sorrow as well as to accept these human feelings in others. The curriculum worker must be aware that his/her feelings are not the same toward all people and that others have different feelings about different persons.[44]

Second, if we accept the notion that persons should have the opportunity to display personal integrity in the context of the school, then the relationships that emerge from informal relationships should be taken into account as persons get together to work on tasks. Persons who profit from others' company might get together to work on data-gathering techniques or to explore some new perspective for their own classrooms.

Opportunities for supervision on a short-term task can be useful in letting persons explore new relationships. What is happening in

[44] For further discussion of authenticity in relationships, see: C. H. Patterson. *Humanistic Education.* Englewood Cliffs, New Jersey: Prentice-Hall, Inc., 1973. pp. 98-106.

the relationship is as important as seeing that the task is accomplished. Peer teaching, friendships, cooperative projects, and brainstorming are necessary if schools are interested in developing communities where collaboration and cooperation are the norm.

Playing as Expressing

Much of what transpires during play is expressed in some way. Something is communicated or expressed when children engage in dramatic play, when a potter makes a bowl, when a guitarist strums some chords. Expression may take the form of words or of body language. What happens during play can also be communicated through some medium such as clay or fabric.

Playing as expressing often involves the total person; it involves responsiveness to the person and/or medium that may be part of the play experience; it may involve conflict and competition. Playing as expressing is also evident when persons come together for some type of festival.

Total person. First it should be noted that in dynamic kinds of play, the total person may be involved in what he or she does. Observe the actress, the child in the sandbox, the flutist, the football player. Many dimensions of the person—the emotional, the intellectual, the aesthetic, the moral, the social and the physical—may be observed in the individual's activities.

In curriculum work, we frequently do not give adequate attention to the total person. The person's intellect may be brought to the fore, but aesthetic, moral, physical, or social strengths given only tangential, if any concern. More questions relative to the aesthetic qualities of a given curriculum design need to be raised. Astute curriculum workers need to ensure that the moral is placed in perspective in the curriculum. Thoughtful persons are aware of the interdependent aspects of today's world and therefore give attention to the interrelationship of persons. Realizing that a healthy body is critical to a full life, curriculum workers try to ensure that in balancing the total program for which they are responsible, adequate attention is given to the physical needs of the person.

It is not enough for teachers, curriculum directors, supervisors, or any others involved in schooling to sit around arm-chairing behavioral objectives—whether they be in the affective or cognitive domains, or both. What is necessary is that what is actually happening in the schools *now* be described and analyzed. When reality is considered in planning for children, descriptions of the here and now will not fall into the neatly packaged lists of objectives. Rather, reality will force us to deal sharply and critically with questions of value. Descriptions of reality coupled with value propositions can help us develop programs which are adventures in living that call forth the best in the individual's moral, ethical, social, aesthetic, and physical development. The programs may be complex, constantly changing, individualized, difficult to design and administer but if we are interested in the schools making a difference we must consider the individuals who frequent them as *total* persons!

Responsiveness. Implicit in the notion of concern for the total person is the idea that curriculum workers as players assist in establishing a responsive environment. Such an environment fosters an individual's expression so that meaning is established in the communication process. Too long have we been concerned that curriculum leaders express themselves lucidly, clearly, and logically. Too little have we been interested that people "listen intelligently, understandingly, and skillfully to another person." [45] Perceptive listening and the intent to respond within the meaning of the other person may mean quite different styles and levels of communicating than we currently advocate. Our problems with community involvement, student disenchantment with schooling, and the sense of fatigue might disappear if we worked within the framework of meanings that others bring to situations.

Conflict and competition. The literature on play gives attention to conflict and competition, which are critical elements of many play situations. We would not have many of our active sports if competition were not encouraged. Dealing with conflict and competition openly, squarely, and positively is extremely critical in the curriculum also.

For example, the solution to value dilemmas is always difficult when basic principles of democracy are honored. The answers ordinarily are not clear-cut. Many times the questions and issues are not even sharply defined. Critical, however, to democratic behavior is the ability to deal with value questions with humility, resolve, skill, and maturity. Individuals need to debate openly, respecting the other person's point of view while constantly clarifying and changing one's own. It is through the vehicle of honest debate that negotiations on critical issues can eventually take place.

[45] For further development of these points see: F. J. Roethlisberger. *Man-in-Organization.* Cambridge, Massachusetts: The Belknap Press of Harvard University Press, 1968. p. 159.

If the curriculum worker is concerned that issues be brought to the fore, that cooperative means be established to deal with them, then the school needs to be conceived as a "gathering place,"[46] a place where persons can meet other individuals representing a variety of persuasions, a place where forums can be conducted. The gathering place can be a center where critical issues are discussed, where possible solutions to problems are played with, and where discussion, reflection, and even silent struggling may be prelude to the resolution of problems—albeit many resolutions may be imperfect.

The diversity which characterizes the school as a gathering place can also characterize the school district. Different priorities in the curriculum, alternative means of staffing, varying ways of grouping children and young people, and unique modes of handling administrative functions might characterize the system. Diversity within a district might lend itself to problem raising and problem solving.

Festival. One has only to examine any culture to find that festival is a common way of expressing one's desire and need to play. People around the world glory in pretending, in celebrating, in carrying out rituals on a systematic basis. Festival is a way of moving out of ordinary living to extraordinary living. Witness the Mardi Gras; anniversaries; college homecomings; the rites in many cultures surrounding birth, puberty, graduations, marriage, retirement, and death.

Curriculum workers as players can examine the expression of festival in the activities in which the school engages. The touches of humor, gaiety, and extravagance inherent in festival are necessary to ease the tensions which may ensue when conflict and competition accompany the resolution of difficult problems.

Festival can take place when routines are established that have an element of fun; when memos become nonroutine; when an individual's accomplishments are brought out into the open, cherished, and praised rather than hidden; when the routine aspects of schooling are periodically called off so that school and community join together in some festive occasion. Play has both its routine and nonroutine aspects. Both are important. Highlighting festival helps

[46] For a discussion of the school as a gathering place, see: Arthur J. Lewis and Alice Miel. *Supervision for Improved Instruction: New Challenges, New Responses.* Belmont, California: Wadsworth Publishing Company, Inc., 1972.

us better appreciate the significance of routine and nonroutine in life and schooling.

Expressing is the coming to life of the internal processes related to play. Thus expressing is the barometer of the extent and quality of what is happening when insights from play are applied to the curriculum.

So What?

The problems confronting schools today are immense. Problems of unequal distribution of resources, of inferior living for many persons, of the inability of persons to collaborate on finding answers to the dilemmas facing us cause us to look to various areas to shed light upon our concerns. It has been suggested that play provides valuable insights which if applied can make real differences in how curriculum workers approach their daily challenges in a time of diversity. In the final analysis the effectiveness of curriculum workers depends upon their striving for maturity as human beings. Curriculum workers, along with all persons of the educational community, can continue to engage in activities which make them feeling, valuing, and growing human beings.

A Word to Administrators

Louise M. Berman

No shifts in curricular emphases, no changes in programs for children and youth are apt to take place on a large scale unless administrators, school boards, communities and others responsible for children and youth wholeheartedly plan for, endorse, and support such changes. It is the contention of these writers and editors that schools can and should plan in a decisive and positive way for youth to feel, value, and grow. If we distill some of the critical themes of the authors we find several ideas which affect the administration of schools. A discussion of a few of the salient points follows.

1. The person acts as a whole and is of infinite worth. His/her ideas are to be respected, honored, and given the opportunity to develop and mature. The school is a place where persons can *transact* with rather than only *react* to what they find in the environment. Because the school cherishes persons, every effort is made for them to act as individuals but also as members of larger communities.

2. Structure and organization are important within a school; however, all who in any way participate in the life of the school should participate in shaping it. Built into the structure of the

school should be planned means for its continuous reshaping. Insofar as possible the organization must accommodate to the persons within it and not vice versa.

3. The school must possess a sense of wholeness even as the persons within it are treated as whole beings. Such a school has a means of formal and informal communication that stresses meaningful dialogue among the parts of the whole. Each part needs to know what the other is doing so that resources can be used fully and fruitfully.

4. A sense of community is important if the affective is considered important. Community can be achieved through opportunities to interact and collaborate with others on meaningful activities.

5. The setting or context should be important to the persons who inhabit it. The setting should not determine the program but rather there should be mutuality between the context and the aspirations, ambitions, and interests of the persons who live within it. School buildings, therefore, must lend themselves to constant reshaping so that what is learned in school is not predetermined by the shaping of space within the school building nor the realia and artifacts which are permanent within the school.

6. Knowledge should be seen as being many pronged. It can include what is found in textbooks or in the packaged materials so frequently found in today's schools. However, that knowledge which is of most worth to the student is the knowledge he/she has had a part in shaping or creating. Since the student is both a creator of knowledge and a user of the knowledge of others, he/she must have the opportunity to consider knowledge from both perspectives. The student probably will be most involved when he or she is creating knowledge.

7. School programs should be shaped in ways that cater to the inner world of the child as well as to the outer demands of those who plan for schooling. The interrelationships among bodies of knowledge should be stressed so that persons see dealing with knowledge as activity involving memory, creativity, and involvement. Staff representing different types of expertise should be encouraged to work together.

8. Time should be thought of primarily as *kairos*, an inner time, rather than *chronos* or clock time. Insofar as possible students should have opportunity to finish a project when a likely termination point occurs rather than when a bell rings.

9. Personnel should value finding pleasure in life, showing interest in the worthwhile, exercising judgment among competing goods and committing themselves to ideals. The range of behaviors necessary to living a full life is frequently taught through example as well as through opportunities for planned experiences. Persons of a variety of ages, ethnic backgrounds, and skills add vitality to a school.

10. Budgeting should be worked out as flexibly as possible. Since new ventures in knowing, new experiences in collaborating, and new opportunities for maturing may be serendipitous of planned activities, funds should be available to implement worthwhile serendipities as well as long-term planned ventures.

11. Legitimate modes of evaluation which go beyond paper-pencil tests should be worked out and given high value in accountability systems. Observational techniques, reflective procedures, photographic data may tell more about the growth of the maturing individual than all the standardized tests in the world.

12. Attention should be given to a very basic community involvement program. The best-laid plans for a program focusing upon the maturing human being may die quickly if parents and community leaders do not understand and consequently do not support what the school is attempting to do.

In summary, the school giving attention to the development of feeling, valuing human beings needs to throw aside the shackles which bind many schools to superficial low-level programs. They need to be daring and venturesome realizing that in the last analysis there is nothing that can destroy a society more rapidly than bored young who are unwilling and unable to live responsible and creative lives.

*Literature Highlighting the Affective**

Louise M. Berman
Cathy Pope Smith

In order to gain a grasp of the affective and its impact on the curriculum, a group of faculty and students conducted a relatively systematic search of the literature. Needless to say the task was not easy, for many curriculum writers, psychologists, and educators in general discuss such areas as feelings, emotions, values and other topics usually associated with the affective domain. Our attempts to define the parameters of our task were further complicated by the wealth of materials in which attention is given to the affective. For example, in the area of values alone, which is commonly categorized as in the affective domain, the amount of material was staggering.

Consequently, we delimited our search primarily to the contemporary scene and to works, for the most part, which have a curricular orientation or that have had a relatively profound influ-

---

* For help on this section we are indebted to a group of University of Maryland graduate students in a curriculum class. They explored the literature and attempted to categorize it. Students included: Elizabeth P. Hansen, Kay Johnson, Judy Johnstone, Mildred Kreider, William D. Monie, Tim Muzzio, Patricia Roche, Linda Schneider, Bettina M. Scott, Bernadine Thomas, Jerry Ward, and Joan Wilson. John Splaine of the faculty of the University gave assistance in reviewing appropriate books from the area of educational technology. Jessie Roderick also provided valuable help.

ence on the curriculum field. Undoubtedly the reader may find glaring errors of commission and omission.

The procedures followed in the literature review included the following: (a) Developing a form for reviewing books on the affective; (b) Summarizing the data found on the forms; and (c) Searching for schemes to make the material useful for curriculum workers.

Since we do not use full bibliographical data in referring to various works later in this section, a selected bibliography follows.

SELECTED BIBLIOGRAPHY

Paul Adams *et al. Children's Rights.* New York: Praeger Publishers, 1971.

Don Allen. *The Electric Humanities.* Dayton, Ohio: Geo. A. Pflaum, Publisher, 1971.

Morton Alpren. *Curriculum Significance of the Affective Domain.* ED 087 666. Bethesda, Maryland: ERIC Document Reproduction Service, 1973.

Vernon E. Anderson. *Principles and Procedures of Curriculum Improvement.* Second edition. New York: The Ronald Press Company, 1965.

Justin Aronfreed. "The Concept of Internalization." In: David A. Goslin, editor. *Handbook of Socialization Theory and Research.* Chicago: Rand McNally and Company, 1969. pp. 263-323.

Kurt Baier and Nicholas Rescher, editors. *Values and the Future: The Impact of Technological Change on American Values.* New York: The Free Press, 1969.

William H. Barber and others. *The Affective Domain: A Sourcebook for Media Specialists.* Washington, D.C.: Communication Service Corporation, 1970.

Walcott H. Beatty, editor. *Improving Educational Assessment & An Inventory of Measures of Affective Behavior.* Washington, D.C.: Association for Supervision and Curriculum Development, 1969.

Louise Berman. *New Priorities in the Curriculum.* Columbus, Ohio: Charles E. Merrill Publishing Co., 1968.

Terry Borton. *Reach, Touch, and Teach.* New York: McGraw-Hill Book Company, 1970.

George Brown. *Human Teaching for Human Learning.* New York: Viking Press, 1971.

Raymond E. Callahan. *Education and the Cult of Efficiency.* Chicago: University of Chicago Press, 1962.

Cathy Pope Smith *attended the Chicago Public Schools and received her bachelor of education degree from Chicago Teachers' College. She received a master of education degree from Towson State College in Baltimore, Maryland, in 1971 and her doctor of philosophy degree from the Department of Administration, Supervision, and Curriculum, University of Maryland, in August 1976. Her dissertation, "A Study of the Influence Exerted by Selected Influentials on the Desegregation Plan Formulated by Baltimore City in 1974–1975," combined the disciplines of education and political science. She plans to continue her research investigating the interrelationship between politics and education. Dr. Smith is presently Acting Regional Specialist in Planning in the Baltimore City Public School System.*

Irvin L. Child. *Humanistic Psychology and the Research Tradition: Their Several Virtues.* New York: John Wiley & Sons, 1973.

Arthur W. Combs. "Accountability for Humanism." Washington, D.C.: Association for Supervision and Curriculum Development, 1973. (Cassette tape.)

Arthur W. Combs, editor. *Perceiving, Behaving, Becoming: A New Focus for Education.* 1962 Yearbook. Washington, D.C.: Association for Supervision and Curriculum Development, 1962.

John Dewey. *Moral Principles in Education.* New York: Houghton Mifflin Company, 1909.

Albert F. Eiss and Mary Blatt Harbeck. *Behavioral Objectives in the Affective Domain.* Washington, D.C.: National Science Teachers Association, 1969.

Edgar Fauré and others. *Learning To Be: The World of Education Today and Tomorrow.* Paris: UNESCO, 1972.

Arthur W. Foshay. *Essays on Curriculum.* New York: Department of Curriculum and Teaching, Teachers College, Columbia University, 1975.

Viktor E. Frankl. *Man's Search for Meaning: An Introduction to Logotherapy.* New York: Washington Square Press, 1959.

Paulo Freire. *Pedagogy of the Oppressed.* New York: Herder & Herder, 1972.

Linda Buchanan Gambrell and Robert M. Wilson. *Focusing on the Strengths of Children.* Belmont, California: L. Seigler, 1973.

Haim Ginott. *Teacher and Child.* New York: The Macmillan Company, 1972.

Thomas Gordon. *Parent Effectiveness Training.* New York: Peter H. Wyden, Inc., 1970.

Herbert Greenberg. *Teaching with Feeling.* New York: The Macmillan Company, 1969.

Ivan D. Illich. *Deschooling Society.* New York: Harper & Row, 1971.

Philip Jackson. *Life in Classrooms.* New York: Holt, Rinehart, and Winston, Inc., 1968.

David W. Johnson. *Reaching Out: Interpersonal Effectiveness and Self-actualization.* Englewood Cliffs, New Jersey: Prentice-Hall, Inc., 1972.

Richard M. Jones. *Fantasy and Feeling in Education.* New York: Harper & Row, 1968.

S. B. Khan and Joel Weiss. "The Teaching of Affective Responses." In: R. M. W. Travers, editor. *Second Handbook of Research on Teaching.* Chicago: Rand McNally and Company, 1973. pp. 759-804.

William Heard Kilpatrick. *Education for a Changing Civilization.* New York: Macmillan Publishing Co., Inc., 1926.

William Heard Kilpatrick. *Education and the Social Crisis.* New York: Liveright, 1932.

Lawrence Kohlberg. "Moral Development and the Education of Adolescents." *Adolescents and the American High School.* New York: Holt, Rinehart, and Winston, Inc., 1970.

Lawrence Kohlberg. "Stage and Sequence: The Cognitive-Development Approach to Socialization." In: David A. Goslin, editor. *Handbook of Socialization Theory and Research.* Chicago: Rand McNally and Company, 1969. pp. 347-480.

Lawrence Kohlberg. "Stages of Moral Development as a Basis for Moral Education." In: C. M. Beck, B. J. Crittenden, and E. V. Sullivan, editors. *Moral Education: Interdisciplinary Approaches.* Toronto: University of Toronto Press, 1971.

Lawrence Kohlberg and Rochelle Meyer. "Development as the Aim of Education." *Harvard Educational Review* 42: 449-96; November 1972.

Jonathan Kozol. *Free Schools.* Boston: Houghton Mifflin Company, 1972.

David R. Krathwohl et al. *Taxonomy of Educational Objectives. Handbook II: Affective Domain.* New York: David McKay and Company, 1964.

Richard A. Lacey. *Seeing with Feeling: Film in Classroom.* Philadelphia: W. B. Saunders Company, 1972.

Susanne K. Langer. *Mind: An Essay on Human Feeling.* Baltimore: The Johns Hopkins Press, 1967.

Robert R. Leeper, editor. *Emerging Moral Dimensions in Society: Implications for Schooling.* Washington, D.C.: Association for Supervision and Curriculum Development, 1975.

George Leonard. *Education and Ecstasy.* New York: Delacorte Press, 1968.

Leon Lessinger. "Outcomes of the Accountability Movement." Washington, D.C.: Association for Supervision and Curriculum Development, 1974. (Cassette tape.)

Harold C. Lyon, Jr. *Learning To Feel, Feeling To Learn.* Columbus, Ohio: Charles E. Merrill Publishing Co., 1971.

George Mandler. *Mind and Emotion.* New York: John Wiley & Sons, Inc., 1975.

Abraham H. Maslow. *New Knowledge in Human Values.* Chicago: Henry Regency Company, 1959.

Abraham H. Maslow. *Religions, Values, and Peak-Experiences.* New York: The Macmillan Company, 1964, 1970.

Lawrence E. Metcalf, editor. *Values Education: Rationale, Strategies, and Procedures.* 41st Yearbook. Washington, D.C.: National Council for the Social Studies, 1971.

Alice Miel and Peggy Brogan. *More than Social Studies: A View of Social Learning in the Elementary School.* Englewood Cliffs, New Jersey: Prentice-Hall, Inc., 1957.

Norman V. Overly, editor. *The Unstudied Curriculum: Its Impact on Children.* Washington, D.C.: Association for Supervision and Curriculum Development, 1970.

Jean Piaget. *The Moral Judgment of the Child.* New York: The Free Press, 1965.

Neil Postman and Charles Weingartner. *Teaching as a Subversive Activity.* New York: Dell Publishing Company, 1969.

Neil Postman and Charles Weingartner. *The School Book.* New York: Delacorte Press, 1973.

David E. Purpel and Maurice Belanger. *Curriculum and the Cultural Revolution.* Berkeley, California: McCutchan Publishing Corporation, 1972.

Thomas B. Roberts. *Seven Major Foci of Affective Experiences: A Typology for Educational Design, Planning, Analysis and Research.* ED 069 215. Bethesda, Maryland: ERIC Document Reproduction Service, 1972.

Jessie A. Roderick. *The Involvement Instrument.* Center for Young Children. Occasional Paper Fifteen. College Park, Maryland: Center for Young Children, University of Maryland, July 1975.

Jessie A. Roderick, Diane M. Lee, and Louise M. Berman. *Observation: Basis for Planning, Implementing, and Evaluating.* Center for Young Children. Occasional Paper Sixteen. College Park, Maryland: Center for Young Children, University of Maryland, 1975.

Carl Rogers. *Freedom To Learn.* Columbus, Ohio: Charles E. Merrill & Company, 1969.

Carl Rogers and others. *Person to Person: The Problem of Being Human.* Lafayette, California: Real People Press, 1967.

Louis J. Rubin. *Facts and Feelings in the Classroom.* New York: The Viking Press, 1973.

Louis J. Rubin, editor. *Life Skills in School and Society.* 1969 Yearbook. Washington, D.C.: The Association for Supervision and Curriculum Development, 1969.

Jean-Paul Sartre. *Existentialism and Human Emotions.* New York: The Wisdom Library, a Division of Philosophical Library, 1957.

Jeffrey Schrank. *Teaching Human Beings: 101 Subversive Activities for the Classroom.* Boston: Beacon Press, 1972.

Flora Rheta Schreiber. *Sybil.* New York: Warner Books, Inc., 1974.

Melvin L. Silberman, Jerome S. Allender, and Jay M. Yanoff. *Real Learning: A Sourcebook for Teachers.* Boston: Little, Brown and Company, 1976.

Anita Simon and E. Gil Boyer, editors. *Mirrors for Behavior: An Anthology of Classroom Observation Instruments.* 14 volumes. Philadelphia: Research for Better Schools, 1970.

B. Othanel Smith, William O. Stanley, and J. Harlan Shores. *Fundamentals of Curriculum Development.* Revised edition. New York: World Book Company, 1957.

Florence Stratemeyer and others. *Developing a Curriculum for Modern Living.* Second revised edition. New York: Teachers College Press, 1957.

Robert D. Strom and E. Paul Torrance, editors. *Education for Affective Achievement.* Chicago: Rand McNally and Company, 1973.

Douglas P. Superka *et al. Values Education Sourcebook.* Boulder, Colorado: ERIC Clearinghouse for Social Studies, Social Science Education, 1976.

David A. Thatcher. *Teaching, Loving, and Self-Directed Learning.* Pacific Palisades, California: Goodyear Publishing Company, 1973.

Theory Into Practice. Total issue on "Moral Education." 145(4); October 1975.

Alvin Toffler, editor. *Learning for Tomorrow.* New York: Random House, Inc., 1974.

Silvan Tomkins. "The Psychology of Commitment." Silvan Tomkins and Carroll E. Izard, editors. *Affect, Cognition, and Personality: Empirical Studies.* New York: Springer Publishing Company, Inc., 1965. pp. 148-71.

Elliot Turiel. "Stage Transition on Moral Development." In: R. M. W. Travers, editor. *Second Handbook on Research in Teaching.* Chicago: Rand McNally and Company, 1973. pp. 732-58.

Wilfred Rusk Wees. *Nobody Can Teach Anyone Anything.* Garden City, New York: Doubleday & Company, Inc., 1971.

Gerald Weinstein and Mario D. Fantini, editors. *Toward Humanistic Education: A Curriculum of Affect.* New York: Praeger Publishers, 1970.

Albert R. Wight. *Toward a Definition of Affect in Education.* ED 069 734. Bethesda, Maryland: ERIC Document Reproduction Service, 1972.

Albert R. Wight. *Affective Goals of Education.* ED 069 733. Bethesda, Maryland: ERIC Document Reproduction Service, 1971.

Kaoru Yamamoto, editor. *The Child and His Image: Self Concept in the Early Years.* Boston: Houghton Mifflin Company, 1972.

Philip Zimbardo and Ebbe B. Ebbeson. *Influencing Attitudes and Changing Behavior: A Basic Introduction to Relevant Methodology: Theory and Applications.* Reading, Massachusetts: Addison-Wesley Publishing Co., 1970.

SUGGESTED FORM FOR REVIEWING BOOKS

The revised version of the review form that follows was used by readers in analyzing most of the listed works in terms of certain critical characteristics. Additional reader input was obtained in readers' responses to requests for a definition of the affective offered in the book, explanations of checks on characteristics, a brief summary of the book, and a statement of what the reader viewed as the work's major contribution to the affective domain.

SUGGESTED FORM FOR REVIEWING BOOKS ON THE AFFECTIVE
(Revised)

Name of reviewer:_____

Address where you
can be reached:_____

_____ Telephone:_____

Title of book:_____

_____

Author:_____

Place of
Publication:_____

Publisher:_____ Date of Publication:_____

Definition of affective: If a definition of the affective is given, please quote
exactly. Give page number.

Characteristics of the book: Check all the items which apply.

_____General curriculum book (deals with school programs at all levels
including elementary and secondary schools).

_____Book geared to specific age, subject, or level in school. Specify.

_____Primarily psychological or philosophical treatment of affective
with little attention to curricular implications. (Include psychological research studies, philosophical treatises, etc.)

_____Primarily curricular treatment of affective with major attention
to school programs.

_____Treatment of specific area of affective such as ethics, morals,
values, feelings from a *philosophical* or *psychological* viewpoint.

_____Treatment of *specific* area of affective such as ethics, morals,
values, feelings from a curricular viewpoint.

_____Retrospective case study of actual situation in which affective or
components of it are critical.

_____Large-scale descriptive study with focus on affective or compo-
nents of it.

_____Longitudinal study of affective or components of it.

_____Criticism of studies which have been conducted on the affective or components of it.

_____Practical suggestions for teachers included.

_____Suggestions for research included.

_____Extensive bibliography included.

One way of typing the affect: Read the five descriptions of the affect developed by Philip Phenix. Do any of the following descriptions characterize your book? Please check.

_____Affect as organic needs: based on impulse, inborn demands, self-preservation.

_____Affect as feelings of delight or pleasure: may be associated with organic needs but go beyond them; passion.

_____Affect as interest or intention: express determination of active nature "rather than a passive response to a want or to a presented sense object."

_____Affect as critical reflection, appraisal, or judgment: subjecting impulses, interest, pleasures "to critical reflection in which alternating compatibilities, and mutual reinforcements of personal realization are explored and decided." Relates reason to other persons, achieves sense of community.

_____Affect as commitment to idealization: unending striving and revision in field to which commitment has been made; comprehensive, transforming activity in achievement of goal.

Explanation: (if appropriate).

Please summarize the book in a paragraph or two.

In a final statement, highlight what you see to be the major contribution of this work to the affective domain.

CHARACTERISTICS OF SELECTED BOOKS

Next follows a table showing characteristics of some of the books in the Selected Bibliography. A brief description of each characteristic follows the table. These descriptions were derived from the characteristics of books listed on the review form and from readers' responses to questions on the forms.

Having received Phenix' manuscript early, we looked for evidences of his way of describing affect. Items 14 through 18 are drawn from his paper.

AUTHORS

CHARACTERISTICS OF BOOKS ON THE AFFECTIVE	Adams	Allen	Alpren	Aronfreed	Baier	Beatty	Berman	Brown	Borton	Callahan	Child	Combs	Dewey	Fauré	Freire	Ginott	Gordon	Greenberg	Jackson	Johnson	Jones	Khan	Kohlberg (Adolescents)	Kohlberg (Goslin)	Kohlberg (Beck & Crittenden)	Kohlberg (Harvard)	Kozol
1. General curriculum	X						X						X	X													
2. Specific books																X		X					X		X		X
3. Psychological or philosophical											X	X		X													
4. Curricular treatment		X							X			X									X						
5. Specific area from philosophical or psychological viewpoint				X	X		X								X		X	X		X	X	X	X	X	X	X	X
6. Specific area from curricular viewpoint		X		X	X			X	X				X				X	X		X	X	X	X	X	X		X
7. Retrospective case study		X						X	X												X	X				X	
8. Descriptive study																		X	X				X	X			
9. Longitudinal study																		X					X	X			
10. Criticism of studies		X			X						X				X	X	X		X			X		X	X		
11. Practical suggestions							X		X				X			X	X	X		X	X		X	X	X	X	
12. Research suggestions			X				X				X	X				X	X	X				X		X	X	X	
13. Extensive bibliography		X	X	X	X	X	X	X	X	X	X	X				X	X		X		X	X			X	X	
14. Affect as organic needs																											X
15. Affect as feelings		X					X																				
16. Affect as interest		X																									
17. Critical reflections		X				X			X				X	X	X												
18. Commitment to idealization	X	X				X								X	X												

CHARACTERISTICS OF BOOKS ON THE AFFECTIVE (continued)	Krathwohl	Lacey	Leonard	Lessinger	Lyon	Maslow (Religions)	Metcalf	Overly	Piaget	Postman	Purpel	Rogers (Freedom)	Rogers (Person)	Rubin	Sartre	Schrank	Schreiber	Strom	Toffler	Tomkins	Turiel	Weinstein	Wight I	Wight II	Yamamoto	Zimbardo
1. General curriculum	X	X			X			X		X	X					X		X				X				
2. Specific books	X						X			X		X				X		X				X				
3. Psychological or philosophical			X	X		X							X										X			X
4. Curricular treatment	X	X			X		X	X				X		X		X		X				X				
5. Specific area from philosophical or psychological viewpoint			X		X				X			X			X				X			X		X		X
6. Specific area from curricular viewpoint		X	X		X			X	X							X					X					
7. Retrospective case study			X		X								X			X					X	X				
8. Descriptive study																				X	X					
9. Longitudinal study					X								X			X										
10. Criticism of studies												X	X		X	X					X	X		X		X
11. Practical suggestions	X	X	X				X					X	X	X		X	X	X	X		X	X			X	X
12. Research suggestions					X							X									X	X			X	X
13. Extensive bibliography	X	X								X	X	X				X	X	X	X		X	X		X		
14. Affect as organic needs		X			X											X	X X									
15. Affect as feelings			X X											X		X						X			X	
16. Affect as interest									X					X			X		X			X			X	
17. Critical reflections							X		X			X			X	X	X	X			X X	X			X	
18. Commitment to idealization						X	X			X X	X X								X							

KEY TO CHART FOR CHARACTERISTICS
OF SELECTED BOOKS

1. General curriculum book (deals with school programs at all levels including elementary and secondary schools).

2. Book geared to specific age, subject, or level in school. Specify.

3. Primarily *psychological* or *philosophical* treatment of affective with little attention to curricular implications. (Includes psychological research studies, philosophical treatises, etc.)

4. Primarily *curricular* treatment of affective with major attention to school programs.

5. Treatment of *specific* area of affective such as ethics, morals, values, feelings from a *philosophical* or *psychological* viewpoint.

6. Treatment of *specific* area of affective such as ethics, morals, values, feelings from a *curricular* viewpoint.

7. Retrospective case study of actual situation in which affective or components of it are critical.

8. Large scale descriptive study with focus on affective or components of it.

9. Longitudinal study of affective or components of it.

10. Criticism of studies which have been conducted on the affective or components of it.

11. Practical suggestions for teachers included.

12. Suggestions for research included.

13. Extensive bibliography included.

14. Affect as organic needs: based on impulse, inborn demands, self-preservation.

15. Affect as feelings of delight or pleasure: may be associated with organic needs but go beyond them, passion.

16. Affect as interest or intention: express determination of active nature "rather than a passive response to a want or to a presented sense object."

17. Affect as critical reflection, appraisal, or judgment: subjecting impulses, interest, pleasures "to critical reflection in which alternating compatibilities, and mutual reinforcements of personal realization are explored and decided." Relates reason to other persons, achieves sense of community.

18. Affect as commitment to idealization: unending striving and revision in field to which commitment has been made; comprehensive, transforming activity in achievement of goal.

SCHEMA FOR MAKING MATERIALS USEFUL
FOR CURRICULUM WORKERS

Our search of the literature and the analysis of the data on the review forms resulted in a set of definitions of affective and several schemes for classifying the literature. The definitions and classificatory schema can be used by curriculum workers in developing their ideas on the affective.

Notes on Definitions of Affective

Although how the affective is defined is alluded to in many of the writings, we found some fairly specific definitions which follow. Again we have only included a sample. Terms such as ethics, values, etc., often included in the affective domain are not included.

Alpren

Provision for growth of attitudes and behaviors that deal with feelings, values, and, in general, the personal concerns of students. (Separates self-knowledge from other kinds of knowledge.)

Brown

The non-intellectual side of learning, the side having to do with emotions, feelings, interests, values, and character (Introduction).

Khan

The evaluative component of attitudes associated with a feeling core of liking or disliking for social and psychological objects (p. 70).

Krathwohl

Objectives which emphasize a feeling tone, an emotion, or a degree of acceptance or rejection. Affective objectives vary from simple attention to selected phenomena to complex but internally consistent qualities of character and conscience. We found a large number of such objectives in the literature expressed as interests, attitudes, appreciations, values, and emotional sets of biases.

Lyon

Feeling or emotional aspect òf experience and learning.

Rubin (Facts . . .)

Pertains to the practical life, to the emotions, the passions, the dispositions, the motives, the moral and aesthetic sensibilities, the capacity for feeling. Concern, attachment or detachment, sympathy, empathy, and appreciation (p. 5).

Wight

Behavior having to do with emotional or feeling responses to an object of experience (thing, idea, process, subject, situation, another person, oneself, etc.) and all the complex perceptions, attitudes, characteristics, and behaviors associated with seeking, accepting, and incorporating or avoiding and rejecting the object (p. 5).

CLASSIFYING THE LITERATURE

Persons have various reasons for searching out particular books. In an attempt to assist the reader, we have developed ways of classifying the books we have read. The classification systems are presented and in some instances a few representative works. We have not attempted completeness but rather ways of thinking about books in this area.

"If . . . Then" Ways of Looking at the Literature

Many persons want books that answer rather basic philosophical or psychological questions. One person came up with the following schema for looking at the literature. It should be noted that three of the sub systems include the Phenix scheme.

IF YOU ARE LOOKING FOR A
GENERAL CURRICULUM BOOK, TRY:

Louise Berman. *New Priorities in the Curriculum.*

John Dewey. *Moral Principles in Education.*

Paulo Freire. *Pedagogy of the Oppressed.*

Harold C. Lyon, Jr. *Learning To Feel, Feeling To Learn.*

Miel and Brogan. *More Than Social Studies.*

Norman V. Overly, editor. *The Unstudied Curriculum: Its Impact on Children.*

David E. Purpel and Maurice Belanger. *Curriculum and the Cultural Revolution.*

Jeffrey Schrank. *Teaching Human Beings: 101 Subversive Activities for the Classroom.*

Stratemeyer *et al. Developing a Curriculum for Modern Living.*

Robert D. Strom and E. Paul Torrance, editors. *Education for Affective Achievement.*

Postman and Weingartner. *The School Book.*

IF YOU NEED A BOOK WITH PRACTICAL SUGGESTIONS FOR TEACHERS, TRY:

Adams *et al. Children's Rights.*

Allen. *The Electric Humanities.*

Louise Berman. *New Priorities in the Curriculum.*

Terry Borton. *Reach, Touch and Teach.*

John Dewey. *Moral Principles in Education.*

Linda B. Gambrell and Robert M. Wilson. *Focusing on the Strengths of Children.*

Haim Ginott. *Teacher and Child.*

Herbert Greenberg. *Teaching with Feeling.*

Richard M. Jones. *Fantasy and Feeling in Education.*

Richard A. Lacey. *Seeing with Feeling: Film in Classroom.*

George Leonard. *Education and Ecstacy.*

Lawrence Metcalf. *Values Education: Rationale, Strategies and Procedures.*

Carl Rogers. *Freedom To Learn.*

Louis J. Rubin. *Facts and Feelings in the Classroom.*

Jeffrey Schrank. *Teaching Human Beings: 101 Subversive Activities for the Classroom.*

Melvin L. Silberman *et al. Real Learning: A Sourcebook for Teachers.*

Elliot Turiel. "Stage Transition in Moral Development." In: *Second Handbook on Research in Teaching.*

Kaoru Yamamoto, editor. *The Child and His Image: Self Concept in the Early Years.*

IF YOU NEED A BOOK WHICH DEALS WITH A PSYCHOLOGICAL OR PHILOSOPHICAL TREATMENT OF THE AFFECTIVE, TRY:

Irvin L. Child. *Humanistic Psychology and the Research Tradition: Their Several Virtues.*

Edgar Fauré and others. *Learning To Be: The World of Education Today and Tomorrow.*

Abraham H. Maslow. *Religions, Values, and Peak-Experiences.*

Jean Piaget. *The Moral Judgment of the Child.*

Carl Rogers. *Freedom To Learn.*

Carl Rogers and others. *Person to Person: The Problem of Being Human.*

Albert R. Wight. *Toward a Definition of Affect in Education.*

Philip Zimbardo and Ebbe B. Ebbeson. *Influencing Attitudes and Changing Behavior: A Basic Introduction to Relevant Methodology, Theory and Application.*

IF YOU ARE LOOKING FOR BOOKS WHICH GIVE ATTENTION TO SPECIFIC AREAS, SUCH AS ETHICS, MORALS, VALUES, FEELINGS, TRY:

Justin Aronfreed. "The Concept of Internalization." In: *The Handbook of Socialization Theory and Research.*

Kurt Baier and Nicholas Rescher, editors. *Values and the Future: The Impact of Technological Change on American Values.*

Terry Borton. *Reach, Touch and Teach.*

Paulo Freire. *Pedagogy of the Oppressed.*

Herbert Greenberg. *Teaching with Feeling.*

David W. Johnson. *Reaching Out: Interpersonal Effectiveness and Self-actualization.*

Richard M. Jones. *Fantasy and Feeling in Education.*

S. B. Khan and others. "The Teaching of Affective Responses." In: *Second Handbook of Research on Teaching.*

Lawrence Kohlberg. "Moral Development and the Education of Adolescents." In: *Adolescents and the American High School.*

George Leonard. *Education and Ecstasy.*

Harold C. Lyon, Jr. *Learning To Feel, Feeling To Learn.*

Abraham H. Maslow. *New Knowledge in Human Values.*

Lawrence Metcalf. *Values Education: Rationale, Strategies and Procedures.*

Jean Piaget. *The Moral Judgment of the Child.*

Carl Rogers. *Freedom To Learn.*

Superka *et al. Values Education Sourcebook.*

Elliot Turiel. "Stage Transition in Moral Development," in *Second Handbook on Research in Teaching.*

Albert R. Wight. *Affective Goals of Education.*

Philip Zimbardo and Ebbe B. Ebbeson. *Influencing Attitudes and Changing Behavior: A Basic Introduction to Relevant Methodology, Theory and Applications.*

IF YOU'RE LOOKING FOR BOOKS WITH SUGGESTIONS FOR FURTHER RESEARCH ON THE AFFECTIVE, SEE:

Morton Alpren. *Curriculum Significance of the Affective Domain.*

Louise Berman. *New Priorities in the Curriculum.*

Irvin L. Child. *Humanism Psychology in the Research Tradition: Their Several Virtues.*

S. B. Khan. "The Teaching of Affective Responses." In: *Second Handbook of Research on Teaching.*

Lawrence Kohlberg and Rochelle Meyer. "Development as the Aim of Education." In: *Harvard Educational Review.*

Harold C. Lyon, Jr. *Learning To Feel, Feeling To Learn.*

Jessie A. Roderick. *The Involvement Instrument.*

Jessie A. Roderick and others. *Observation: Basis for Planning, Implementing, and Evaluating.*

Kaoru Yamamoto. *The Child and His Image: Self Concept in the Early Years.*

IF YOU WANT A MORE ORDERLY, SYSTEMATIZED VIEW OF THE AFFECTIVE, SEE:

Walcott H. Beatty. *Improving Educational Assessment: An Inventory of Measures of Affective Behavior.*

Lawrence Kohlberg. All works.

David Krathwohl. *Taxonomy of Educational Objectives, Handbook II.*

Jean Piaget. *The Moral Judgment of the Child.*

Silvan Tomkins. *The Psychology of Commitment.*

Elliot Turiel. "Stage Transition in Moral Development," in *Second Handbook on Research in Teaching.*

The Phenix Scheme

One of our group took a few of the readings and tried to place them on the Phenix continuum. She came up with the following. It should be noted that of the books selected only the Stratemeyer book seems to fall into the five categories designated by Phenix.

Organic Needs	Feelings	Interests	Judgments	Identification
			Dewey	
		Kilpatrick		
			Piaget	
		Stratemeyer		
				Smith, Stanley, Shores
			Kohlberg	
	Roberts			
	Alpren			
	Wight			
	Toffler		Toffler	
		V. Anderson		
	Yamamoto			
	Brown			
	Lyon			

If you are interested in developing experiences for children and youth based upon the Phenix schema, you might be interested in reading some of the works by the authors listed below and carrying out certain of the suggestions.

1. If you feel that affect is based on organic needs such as impulse read Kozol, Lacey, Lyon, Maslow, Rubin, and Schrank. Then develop five experiences for children based upon insights derived from these works. Attempt to gather information about what children and youth are doing as they engage in these experiences. Do you get any new insights about affect as related to organic needs?

2. If you feel that affect is based upon feelings of delight or pleasure, read Allen and Schrank. Develop two experiences for children and youth based upon insights from these readings. Implement the experiences. What do you learn about children and youth as they engage in these activities?

3. If you feel that affect is interest or intention, that there is a factor of determination in it, then read Allen, Krathwohl, Metcalf, Piaget, Rogers, Schreiber, Wight, Yamamoto, and Zimbardo. What characterizes a person who sees affect as interest? How does this level differ from other levels? What experiences would give children the opportunity to understand the intentional qualities of affect?

4. If you feel that affect involves critical reflection and judging of alternatives, then Allen, Beatty, Borton, Dewey, Freire, Greenberg, Johnson, Khan, Kohlberg, Kozol, Krathwohl, Lacey, Metcalf, Purpel, Rogers, Schreiber, and Sartre are persons whose works you will want to read. Do any of these writers suggest looking at persons in the process of making critical judgments? How can you find out when persons actually carry out decisions based upon critical reflection?

5. If you feel that affect is commitment to idealization, then read Allen, Berman, Jackson, Kohlberg, Lacey, Maslow, Metcalf, Purpel, and Sartre. How can you determine whether a person is really committed to an ideal? What would you look for?

6. If you are attempting to formulate your own levels or types of affect, read Krathwohl, Kohlberg, Maslow, Wight. What tentative types of affect do you come up with?

Educational Outcome. Sometimes we need to locate books which deal with specific educational functions. Listed here are a few suggestions about books which might shed light on research, supervision, teacher education, and parent-community education.

Research	Supervision	Teacher Education	Parent/Community Education
Aronfreed	Alpren	Adams	Adams
Baier	Berman	Allen	Berman
Beatty	Borton	Aronfreed	Borton
Berman	Callahan	Baier	Ginott
Borton	Dewey	Berman	Gordon
Child	Fauré	Borton	Greenberg
Fauré	Freire	Brown	Jackson
Freire	Greenberg	Callahan	Kozol
Jackson	Jackson	Dewey	Lacey
Khan	Johnson	Ginott	Postman
Kohlberg	Kozol	Greenberg	Rogers
Krathwohl	Krathwohl	Jackson	Schreiber
Leonard	Lyon	Jones	Thatcher
Metcalf	Maslow	Kahn	Yamamoto
Roderick	Piaget	Kohlberg	
Rogers	Rogers	Kozol	
Rubin	Sartre	Krathwohl	
Thatcher	Thatcher	Lacey	
Tomkins	Turiel	Leonard	
Wight	Yamamoto	Lyon	
Zimbardo	Wees	Postman	
	Wight	Overly	
		Piaget	
		Purpel	
		Rogers	
		Rubin	
		Schrank	
		Schreiber	
		Sartre	
		Strom	
		Thatcher	
		Yamamoto	

In conclusion, an attempt was made in this section to suggest some readings in the affective. A bibliography was followed by some suggested ways of organizing the literature. If this chapter does nothing more than to assist the reader in his/her efforts to get some handles on the diversity of literature in the area, the section will have served a useful purpose.

ASCD 1977 Yearbook Committee Members

Louise M. Berman, *Co-Chairperson and Co-Editor,* Department of Administration, Supervision, and Curriculum, College of Education, University of Maryland, College Park

Jessie A. Roderick, *Co-Chairperson and Co-Editor,* Department of Early Childhood-Elementary Education, College of Education, University of Maryland, College Park

William D. Hedges, Department of Childhood Education, College of Education, University of Florida, Gainesville

Marian L. Martinello, Division of Education, College of Multidisciplinary Studies, University of Texas at San Antonio

Kaoru Yamamoto, College of Education, Arizona State University, Tempe

The Authors

Kenneth R. Beittel, The Pennsylvania State University, University Park

Louise M. Berman, Department of Administration, Supervision, and Curriculum, College of Education, University of Maryland, College Park

Charles M. Fair, Cambridge, Massachusetts

William D. Hedges, Department of Childhood Education, College of Education, University of Florida, Gainesville

Madeleine L'Engle, Cathedral Heights, New York, New York

Marian L. Martinello, Division of Education, College of Multidisciplinary Studies, University of Texas at San Antonio

Cecil H. Patterson, College of Education, University of Illinois at Urbana-Champaign

Philip H. Phenix, Teachers College, Columbia University, New York, New York

Jessie A. Roderick, Department of Early Childhood-Elementary Education, College of Education, University of Maryland, College Park

Elizabeth Léonie Simpson, Santa Monica, California

Cathy Pope Smith, Baltimore City Public Schools, Maryland

Rodman B. Webb, Foundations of Education, University of Florida, Gainesville

Kaoru Yamamoto, College of Education, Arizona State University, Tempe

ASCD Board of Directors

303

Edward A. Karns, Director of Elementary Education, Parma City Schools, Parma, Ohio

Charles G. Kingston, Jr., Principal, Thomas Fowler Junior High School, Tigard, Oregon

S. Elaine Kohn, St. Anthony Convent, Indianapolis, Indiana

Dolores Silva, Professor of Curriculum Theory and Development, Temple University, Philadelphia, Pennsylvania

Bette W. Treadwell, National League of Cities, Washington, D.C.

Board Members Elected at Large

James A. Banks, University of Washington, Seattle (1980)

Julianna Boudreaux, New Orleans Public Schools, Louisiana (1977)

Gwyn Brownlee, Education Service Center, Region 10, Richardson, Texas (1979)

Joseph W. Crenshaw, State Department of Education, Tallahassee, Florida (1977)

Theodore Czajkowski, Public Schools, Madison, Wisconsin (1980)

Ivan J. K. Dahl, University of North Dakota, Grand Forks (1979)

Lawrence S. Finkel, Northeast Bronx Education Park, Bronx, New York (1979)

Ben M. Harris, University of Texas, Austin (1980)

Edward A. Karns, Parma City Schools, Parma, Ohio (1977)

Lucille G. Jordan, Atlanta Public Schools, Georgia (1978)

Milton Kimpson, Community Relations Council, Greater Columbia Chamber of Commerce, Columbia, South Carolina (1977)

Chon LaBrier, Dulce Independent School, New Mexico (1978)

Norman V. Overly, Indiana University, Bloomington (1978)

Marshall Perritt, Shelby County Schools, Memphis, Tennessee (1980)

James A. Phillips, Jr., Kent State University, Kent, Ohio (1977)

James Raths, University of Illinois, Urbana (1978)

Mary-Margaret Scobey, Educational Consultant, Eugene, Oregon (1979)

Dolores Silva, Temple University, Philadelphia, Pennsylvania (1978)

Georgia Williams, Berkeley Unified School District, California (1980)

Mary J. Wood, Las Cruces Public Schools, New Mexico (1979)

Unit Representatives to the Board of Directors

(Each Unit's President is listed first; others follow in alphabetical order.)

Alabama: James B. Condra, University of Alabama, Gadsden; Alvis Harthern, University of Montevallo, Montevallo; Dorthea Grace Rockarts, University of Alabama, University.

Arizona: Thelma Peterson, Public Schools, Phoenix; Carl B. Furlong, Kyrene School District, Tempe; James J. Jelinek, Arizona State University, Tempe.

Arkansas: Phillip E. Powell, Arkansas Department of Education, Little Rock; James C. Williams, Public Schools, Dumas.

California (liaison): William Georgiades, University of Southern California, Los Angeles; Jessie Kobayashi, Whisman Elementary School District, Mountain View; David Martin, Mill Valley School District, Mill Valley.

Colorado: Jack Nold, Aurora School District 28J, Aurora; Dale F. Graham, Adams School District 14, Commerce City; P. L. Schmelzer, Poudre School District R-1, Fort Collins.

Connecticut: Joan D. Kerelejza, West Hartford Public Schools; Philmore Wass, University of Connecticut, Storrs.

Delaware: Pat O'Donnell, Jr., Newark School District; William J. Bailey, University of Delaware, Newark.

District of Columbia: Inez Wood, E. A. Clark School; Bessie D. Etheridge, Spingarn Instructional Unit; Lorraine H. Whitlock, Woodson Senior High School.

Florida: Mabel Jean Morrison, Okaloosa County Schools, Crestview; Charles Godwin, Palm Beach County Schools, West Palm Beach; Patrick Mooney, Dade County Public Schools, Miami Springs; Richard Stewart, Lee County Schools, Ft. Myers; Charlotte Eden Umholtz, Hillsborough County Schools, Tampa.

Georgia: George Stansbury, Georgia State University, Atlanta; Martha Sue Jordan, University of Georgia, Athens; Joseph A. Murphy, Jr., DeKalb County Schools, Decatur.

Hawaii: Elmer S. Dunsky, Chaminade College, Honolulu; Albert Tamaribuchi, Kailua Intermediate School, Honolulu.

Idaho: Claude A. Hanson, Boise Public Schools; David A. Carroll, Boise Public Schools.

Illinois: Raymond E. Hendee, Park Ridge School District 64; Leone Bergfield, Litchfield School District 12; R. Kim Driggers, Centralia City Schools; Blanche Martin, Rockford Public Schools; Donald W. Nylin, Aurora Public Schools; Mildred Hindman Phegley, Public Schools, Collinsville; Luceille Werner, Public Schools, Peotone.

Indiana: Clive C. Beattie, Public Schools, Portage; Donna Delph, Purdue University, Hammond; Charles E. Kline, Purdue University, West Lafayette; James H. McElhinney, Ball State University, Muncie.

Iowa: Luther Kiser, Ames Public Schools; Virginia Cooper, Sioux City Community School District; Robert Wrider, Waterloo Public Schools.

Kansas: Glenn Pyle, McPherson Public Schools; Walter L. Davies, Kansas City Public Schools; Harlan J. Trennepohl, Kansas State University, Manhattan.

Kentucky: Juanita K. Park, Western Kentucky University, Bowling Green; William Bolton, Clark County Public Schools, Winchester; Ernest H. Garner, Bowling Green City Schools.

Louisiana: Louise M. Bouise, New Orleans Public Schools; Darryl W. Boudreaux, St. Mary Parish Schools, Morgan City; Edwin H. Friedrich, retired, New Orleans; Katye Lee Posey, Caddo Parish Schools.

Maine: Arthur K. Hedberg, Jr., School District 71, Kennebunk; Phillip Gonyar, Bangor Public Schools.

Maryland: Janice Wickless, Maryland State Department of Education, Baltimore; Ruth Burkins, Harford County Board of Education, Bel Air; Benjamin Ebersole, Baltimore County Board of Education, Towson; L. Morris McClure, University of Maryland, College Park.

Massachusetts: C. Louis Cedrone, Westwood Public Schools; Paul V. Congdon, Springfield College, Springfield; Julian Demeo, Jr., Braintree Public Schools; Carolyn Teixeira, Public Schools, Wellesley Hills.

Michigan: Stuart C. Rankin, Detroit Public Schools; William Cansfield, Mt. Clemens Community Schools; LaBarbara Gragg, Detroit Public Schools; David Newbury, Hazel Park Public Schools; Virginia Sorenson, Western Michigan University, Grand Rapids; Jack Wickert, Kalamazoo Public Schools.

Minnesota: Jack Sjostiom, Independent School District 77; Marjorie Niehart, St. Paul Public Schools; Richard D. Kimpston, University of Minnesota, Minneapolis.

Mississippi: Robert J. Cagle, Jr., Public Schools, Greenwood; Norvel Burkett, Mississippi State University.

Missouri: Howard Lowe, Springfield Public Schools; William Anthony, Jefferson City Public Schools; Patricia Rocklage, Normandy School District, St. Louis; Frank Morley, Ladue School District, St. Louis.

Montana: Ethel Picton, Dillon Public Schools; Lloyd B. Ellingsen, Billings Public Schools.

Nebraska: Ron Brandt, Lincoln Public Schools; Gerald Bryant, Grand Island Public Schools.

Nevada: Edward Howard, State Department of Education, Reno; Glenn Duncan, Washoe County School District, Reno.

South Dakota: Maizie R. Solem, Sioux Falls Independent School District 1; A. Joyce Levin, South Dakota State Department of Education, Pierre.

Tennessee: Barbara G. Burch, Memphis State University, Memphis; Jerry C. McGee, Middle Tennessee State University, Murfreesboro; Ken Thornton, Lakeway Educational Cooperative, Jefferson City.

Texas: Virginia Cutter, Texas Education Agency, Austin; R. C. Bradley, North Texas State University, Denton; Rita Bryant, Texas Eastern University, Tyler; Dwane Russell, Stephen F. Austin State University, Nacogdoches; James L. Williamson, Pan American University, Edinburg.

Utah: Phyllis Bennett, Jordan School District, Sandy; Nellie T. Higbee, Murray Public Schools.

Vermont: John O'Brien, Washington Northeast Supervisory Unit, Plainfield.

Virginia: Edwin White, State Department of Education, Charlottesville; Margaret B. Moss, State Department of Education, Richmond; Gennette Nygard, Arlington Public Schools; Russell L. Watson, Campbell County Schools, Rustburg.

Washington: Robert H. Williams, Spokane Public Schools; Roy Duncan, Pasco School District; Donald Hair, State Office of Public Instruction, Olympia.

West Virginia: Ronald Cook, Wyoming County Board of Education, Pineville; Betty Livengood, Mineral County Schools, Keyser.

Wisconsin: Ronald Sime, Plattville Public Schools; Myron Anderson, Whitefish Bay Public Schools; James Ticknor, Sparta Public Schools; Russell Mosely, Department of Public Instruction, Madison.

Wyoming: Margaret J. Dobbs, Laramie County School District 1, Cheyenne; Leo Breeden, Cheyenne Public Schools.

ASCD Review Council

ASCD
Headquarters Staff

Executive Director: Gordon Cawelti
Associate Director; Editor, ASCD Publications: Robert R. Leeper
Associate Director: Geneva Gay
Associate Director: Charles A. Speiker
Business Manager: John H. Bralove
Administrative Assistant: Virginia O. Berthy

Staff Assistants:

Elsa Angell
Sarah Arlington
Ruth Block
Barbara Collins
Patsy Connors
Melea R. Epps
Anita Fitzpatrick
Teola T. Jones
Polly Larson

Frances Mindel
Nancy Olson
Alice H. Powell
Charlene Rothkopf
Carolyn Shell
Barbara J. Sims
Christine Smith
Myra K. Taub
Collette A. Williams
Linda Wysocki

ASCD Publications, Spring 1977

Yearbooks

Balance in the Curriculum (610-17274)	$5.00
Education for an Open Society (610-74012)	$8.00
Education for Peace: Focus on Mankind (610-17946)	$7.50
Evaluation as Feedback and Guide (610-17700)	$6.50
Feeling, Valuing, and the Art of Growing: Insights into the Affective (610-77104)	$9.75
Freedom, Bureaucracy, & Schooling (610-17508)	$6.50
Leadership for Improving Instruction (610-17454)	$4.00
Learning and Mental Health in the School (610-17674)	$5.00
Life Skills in School and Society (610-17786)	$5.50
A New Look at Progressive Education (610-17812)	$8.00
Perspectives on Curriculum Development 1776-1976 (610-76078)	$9.50
Schools in Search of Meaning (610-75044)	$8.50
Perceiving, Behaving, Becoming: A New Focus for Education (610-17278)	$5.00
To Nurture Humaneness: Commitment for the '70's (610-17810)	$6.00

Books and Booklets

Action Learning: Student Community Service Projects (611-74018)	$2.50
Adventuring, Mastering, Associating: New Strategies for Teaching Children (611-76080)	$5.00
Beyond Jencks: The Myth of Equal Schooling (611-17928)	$2.00
The Changing Curriculum: Mathematics (611-17724)	$2.00
Criteria for Theories of Instruction (611-17756)	$2.00
Curricular Concerns in a Revolutionary Era (611-17852)	$6.00
Curriculum Leaders: Improving Their Influence (611-76084)	$4.00
Curriculum Materials 1974 (611-74014)	$2.00
Degrading the Grading Myths: A Primer of Alternatives to Grades and Marks (611-76082)	$6.00
Differentiated Staffing (611-17924)	$3.50
Discipline for Today's Children and Youth (611-17314)	$1.50
Early Childhood Education Today (611-17766)	$2.00
Educational Accountability: Beyond Behavioral Objectives (611-17856)	$2.50
Elementary School Mathematics: A Guide to Current Research (611-75056)	$5.00
Elementary School Science: A Guide to Current Research (611-17726)	$2.25
Eliminating Ethnic Bias in Instructional Materials: Comment and Bibliography (611-74020)	$3.25

Emerging Moral Dimensions in Society: Implications for Schooling (611-75052)	$3.75
Ethnic Modification of Curriculum (611-17832)	$1.00
Global Studies: Problems and Promises for Elementary Teachers (611-76086)	$4.50
The Humanities and the Curriculum (611-17708)	$2.00
Humanizing the Secondary School (611-17780)	$2.75
Impact of Decentralization on Curriculum: Selected Viewpoints (611-75050)	$3.75
Improving Educational Assessment & An Inventory of Measures of Affective Behavior (611-17804)	$4.50
International Dimension of Education (611-17816)	$2.25
Interpreting Language Arts Research for the Teacher (611-17846)	$4.00
Learning More About Learning (611-17310)	$2.00
Linguistics and the Classroom Teacher (611-17720)	$2.75
A Man for Tomorrow's World (611-17838)	$2.25
Middle School in the Making (611-74024)	$5.00
The Middle School We Need (611-75060)	$2.50
Needs Assessment: A Focus for Curriculum Development (611-75048)	$4.00
Observational Methods in the Classroom (611-17948)	$3.50
Open Education: Critique and Assessment (611-75054)	$4.75
Open Schools for Children (611-17916)	$3.75
Personalized Supervision (611-17680)	$1.75
Professional Supervision for Professional Teachers (611-75046)	$4.50
Removing Barriers to Humaneness in the High School (611-17848)	$2.50
Reschooling Society: A Conceptual Model (611-17950)	$2.00
The School of the Future—NOW (611-17920)	$3.75
Schools Become Accountable: A PACT Approach (611-74016)	$3.50
Social Studies for the Evolving Individual (611-17952)	$3.00
Supervision: Emerging Profession (611-17796)	$5.00
Supervision in a New Key (611-17926)	$2.50
Supervision: Perspectives and Propositions (611-17732)	$2.00
The Unstudied Curriculum: Its Impact on Children (611-17820)	$2.75
What Are the Sources of the Curriculum? (611-17522)	$1.50
Vitalizing the High School (611-74026)	$3.50
Developmental Characteristics of Children and Youth (wall chart) (611-75058)	$2.00

Discounts on quantity orders of same title to single address: 10-49 copies, 10%; 50 or more copies, 15%. Make checks or money orders payable to ASCD. Orders totaling $10.00 or less must be prepaid. Orders from institutions and businesses must be on official purchase order form. Shipping and handling charges will be added to billed purchase orders. **Please be sure to list the stock number of each publication, shown in parentheses.**

Subscription to **Educational Leadership**—$10.00 a year. ASCD Membership dues: Regular (subscription and yearbook)—$25.00 a year; Comprehensive (includes subscription and yearbook plus other books and booklets distributed during period of membership)—$35.00 a year.

Order from: **Association for Supervision and Curriculum Development
Suite 1100, 1701 K Street, N.W., Washington, D.C. 20006**